Christian Ethics and Imagination

A Theological Inquiry

Philip S. Keane, S.S.

PAULIST PRESS
New York/Ramsey

Library of Congress
Catalog Card Number: 84-81659

ISBN: 0-8091-2647-8

Published by Paulist Press
545 Island Road, Ramsey, N.J. 07446

Printed and bound in the
United States of America

Contents

Preface   1

1. Why Ethics and Imagination?   3

2. Historical Perspectives on the
    Non-Discursive Aspects of Christian Thought   21

3. Some Contemporary Insights Supporting
    a Moral Theology of Imagination   47

4. The Meaning and Purpose of Moral Imagination   79

5. Some Examples of Moral Imagination   110

6. Imagination and Education for Moral Living   147

    Notes   173

    Abbreviations   204

    Index   207

To
Rev. Msgr. A. Robert Casey
On the Occasion of His Fortieth Anniversary
With Gratitude

Preface

The present book was written during my 1983 calendar year sabbatical. In that context it strikes me that moral theology can be written from several different perspectives. It can be written to explain traditional and valuable moral standards more clearly. It can be written to critique inadequate understandings of traditional moral standards. Or it can be written to ask new questions, questions which the tradition may not have asked, or at least not asked as clearly as they should have been asked.

While all three of these perspectives overlap, it seems to me that the third perspective—seeking to ask new questions—is especially appropriate for a year of sabbatical leave. Thus I have written this book on an issue which, for me at least, is something of a new question, i.e., the question of the place of imagination in moral theology. Were I giving the book a subtitle, I might well subtitle it "moral theology and the right side of the brain."

For the sabbatical year itself, I am especially grateful to Father Edward Frazer, Provincial Superior of the American Province of the Society of St. Sulpice, and to Father Robert Leavitt, President-Rector of St. Mary's Seminary, Baltimore. I am also grateful to Thomas Ulshafer, S.S. and Patricia Smith, R.S.M. who formerly held the offices of Vice Rector and Academic Dean at St. Mary's. All of these persons helped work out the time for my sabbatical and helped arrange for coverage of my various tasks during my year of leave.

During the course of the sabbatical, I have been helped by many persons who offered me services which included reading drafts of my text, suggesting resources, and providing me with quiet havens at which to read and write. Without naming each person's specific contribution, I would like to thank Archbishop William D. Borders, John Bowen, S.S. and the Sulpician Community at Paca Street, Ms. Rosann Catalano, Gerald D. Coleman, S.S., Marie Egan, I.H.M. and the Community of the I.H.M. Center for Spiritual Renewal at Montecito, California, Richard M. Gula, S.S., Mr.

1

James Harkness, Dr. A. Vanlier Hunter, Mrs. Harriet Keane, Robert Leavitt, S.S., Mr. Donald Kemple, Ms. Mary Agnes Eagen, Mr. John McCarty, Mrs. Rosemary McCarty, Dr. Ann Neale, Paul Philibert, O.P., Louis Reitz, S.S., and Thomas Schindler, S.S.

I wish also to express my gratitude to Fr. Kevin A. Lynch, C.S.P., and to the staff of the Paulist Press for their encouragement and help in bringing this book to completion.

Friendsville, Pennsylvania
February 25, 1984

1

Why Ethics and Imagination?

THE POSITIVE STATE OF MORAL THEOLOGY TODAY

Without doubt, many significant advances have been made in moral theology over the course of the past generation. To help set our context, we shall briefly consider these advances as they have occurred in three categories: Roman Catholic fundamental moral theology, Roman Catholic thinking on special questions in ethics, and ecumenical advances in ethics.

Catholic Advances in Fundamental Moral Theology

In Roman Catholicism, the Vatican II and post-Vatican II years have seen the development of a moral theology which is much more conversant with biblical themes than was the case in previous generations.[1] The use of biblical themes has resulted in a moral theology which is much more alive and vital than some former approaches were. Roman Catholic moral theology has also become a great deal more united with spiritual theology or asceticism. The old split between moral and spiritual theology separated many persons' moral decisions from prayerfulness and liturgical piety and sometimes led to an undue legalism. Today, the theme of discernment of spirits, once again prominent, helps many believers make their life decisions in a highly prayerful and spiritual fashion.[2] A new sense of the true meaning of sin and of our need for ongoing and daily conversion has also enriched today's moral theology both in theory and in the practice of many believers. An awareness of the importance of the contemporary research into moral development has helped many Catholic authors and teachers work out more creative patterns for the education of our young people.[3]

Besides these advances in fundamental moral theology, the

3

Vatican II and post-Vatican II era has seen the revitalization of some of our most important traditional moral themes such as natural law and the principle of the double effect.[4] A dialogue with contemporary philosphical systems such as transcendental Thomism, existential phenomenology, historical critical methodology, and hermeneutical methodology has been a key factor aiding development in areas such as natural law and double effect reasoning. The advances in natural law and double effect thinking have not been without controversy, and more refinement is still needed on these two issues. But nonetheless a great deal of progress has been made, especially in dealing with the excessive preoccupation with physical and biological realities which marked some (but not all) past natural law and double effect thinking.

Other advances in Roman Catholic fundamental moral theology could be added to those just cited, but the point is clear: notable advances have been made in recent moral theology. One of the clearest signs of the recent progress is that within the past five years several significant full-length treatises on fundamental moral theology have been published.[5] Up to these past few years, there had been very few major full-length fundamental moral treatises since Vatican II. The appearance of these full-length books suggests that enough significant gains have been made since Vatican II to make full-length efforts at consolidation worthwhile.

Catholic Advances on Particular Moral Issues

Forward moving steps in Catholic moral theology have not been limited to fundamental issues. To illustrate this point some comments can be made on sexual ethics, medical ethics, and social ethics. In sexual ethics, four important developments can be mentioned. First, there is a renewed sense of the goodness of human sexuality. Second, there is an understanding that sexuality is profoundly interrelated with the whole fabric of our humanity instead of being limited only to certain levels of our personality. The third development is a greatly increased pastoral sensitivity to persons dealing with difficult sexual dilemmas. Finally, and perhaps most notably, current approaches to sexual ethics include a much deeper understanding of women as truly co-equal sharers with men in a common humanity.[6] Of course there remain some controversies in Roman Catholicism on specific sexual questions, but these controversies, legitimate and honest though they be, should not obscure the great progress which has been made in Roman Catholic sexual ethics. A perusal of statements on homosexuality made by some American Catholic bishops over the course of the past decade ought to convince most anyone that moral theology has taken on a much different tone than it had a generation or two ago.[7]

In medical ethics, recent Roman Catholic thinking has continued the traditional leadership which Roman Catholicism has offered on issues such as death and dying and the right to life.[8] But new themes are beginning to appear in Roman Catholic writing and teaching about medical ethics. These new themes include the rights of patients, the question of how we should finance the costs of health care, and the establishment of adequate guidelines for medical research and experimentation.[9] Roman Catholic medical ethics has also become much more of a "hands on" reality than was the case in the past. A fair number of the Catholic religious communities involved in health care now employ full-time ethical consultants. Many individual Catholic hospitals now have human values committees and draw upon the services of nearby moral theologians or philosophical ethicists. Hopefully the result of all this is a deeper commitment to moral values on the part of Catholic health care systems. Hopefully, too, this kind of direct involvement has given moral theologians and ethicists a much more concrete sense of the many moral issues which exist in the health care field.

The renewal of Roman Catholic social ethics began with *Rerum Novarum* in 1891 and thus pre-dates the Vatican II period. Nonetheless, a deepening of the Roman Catholic approach to social questions has been a key aspect of the recent renewal of Roman Catholic moral theology.[10] Catholic social ethics today is more inductive, more biblical and perhaps more ready to address the really difficult questions. Pope John Paul II has given excellent leadership in the field of economic ethics, especially with his encyclical *Laborem Exercens*,[11] a document which, if read without automatic pre-conceptions in favor of a free market, could lead Catholics in the Western countries to a major reassessment of some aspects of their approaches to economic systems and social justice. The effort of the American Catholic bishops in issuing a pastoral letter on the nuclear arms question could prove to be one of the most remarkable events in the entire history of American Catholicism.[12] The style which the bishops employed in developing the pastoral (broad consultation, etc.) may become a paradigm for the Church's future handling of many complex ecclesial and social issues.

In reviewing these very notable advances in Roman Catholic moral theology, we should not lose sight of another different sort of advance—an advance in who does moral theology on a professional level. A generation ago, almost all Catholic moral theology was done by clerics, many of whom were canon lawyers who were only secondarily interested in and educated to do moral theology per se. Nowadays, there are religious women and men, married persons of both sexes, and single persons who are making significant contributions to the developments described in the last few paragraphs.[13] This diversity among the contributors to moral theology has greatly enriched the discipline of moral theology.

Protestant Moral Advances

I write as a Roman Catholic, and thus with a special awareness of the progress Roman Catholic moral theology has made in recent decades. It would be wrong, however, not to acknowledge that equally important accomplishments have also been made in recent Protestant writing on Christian ethics. Because both Protestant ethics and Catholic moral theology share many of the same basic concerns, it should not be surprising that much of the progress in Protestant ethics has been of a similar nature to what we have already seen in Roman Catholicism. In these areas of similar accomplishment, both Protestant and Catholic scholars have contributed with genuine originality, so that it is not a case of Protestant ethics being derived from Catholic ethics or vice versa.

On fundamental moral issues, several Protestant developments similar to those in Roman Catholicism can be mentioned. Modern biblical scholarship has had a marked influence on Protestant ethics. The area of spirituality, especially the theme of discernment of spirits, has emerged as a major concern for some Protestant ethicians. Important full-length Protestant books on fundamental Christian ethics are appearing such as the major new work by James Gustafson.[14]

Recent Protestant ethics also offers parallels to Roman Catholic thought on specific moral issues. Medical ethics, for instance, has become a major area of research for some leading Protestant scholars. This development is particularly remarkable since Protestant medical ethics was almost unheard of before the mid-1950's.[15] Protestantism has also accomplished much in recent decades in the area of social justice. As with Catholicism, a renewed Protestant social ethics began around the turn of the century. But specific progress has taken place in recent years, with the nuclear arms issue again being a key example.[16]

Although these examples are similar to what has been happening in Roman Catholicism, there are also developments in Protestant ethics which are more unique. From the great hostility to natural law which existed in the Barthian era and earlier, certain Protestant scholars have begun a much more serious and intensive dialogue with the natural law tradition, so that, in the opinion of some contemporary observers, Protestantism and Catholicism can be said to be moving from two very different starting points towards a common middle ground on the natural law.[17] To get to this common ground Catholics have moved from static and sometimes overly physical approaches to natural law, while Protestants have moved from a tendency to rely on Scripture and to disregard philosophy and science as sources of moral knowledge.

Protestant authors have also contributed most notably to the development of a contemporary ethics of virtue.[18] This Protestant concern for virtue (which is beginning to be echoed by some Catholic authors) is ironic since in the past virtue was always such a key concept in Roman Catholic moral thought. As Catholic writers in the Vatican II period dealt with virtue ethics much less than before, some Protestant authors significantly revived the theme of virtue. Some older Protestant scholars saw the life of faith and justification as rather extrinsic to our human nature and human actions. The newer Protestant concern for virtue sees human interiority and the life of faith as important sources for moral life and action.

THREE PERSISTING PROBLEMS IN MORAL THEOLOGY

Based on the considerations mentioned so far, it seems that today's moral theology can be given a good deal of positive praise. At the same time however, any vital discipline always stands in need of further renewal, with moral theology being no exception. To set a context for this book on imagination and moral theology, I would like to describe three problems which I see as present in today's moral theology, three problems which have caused me increasing concern over the fifteen years during which I have taught moral theology. These problems in no way gainsay the progress outlined earlier, but they are very real and they help explain the need for a book on imagination and moral theology.

What Do Moral Principles Mean?

To explain the first problem, we must begin with one of the greatest strengths of Roman Catholic moral theology, i.e., its insistence on clear and definite principles for moral behavior. Roman Catholicism should be deeply proud of its devotion to moral principles, and nothing to be written in this book will question our need to make decisions on the basis of clear and well-articulated moral principles. However, there is a serious problem in that, while many believers know what our moral principles are, rather few believers know what many of these moral principles really mean. Perhaps part of the problem is that some of our moral principles have been around for so long that many people have forgotten the once hard-earned lesson of what these principles really mean.[19]

This forgetfulness of the real meaning of moral principles has created two quite opposite responses. Some persons, often including conservatives and/or authority figures, realizing that many moral principles are no longer understood, insist on an inflexible and sometimes legalistic following of our principles. Such an approach leaves very little room for the openness in interpreting principles which marked the work of many traditional scholars such as Aquinas with his teaching on *epikeia*. In some respects, our present situation makes a legalistic approach to principles understandable, and I for one can sympathize with the goals of those who proceed in this fashion. If many people have forgotten what our principles mean, there is logic to insisting on inflexible descriptions of moral principles. People who do not understand the principles they practice are more likely to make mistakes in their practice of the principles. The conservative position helps avoid such mistakes. There is, of course, an unacceptable paternalism in the conservative approach to defining moral principles, a paternalism which assumes that since persons do not now understand the meaning of many moral principles, they never will be able to understand them. But the cautious approach clearly has its own inner consistency and logic.

The second response to the fact that many moral principles are not well understood at a core level is the response taken by those who largely or completely abandon the use of moral principles in decision making. These persons find the routine and often shallow presentations of moral principles to be frustrating, and they see no course open to them other than to give up relying very much on moral principles. As with the first response, it is easy to see why persons with limited understandings of moral principles take this second response. However, the second response is ultimately unacceptable because of its antinomianism. It cuts itself off from the very real help which moral principles can offer. What is really needed is neither a legalistic nor an antinomian approach to principles. What is really needed is a deeper grasp of what our principles mean in the first place.

To give just one example of a moral principle with a forgotten meaning, consider one of our best known traditional principles, namely that genital sexual activity belongs in marriage and not elsewhere. It is a principle which seems to be observed as much today in its breaching as it is in actual practice. I doubt that we will have very much success in helping people in our society to practice this basic principle of sexual ethics unless we can find some ways to convey to people a whole new sense of what this principle really means. I also doubt that we will have much universal success in considering whether or not this principle might ever admit any objectively moral instances of genital sexual activity outside marriage unless we can come to a better grasp of what this principle means at its heart. Later in this book, after working out a moral theology of imagination, I shall attempt a fresh articulation of the sex-belongs-in-marriage principle.[20] This articulation will rest heavily on the biblical notion of covenant, and hopefully it will be sounder and more inspiring to many people.

How Do We Apply Our Moral Principles?

A second problem which concerns me in today's Christian ethics or moral theology has to do with how we go about applying our moral principles to particular cases. The fact that we are so often unsure of the deepest meaning of our principles is one clear reason why applications can be difficult. But even when our principles are fairly well understood, applications can be difficult. So often we can face cases in which two or more of our central moral principles collide or at least appear to collide. So often, too, we get bombarded with new information which makes it hard for us to know which of our principles are relevant to a given situation and how we should apply the principles which are in fact relevant.

Two examples of this difficulty in applying moral principles come quickly to mind. In the current debate over nuclear arms, relatively few persons have doubts about the classic strength and validity of the just war theory. The principles of the just war theory developed by Augustine of Hippo still seem sound in themselves to many scholars. The traditional applications of the just war theory to ancient, medieval, and pre-nuclear modern wars were acceptable to many. But can a nuclear war ever be just? Or would a sound application of the just war theory in our changed, post-nuclear era call on us to reject all nuclear wars or even all wars in general as unjust? These are ''application of known principles'' questions and they are tough questions.[21]

The second example comes from medical ethics. One of the better accomplishments of traditional Roman Catholic morality was the set of principles pertinent to care for the dying.[22] We knew clearly that life was a value to be protected. But we also knew clearly that we did not always have to prolong life. We had a good distinction between ordinary means of preserving life (which we were obliged to use) and extraordinary means of preserving life (which we were not always obliged to use). Today however, in spite of all these clear principles, Catholic hospitals sometimes have a most difficult time in fostering good decisions in death and dying cases. There are so many new medical technologies that it is often unclear how we should go about rendering appropriate medical care. Doctors fear lawsuits and thus are very hesitant not to treat all patients vigorously, even when there are surely good reasons not to treat a given patient vigorously. People in general find it hard to talk about death (is this another instance of our not really grasping basic Christian values?), with the result that the patient, the doctor, the family, the pastoral minister, *et al.* can find it hard to begin a dialogue on what treatment is in the best interest of the patient. Even with our clear principles, the factors just mentioned can sometimes lead to less than satisfactory death and dying decisions. Where ethics committees exist in Catholic hospitals, they seem to struggle with this issue more than with any other single question.

In general two responses can be made to this difficulty in applying moral principles, two responses which basically parallel the earlier described responses to the problem of understanding principles well. One response is more cautious and opts for only carefully agreed upon applications of principles. At certain stages in our moral development, carefully worked out applications may well be all we can handle. But in the challenging crises of life, people will often have to move toward new and not so standard applications, applications which do not deny our principles but rather apply them in new ways to new cases. Many persons' moral development will not be able to proceed adequately if they cannot learn to move beyond the cautious applications to more creative ones.

The opposite response to the cautious standard-applications-only approach is the approach of those who will make esoteric and sometimes highly personalistic applications of principles, applications which are often mere rationalizations which undercut the essential meaning of principles. Such an approach is obviously not an acceptable application of principles, even if one can understand why it happens in an age in which many persons find it so difficult to apply principles.

In describing these two opposing approaches to the applying of moral principles, I am not trying to suggest that an acceptable and moderate middle ground is as of now completely unavailable. But we do find the middle ground difficult to hold today. One purpose of this book, as it deals with the theme of imagination and ethics, will be to help us hold that middle ground more securely.[23]

Seeing the Social Side of Moral Issues

The third difficulty which strikes me concerning the state of moral theology today is that so many people have trouble in grasping the social dimensions of moral issues. In a general sense many believers have a hard time in making connections between their lives of prayerful openness to the Spirit and the social problems of the world around them. Such believers see prayer and spirituality as belonging in church while social problems are the world's business. Such believers find it hard to understand why Catholic bishops have spent so much time reflecting on nuclear arms. Once such a mindset is adopted, and social problems are detached from religious experience, it becomes quite difficult for social problems to be viewed as moral issues.

This difficulty can appear in various ways. Sometimes people can tend to think that only personal issues are true moral issues. Sometimes people will look at a moral issue which is both personal and social, but only be able to appreciate the personal moral aspects of the issue. Still other times, people will be aware of a given social issue, but without understanding that the issue is moral, as well as social, and therefore crucially important. In all these different cases there is a common root problem, namely the failure of people to see the social side of moral issues.

Several examples can serve to illustrate the difficulty many have in seeing the social side of moral issues. The first example will show the tendency to limit moral concern to personal issues alone. Very often when someone who was educated in traditional moral theology uses the phrase "moral problem," the phrase clearly refers to a sexual or a medical problem and to nothing else. When a program for a study week for priests states that a day will be devoted to moral problems, what is often meant is that the day will be devoted to sexual issues, or possibly to sexual and medical issues. This common and exclusively personal view of the term "moral problems" represents a serious failure to see the social side of human morality.

Two further examples show how people will look at issues which are both personal and social, but see only the personal side of such issues. In courses which deal with the problem of rape, many students tend to see rape as a sexual problem and nothing more. Such students cannot see that rape is profoundly connected to the way in which we organize society and to the many ways in which society systematically oppresses women. These students see rape only as the failure of certain isolated individuals to control their sexual instincts.[24] Similarly, in courses dealing with death and dying decisions, many students have a tendency to base death and dying decisions only on the suffering of the patient and/or on the anguish the situation is creating for the patient's family. Surely the needs of the patient and of his or her family are crucially important in death and dying cases. But the practice of medicine in death and dying cases is also very important for society as a whole and for the trust (or lack thereof) which all persons in society place in the medical profession. While direct mercy killing might appear to some to be reasonably justified based on the needs of the patient alone, the social dimensions of medicine raise a whole new series of questions about mercy killing, questions which cannot be ignored.[25]

A final example will show that people sometimes know about a social issue but fail to see that the issue is a moral issue. Perhaps the best current example of this type is unemployment. For years people have seen the growing statistics on unemployment and have known that it is a social problem. Especially today, when there are so many unemployed persons, there is much awareness that high unemployment is a social problem. However, the social problem of unemployment has not really struck most persons as a moral issue. Even when people know about unemployment, they fail to see that the lack of a job has a profound effect on the human dignity and worth of the unemployed persons and thus stands out as a major moral crisis. Government leaders are of course concerned about unemployment, but the comments of such leaders often seem to lack a grasp of the human dignity or moral side of the unemployment issue.

RATIONALITY AND IMAGINATION

A Common Source for the Three Problems?

Without doubt, other problems could be cited in today's moral theology. But the three problems described above all support my contention that, for all its recent gains, today's moral theology still has some significant limitations when it is used in teaching, preaching, and counseling. Ongoing work is essential on what moral principles mean, on how we apply them, and on how we see them as social.

To pursue this question a bit further, it might be asked whether these three problems have any common root or source. Obviously, each of the three problems has unique factors. But is there a common thread to the three problems? A survey of recent moral literature suggests one very important common thread, namely that each of the three problems is rooted in the tendency of moral theology to rely too heavily on forms of moral argument which are logical, discursive, and positivistic. We will not fully understand our moral principles on a discursive basis. Nor will we adequately apply our principles or see their social side if we proceed only with logical arguments. A substantial number of moral authors have recognized this common thread of over-reliance on discursive reasoning. These authors have begun to search for other means which can help us achieve moral wisdom.

One point must be clear from the outset: the turn to other elements of morality besides the discursive does not mean that logical clarity and discursive thinking are wrong or unnecessary in moral theology. Indeed, moral theology very much needs clear logical thinking as a means of explicating moral principles. The point therefore is not that we should abandon discursive moral thinking. The point is that we need more than discursive logic to successfully address the kinds of problems noted above. The major purpose of this book will not be to attack moral principles; the major purpose will be to get at the "more" which we all need, especially at the "more" which imagination can help offer us.

As an illustration of our need for more than the discursive in moral theology, let us consider one of the most interesting developments in moral theology in recent years: the effort to reinterpret the double effect principle.[26] Many scholars including myself have taken this issue up over the course of the past two decades. The contemporary investigation into the principle of double effect has had some very worthwhile results, although more discursively oriented research into the double effect is still needed to help clear up some of the questions which remain unanswered in the recent research. However, and most importantly in the present context, the key moral controversies which rage in the Church today will not be solved only on the basis of continued research into the principle of double effect. We also must turn in other, less logically oriented directions.

Efforts To Move Beyond the Discursive

The move in less discursively oriented directions has already been taken up by a number of moral theologians and philosophical ethicists. Authors such as Hauerwas and MacIntyre have stressed the importance of story (whether narrative, or drama, or journal) for moral theology. The same authors have also emphasized the role of character and virtue in the moral life.[27] Edward Shils and Daniel Callahan have emphasized the theme of tradition.[28] Paul Ramsey and a number of others have begun to explore the question of liturgy and ethics.[29] Bernard Häring and those who have been inspired by him have sought to tie Christian spirituality and ethics much more closely together. Häring has also introduced the notions of beauty and glory into moral theology, thereby opening up the whole question of moral theology and aesthetics.[30] Daniel Maguire has specifically raised the issue of imagination and moral thinking.[31] Maguire and Hauerwas have reflected upon the importance of the tragic and the comic as sources for Christian ethics.[32] All of these authors and themes will be considered in more detail later. For now we simply note the basic point: the move beyond an exclusively logical approach in moral thinking is clearly underway in an impressive group of ethical scholars.

Similar and helpful moves in less discursively oriented directions can also be found in philosophy, systematic theology, and Scripture.[33] In philosophy, the hermeneutic or interpretation theories of scholars such as Gadamer and Ricoeur point to notions such as a ''surplus of meaning'' to be found in literary and artistic classics.[34] In systematic theology, David Tracy has articulated a theology of the analogical imagination.[35] In Scripture, frustration with positivist approaches to studying the Bible is beginning to produce some important new schools of biblical interpretation such as rhetorical criticism and literary criticism (in the new sense which views the Bible as literature). All this suggests that the recent problems of moral theology and the efforts to address these problems are not an isolated case but part of a larger whole. In what follows we will need to give a good deal of attention to the larger whole.

So far, in describing a common source for the three problems, I have made use of the two terms logical and discursive, but I have not used the term rational. Critics who hold that moral theology is sometimes one-sidedly logical or discursive are also prone to say that moral theology can be excessively rational or rationalistic. If the word rational is understood as a term equivalent to logical or discursive, it can be appropriate to critique some moral theology as excessively rational or as rationalistic. Sometimes in this book the word rational will be used in this critical sense. It must be remembered, however, that, in a deeper sense, the word rational can and should be used to describe all of our human thought processes, not simply our logical processes. With this deeper sense in mind, it is not accurate to describe imagination as anti-rational or as critiquing rationality. Instead, the book will argue that imagination is indeed a rational process even though it involves a different kind of rationality from what we find in logical thought.

Why Imagination?

The last few paragraphs have suggested a common root problem in moral theology today and a variety of responses involving themes such as virtue, tradition, beauty, literature, and imagination. Surely these varied responses all belong in a common framework, and surely this book will need to look at all the elements in the common framework: the elements are part of a whole. Why then does this book plan to focus on the specific area of imagination and creativity? There are three main reasons. First, while there has been some writing on imagination and moral theology, this theme has not been treated as extensively as some of the related themes such as story, virtue, character, and vision. It is clearly a theme which deserves further investigation. Second, imagination as a moral theme appears to offer some specific benefits not available in the related themes. For instance, imagination might help us focus on how we grasp the Christian story in the first place and on how we relate our knowledge of the Christian story to the specific moral dilemmas we face. Similarly, imagination might help us to more accurately assess how we become virtuous and how we act concretely on the basis of our virtue. These questions have not yet been addressed in the contemporary literature as well as might be desired, with the result that the move beyond more logical categories in moral thinking may not yet have reached all of its potential in terms of practical or concrete impact.

Third, by taking up the theme of imagination we will also be able to attend to the theme of aesthetics and moral theology, a theme which offers much potential for our effort to work out a moral theology which moves beyond the discursive. Connected with this, it can be argued that music, art, literature, and beauty are always highly precious realities in themselves and that a sensitivity to them can contribute much to moral perception and judgment. Even many forms of athletic activity can be said to be beautiful and thus to have an important impact on human development and moral awareness. Some of our greatest theologians such as Karl Rahner have sensed all of this and written impressively on poetry and art.[36]

As our considerations unfold, the issue of aesthetics and moral theology will prove to be both fascinating and troubling. The fascination will come from an awareness of the potential benefits which the whole area of aesthetics might bring to moral thinking. The trouble will come from the fact that in our highly technical era, fewer and fewer of our young people get very many of the traditional opportunities for aesthetic experience. While not all of these concerns will be fully addressed in this book, the basic theme of imagination and moral theology may well help open up some of the aesthetic issues which are so important for human moral growth and development.

While the notion of imagination (and with it the related theme of aesthetic creativity) will be the focal point for this book's search for an ethics which includes but moves beyond the logical, imagination will not be considered apart from or in opposition to the other themes such as virtue, narrative, liturgy, and beauty. We will work with the whole picture of what is happening in moral theology today, but with a special emphasis on the issue of imagination.

THE PLAN OF THE BOOK

The Basic Outline

In addition to this first introductory chapter, the book will include five more chapters. The ''game plan'' for these chapters will be as follows: Chapter 2 will take a look at the history of Christian philosophy and theology, especially as these disciplines relate to moral theology. The chapter will show that, while principles and deductions have for centuries been crucial in moral theology, there has been a surprising and sometimes neglected theological interest in moving beyond the discursive, both in philosophy and theology in general, and in moral thinking in particular. The second chapter will root today's concern for moral theology and imagination in our tradition. Chapter 3 will survey the contemporary philosophical, theological, and moral literature which relates to our theme of the non-discursive and the imaginative. The authors cited above and a number of others will be discussed so as to give us an overall picture of the contemporary discussion. This chapter will not only address imagination, but related themes as well.

Chapter 4 will be the most important. It will attempt to articulate a fundamental theory of how imagination functions in moral theology. While this chapter will address many issues, one of the chapter's special concerns will be to show how imagination as a moral theme and method is mutually interactive with principled moral thinking instead of rejecting principled moral thinking. The chapter will argue that making moral decisions is an art, but it will not deny that the making of moral decisions is also a science.

Chapter 5 will reflect on a number of issues in sexual ethics, medical ethics, and social ethics. The first half of this chapter will suggest some ways in which a moral theology of imagination might help us deal with sexual and medical issues. The sexual and medical examples to be cited will seek to address two of the problems noted earlier by showing how imagination can enhance our understanding of moral principles and how it can assist us in making suitable applications of these principles. The second half of Chapter 5 will discuss some key issues in social ethics and explore how imagination can aid us in taking social issues more seriously and in arriving at more adequate approaches to social issues.

Chapter 6 will turn to the theme of moral education and point out some ways in which our approaches to the teaching of morality might be enriched on the basis of a moral theology of imagination. The three problems described earlier are all, in many respects, problems in moral education, problems in how we teach people to grasp and apply moral principles or problems in how we educate people to see that moral issues are social as well as personal. The chapter will be concerned about the moral education of young people, but it will also be interested in the moral education of adults.

Three Underlying Divisions

A reflection on the outline just described shows that, from the point of view of methodology, the following five chapters of this book will fall into three major divisions. Chapters 2 and 3 might be considered to be positive theology, since they will seek to report on and to summarize some of the key resource materials, both historical and contemporary, which pertain to the book's purpose. Chapter 4 will be in the nature of systematic theology in its effort to articulate a fundamental over-view of morality and imagination. In this context it is well to note that, in spite of past tendencies to view it as a fully independent kingdom, fundamental moral theology is best understood as a branch of systematic theology. Chapter 4, this book's key chapter, will be asking systematic questions about moral theology.

Chapters 5 and 6 will be an exercise in practical theology as they address specific ethical problems and then the issue of moral education. The authors who have begun to move beyond discursive reasoning in their approach to Christian morality have not yet addressed questions of practical application in very much detail. Moreover, the final worth of the effort to move beyond (but not to forget) discursive moral thinking will not be able to be assessed adequately until there is some investigation of how this effort deals with practical moral questions. Thus the practical theology of the last two chapters will be an integral and important part of this book.

Final Notes on the Outline

Two final comments need to be made relative to the plan of this book. First, I write as a Roman Catholic, and thus as someone who is especially familiar with the Roman Catholic tradition and with moral issues which create difficulty for Roman Catholics today. Thus, a great deal of what this book contains will relate to the Roman Catholic context. At the same time, however, much that is going on in Roman Catholic moral theology (and in the related disciplines) has very instructive parallels in Protestant theology and ethics and in several major schools of contemporary philosophy. The book will of necessity draw from this ecumenical base of materials and could not be adequate if it did not draw from this base. Unless there is some special need, I will not take time to state whether a given concern or approach is ecumenical or more specifically Roman Catholic; the context will make this clear. To paraphrase James Gustafson, I will write with "a preference for the Roman Catholic tradition."[37] But I hope that my work can be ecumenically relevant as well. One of the most refreshing things about recent moral theology or Christian ethics has been its ecumenical character, and I intend for this book to reflect that character.

The second comment is that, both historically and at present, there is an enormous amount of research material which is pertinent to the theme of this book. I intend to draw upon this material, and to give a brief overview of its major themes, especially in Chapters 2 and 3. However, it is not my purpose to offer a full-length critical evaluation of all the pertinent research material. My basic intent is more constructive: to move beyond the available material and in my own way contribute to the development of a theology of imagination and ethics which is both systematic and practical. The research material will be cited only briefly as a preparation for this systematic and practical project. A complete exposition and evaluation of all the sources is not my intention.

Hopefully this chapter has made clear the project of the book. We can now move on to Chapter 2 with its historical investigation of imagination and other "beyond the discursive" themes in philosophy, theology, and Christian ethics.

2

Historical Perspectives on the Non-Discursive Aspects of Christian Thought

It is clear that in Christian thought in general and in Christian ethics in particular, there has been a great deal of concern for working out clear principles and using these principles to resolve difficult ethical dilemmas. But at the same time, Christian history also shows us a quite regular and consistent concern for other types of human learning and experience in addition to discursive and principle oriented approaches. The present chapter will briefly review this consistent concern for other forms of learning with a view to showing that a concern for an imagination-oriented moral theology has some sound historical precedents.

To explain the historical interest in some of the non-discursive types of human learning and experience, this chapter will consider five major themes—epistemology, aesthetics, sacramental theology, spirituality, and ethics. To get at these themes, we will look not only at significant Christian thinkers who dealt with them; we will also mention some of the major non-Christian philosophers such as Plato and Aristotle who contributed so much to the shaping of the Christian tradition. In general our historical considerations will take us up to the earlier part of the twentieth century, with more recent developments being treated in the next chapter.

EPISTEMOLOGY

Plato, Augustine, and Kant

When we think of Plato's approach to knowing, the first theme to come to mind is Plato's notion of forms. Plato had a deep mistrust of sense knowledge which he thought could offer us at best approximations of truth. Thus he insisted that real truths were timeless and that they existed in the mind. More specifically, Plato held that there was a world of pre-existing forms or ideas. These forms are for Plato immutable and timeless; they exist completely independently of our experience here on earth.[1] Such an approach obviously gave Plato a disdain for anything other than a narrowly rational approach to life. His well-known attack on the arts in *The Republic* is one good example of his fear of leaving deductive arguments to seek other ways of dealing with human experience.[2] In his later writings, Plato came to see some of the difficulties of his own position and spoke against an overly sharp distinction of concepts from experiences,[3] but the theme of opposing deductive reasoning to other forms of human experience was well established in Plato's theory of forms. There is of course an underlying value to Plato's theory: we need to remember that we can never give a fully adequate concrete expression to our underlying ideas. But at the same time, we must remain critical of the Platonic tendency to a one-sided rationalism. It is a tendency which has kept appearing across the centuries.

A major early Christian thinker who adopted many elements of Plato's thinking was Augustine of Hippo who was especially attracted to the neo-Platonism of his own times.[4] In his theory of knowledge, Augustine regarded sense knowledge with the same distrust as Plato. Augustine basically saw the senses as instruments working under the control of the mind.[5] Thus the body could have no influence on the soul whereas the soul could influence the body. Like Plato, Augustine was enough of a genius not to let his theory of senses and intellect lead him to a complete rationalism in his approach to knowing. Thus, he followed many of the neo-Platonists of his age in working out a notion of God divinely illuminating our intelligence. He thought that God placed traces (*vestigia*)[6] of himself in the world around us which we could recognize through our experience. Somewhat similarly he acknowledged an evolutionary dimension to creation by asserting that God had bestowed various *rationes seminales* (seminal sources)[7] in the initially created world so that, under God, new forms could develop across the ages. Thus, while Augustine never abandoned his interest in rational deductions from Platonic forms, he did have a clear openness to other levels of human knowing. In the Middle Ages, the Victorine theologians especially developed these more broadly contemplative aspects of Augustine's approach.

In the seventeenth century René Descartes promoted his idea of a real distinction between mind and body (i.e., between *res cogitans* and *res extensa*).[8] While Descartes was aware of some of the problems contained in the approaches of Plato and Augustine, he clearly continues the rationalist and anti-experiential bent which is found in their epistemologies. His insistence on clear, logically persuasive explanations as to why humans like works of art shows the preoccupations of his thought system.

Like Plato and Augustine, Immanuel Kant's genius was such that he did not limit himself to rationalist or formalist categories alone. His efforts to unify imagination and understanding in a transcendental deduction, and his development of the notion of synthetic *a priori* judgments are examples of his work to unify experience and understanding.[9] But the dualism or separation of sense experience and rational understanding remained the dominant note in Kant's thought, and in the opinion of many critics, Kant never ultimately succeeded in bridging his dualism. Kant's ethics, while brilliant and moving in its description of our duty to one another,[10] is not able to deal with our experiencing meaningful purposes rooted in our actions so that we can choose on the basis of these goals or purposes.

Aristotle, Aquinas, and Newman

So far we have cited the epistemologies of some of history's greatest thinkers. We have noted some indications of moves beyond logical deduction (Augustine's concern with illumination, Kant's transcendental union of imagination and understanding). Thus the authors cited do offer some resources for a moral theology of imagination. Nonetheless, a concern for rational deductions has been the dominant note in the authors thus far mentioned. It is rather unlikely that a Christian ethics strongly based on human creative imagination as well as on logic will emerge from the epistemologies we have mentioned. However, Plato, Augustine, and Kant are not the whole of the history of epistemology. There is another line of approach to epistemology to be found in the works of authors such as Aristotle, Aquinas, and Newman. In my judgment the epistemology of these authors has proven more successful over the course of history.

Moreover, the epistemology of this second group of authors does provide a stronger basis for an ethics of imagination and creativity, as well as an ethics based on reason.

Aristotle was a generation younger than Plato. He found Plato's approach, i.e., that knowledge must be clear and unchanging (because of its basis in the forms) to be unacceptable. In his rejection of Plato's approach, Aristotle insisted on a very close unity of our bodies and our souls. He rejected the notion of pre-existing forms detached from all sense experience, and asserted that we know the forms in knowing the concrete individuals in whom the forms are embodied. We do not have a pre-existing form such as "man" into which we fit an individual such as Socrates. We know the form "man" in knowing the individual Socrates. Thus we can have a true intellectual knowledge of concrete realities, in a way that was not possible for Plato (at least for the Plato of the theory of forms) and his intellectual successors.[11]

Aristotle's close union of matter and spirit, sense and intelligence, universal forms and concrete experiences, etc., in no way led him to deny the importance of reason and logical thinking. Indeed, acting on the basis of reason is one of the keystones of Aristotle's *Ethics*.[12] But Aristotle's concept of reason has broader dimensions to it. It is reason based on the whole range of concrete human experience. We mentioned this broader notion of reason in the last chapter. Thus Aristotle's thought system seems to approach the moral life in a more concrete and experiential manner than does the Platonic tradition.

In the thirteenth century, after medieval Europe's rediscovery of Aristotle's long missing works, Thomas Aquinas strove to reaffirm and to continue Aristotle's achievements. Thomas began his approach to knowledge by insisting that all knowledge begins with sense knowledge. He described sense knowledge at quite some length, stating that we have five external senses and four internal senses. Thomas' four internal senses were the common sense (which forms one sense impression out of the data of the various external senses), the sense memory (which stores sense data for future recall), the imagination (which presents the combined sense data [from immediate impressions, from memory, from combinations of data] to the intelligence), and the *vis aestimativa* (in humans called the *vis cogitativa*) which evaluates the sense data in an instinctual as opposed to a reflective manner.[13]

Before moving on to Thomas' description of how imagination and intelligence are related, two notes can be made on his approach to the internal senses. First, while many would not agree with Thomas' division of four internal senses, a surprising number of authors in later centuries either spoke of several types of imagination or made some other division which at least partially parallels Aquinas' approach. Second, by using the word *cogitativa* in talking about human instinct, Thomas seems aware that the higher internal senses have a quasi-intellectual or spiritual character about them. He clearly insists on making the distinction between sense experience and intellection, but perhaps he also partially anticipates the work of later authors who include the operations of intelligence on sense images in their description of imagination. The next section of this chapter will be on aesthetics and it will follow up some of these imagination issues.

Perhaps most interesting in Thomas' own work on imagination is his way of explaining the relationship between sense images and our intelligence. Like Aristotle, Thomas insists that there are two operations involved in human intelligence, passive intellect and agent intellect.[14] In many later commentators on Thomas, the agent intellect is given only a very minimal role. The result of this minimal role is that the data of sense imagination is understood to be more or less automatically programed into our passive intelligence in a clear logical fashion, similar to the manner in which information is keyed into a computer. If Thomas is read more carefully, however, the act of abstracting intellectual data from our imagination is a process involving the agent intellect and therefore involving human insight and creativity. As Thomas himself puts it, the agent intellect functions on the basis of an *excessus ad esse*, an excess or openness toward being, toward God.[15] Such an approach makes the activity of imagination in offering us data for reflection and our process of reflection on imagination to be a much more dynamic process. This process opens up the whole question of mystical and intuitive knowledge. Imaginatively, we can be open to experiences of faith and trust in God, experiences that would not be possible at the level of systematic philosophical or theological discourse.

If we interpret Thomas along these lines, his epistemology clearly seems to offer high possibilities for approaches to ethics which emphasize more than deductive elements. Surely this does not mean that Thomas was against logic or against moral principles, but it does mean that there may be more possibilities for an ethics of imagination in Thomas than were realized by some later Thomist scholars who had a very rationalistic understanding of Thomas. In our own century both neo-Thomist thought (in someone such as Maritain) and transcendental Thomist thought have moved toward a more dynamic and creative understanding of Thomas' epistemology.[16] Rahner has gone so far as to call for a metaphysics of imagination, based on his approach to Thomas.[17]

John Henry Newman should also be mentioned here since his epistemology follows in the tradition of the work of Aristotle and Aquinas, even though Newman's specific terms and arguments differ. In his classic work, *An Essay in Aid of a Grammar of Assent*, Newman distinguishes two kinds of inference, formal and informal.[18] Formal inference has its place in mathematics and logic, but it is not suitable for concrete human experiences which call for informal inference as the way to certitude. Informal inference achieves certitude on the basis of what Newman calls an "illative sense."[19] For Newman, "the mind is more versatile and vigorous than any of its works,"[20] and thus able to make true judgments even when these judgments cannot be accounted for logically. Newman is of course relating his work to British empiricism; nonetheless he explicitly compares his work on the illative sense to Aristotle's notion of *phronesis* or moral judgment,[21] and, at least implicitly, his illative sense seems to compare with Aquinas' agent intellect. Newman's language also has echoes of the concept of *ratio practica* (practical reason) which we will be mentioning later in this chapter.

To summarize, we have looked at two main historical streams of epistemology or theory of knowing. One of these streams, while having some important openings beyond the discursive, tends to be highly deductive in its methods. A good deal of the discussion in ethics today is dominated by this stream. The second stream, while it continues to prize norms (in ethics and elsewhere), is also quite open to a broader range of human learning, to experiences involving the senses, involving imagination, intuition, and creativity. For Roman Catholics, this second epistemological stream is ultimately closer to the heart of our tradition. It is a critically important historical building block for an ethics of imagination.

AESTHETICS

The term aesthetics as we know it today only originated with the work of Alexander Gottlieb Baumgarten in 1735. Beyond the Scholastic work on imagination done by Thomas and others, serious work on imagination did not occur until the appearance of Francis Bacon's *Advancement of Learning* in 1605. However, concern about the arts and their meaning reaches back into ancient Greek philosophy, with the ancients asking many of their deepest questions about art through inquiries into the concept of beauty. In what follows we shall look at some of the great themes which have recurred in the philosophy of art across the centuries, and we shall see that the philosophy of art rather consistently points to forms of human knowing which go beyond logical or discursive thought patterns.[22] By art and the arts we will consistently mean the arts in general, not simply the visual arts such as painting.

Fear of the Arts

Plato, in *The Republic*, showed a great deal of concern about the arts. If an idea-form, e.g., of a bed, existed independently of a concrete specific bed, the bed made by a carpenter was already an imitation of the idea-form, once removed from true reality. The artist, who paints a picture of a bed built by a carpenter, is thus imitating an imitation, so that his work is even further removed from reality.[23] Moving from this viewpoint, Plato was well aware that the arts could be used both to morally educate people about the meaning of life and to lead them astray by portraying reality falsely. This explains why Plato was favorably inclined toward censorship of the arts.[24] Plato's concern about art was re-echoed on numerous occasions across the ages. David Hume, for instance, thought that art was based on fancy (the negative side of imagination),[25] and could thus distract us from getting at the truth. The efforts of some modern forms of socialism and Marxism to rigidly control the arts, so that only established views are expressed in the arts, show a continuance of this same anxiety.

Art and Formalism

The fear of the arts just described was never great enough to keep philosophers from thinking about the true meaning of art and beauty. Plato himself recognized that art had some direct relationship to the idea-form of beauty.[26] While it would be impossible to come up with a simple classification of all the schools of thought about the meaning of the arts, it does strike me that the theories about the meaning of art can be divided into two main families. First is the school of thought of those who hold that works of art are valuable only because they embody clear principles of form or unity. Such principles enable us to appreciate works of art in and for themselves without reference to any other issues or values. The philosophers of art who emphasize clear principles of artistic unity might be called formalists. The familiar expression "art for art's sake" is often associated with the formalist view. The second school on the meaning of art is composed by those who appreciate form in art, but who also hold that art expresses deeper meanings about the nature of human life. This second school can be broken down into a great many sub-groups.

In ancient times, formalism can be found in the works of the Stoics who held that order or arrangement of parts is the source of artistic beauty, and even more so in Epicurean thinking such as the work of Philodemus who held that artistic goodness was based only on the unity of form and content in a work, and that a work without form (e.g., music without words) could have no meaningful effect on humanity. In the Cartesian period, there was a strong insistence on clear rules intrinsic to the art objects themselves as the basis for evaluating works of art.[27] Early in our own century, the critic Clive Bell strongly supported a formalist approach to art and music, though not to literature.[28]

A one-sided formalism as an approach to the meaning and value of art deserves criticism, since formalism does not seem to adequately reflect the human experience of art. In the final analysis human experience suggests that art is valuable for more than simply its own sake. But in criticizing we should also remember that there is an important value which formalism seeks to uphold. So often across history, art has been used as propaganda or subjected to various forms of social control. The effort to assess the value of works of art in and of themselves stands as an effort to resist such propagandizing. We may well choose to move beyond the formalist approach, but it does help to recall the point that formalism makes.

Meaning Approaches to the Arts

Granted the value of formal assessments of works of art, most philosophers of the arts, while retaining some formal considerations, have argued for an aesthetics which sees deeper levels of meaning in works of art. This is important in the context of this book. If creative artistic expressions do in fact help us to see the deeper meaning of life, it may very well be that aesthetic experiences can assist us in making good judgments on moral matters. We will see later that some scholars have held that art directly teaches morality. But, first and more fundamentally, art inspires us to be creative and imaginative. Such creativity and imagination can in turn enable us to come to better moral decisions.

Of the many meaning-centered approaches to the arts, there are eight which have struck me in my own reading: (1) art is imitation giving universal insight, (2) art is participation in the idea-form of beauty coupled with an intuitive illumination of the human understanding, (3) art unifies human experience and understanding, (4) art is the symbolic expression of meaning, (5) art is an expression of taste, (6) art is an expression of the artist's intuitive intentional insight into life, (7) aesthetic experience is the basis for refining and interpreting all human experience, and (8) art fosters human growth and integration by moving human beings psychologically and emotionally. To give a sense of the wide range of art-gives-meaning approaches, each of these eight will be mentioned briefly. There is some overlapping of the eight approaches, and it will not be our purpose to evaluate the adequacy of each approach, or to compare and contrast them. After considering the eight approaches we will divide them into three main groups so as to give the meaning approaches to the arts a bit more organization.

Aristotle is perhaps the best representative of the imitation-gives-universal-insight approach. He holds that we find imitation enjoyable because it helps us to see the sorts of things certain persons would do under certain circumstances. Once we have this kind of knowledge, we have an insight into the nature of humanity, an insight which can enhance our human growth and development.[29] Moral theology has always been concerned with human nature so that art's ability to give us insight into our humanity is an ability with clear moral implications. In subsequent centuries many thinkers have built on this Aristotelian approach by arguing that imagination moves us by enabling us to make associations between a number of different human experiences. Some, such as Locke, have mistrusted the associative capacity of imagination.[30] But the Aristotelian tradition would tend, I believe, to see association as a positive force which enhances human learning.

The second approach, i.e., that in the experience of beauty we participate in the idea-form of beauty, was present in Plato, but especially developed by Plotinus and Augustine. Augustine described our participation in beauty as possible because in experiencing beauty we experience a divine illumination.[31] Such an outlook raises some interesting considerations for the relationship between artistic experience and mystical experience. Aquinas speaks of brightness or clarity as one of the major conditions necessary for us to experience beauty, and he (or his teacher Albert the Great)[32] states that beautiful things shine with a splendor of form (*"resplendentia formae"*). Henri Bergson's notion of an artistic intuition into the *élan vital* or ultimate reality which our spatializing intellects cannot grasp seems to have some similarities to the earlier notions of participation and illumination.[33]

The third approach holds that, in the experience of great art, our imagination's grasp of beauty and our intellect's grasp of truth are unified transcendentally. The Thomist tradition held that there were several transcendental notions (oneness, truth, goodness, and beauty) which could be predicated of all being. While these transcendentals had different forms, Thomas' followers saw them as really the same.[34] Kant argued that the unity of imagination and understanding was a transcendental necessity.[35] In this approach, which is the most metaphysical of the meaning centered approaches to the arts, the fact that goodness and beauty are transcendentally one suggests that our effort to unify moral thinking and aesthetic thinking may be well founded.

The fourth approach to the arts and meaning stems from one of the most important questions for the Church across the centuries (and today), the question of interpreting Scripture. Origen in the third century distinguished three senses of Scripture: the literal, the spiritual, and the mystic. In the medieval period, Scripture was seen to have literal, typical, tropological, and anagogical senses.[36] The fact that so much symbolism was seen as present in most of these senses of Scripture helped create a significant awareness of the role of symbol in aesthetic experience, i.e., an awareness that art forms move us by symbolizing much more than they say. This symbolic approach to aesthetics was highlighted in the 1920's by Ernst Cassirer in his *Philosophy of Symbolic Forms*.[37] Interestingly, some of the best work on imagination and symbolism in our own times is still being done by those working on issues of biblical interpretation. Some of this work will be mentioned in our next chapter.

The fifth approach which suggests more than ordered form as the meaning of the arts has to do with taste theories. Some approaches to artistic taste (why we like some works of art and dislike others, why we differ in our artistic likes and dislikes) stress objective or logical criteria very strongly. While objective criteria will always be a factor, the more dominant theory holds that there is no objective way to account for differences in artistic taste. The work of David Hume is a good example of the more common approach to taste.[38]

The sixth approach holds that the deeper meaning we find in works of art is that which the artist intuitively grasps and then expresses. This approach, which is often called metaphysical, is especially associated with the writings of Benedetto Croce and Robin Collingwood.[39] This approach places a great deal of stress on the intentionality of the artist.

The seventh approach which speaks of aesthetic quality as the basis for refining human experience has some roots in British empiricism, but is especially found in John Dewey's book *Art as Experience*, written in 1934.[40] Dewey wished to stress the experiential character of human knowing based on experimental inquiry. He thus disagreed with epistemologies which conceive of us as looking at or gazing at the truth, i.e., with epistemologies which hold that we have a direct intuition into truth. Dewey's goal was to help people move from more conflictual experiences to more harmonious experiences. He viewed all of life as artistic, and thought that people could move to more harmonious experiences by finding the pervasive aesthetic quality which he saw as present in all experience.

Dewey's theory clearly seems to lend itself to a moral theology of imagination. In his theory aesthetic qualities in an experience emerge as centrally important to moral decision making.

The eighth approach has to do with the emotional or psychological impact which works of art have on persons who experience them. Some of the earlier described approaches have related aesthetic experience to contemplation, intuitive knowledge, and universal understanding. But art also influences our emotions. Care is needed here, since art can be used to manipulate emotions in a dehumanizing manner. Great art, however, can liberate or release our emotions and thus be of genuine benefit to our humanity. This approach to the value of art goes back to Aristotle with his notion of art as offering us an opportunity for catharsis.[41] Much of the work done on the sublime in the eighteenth century by Edmund Burke and others opened up this same theme.[42] These authors inquired into why we appreciate the depiction of tragedy and danger and into why we understand the depiction of tragedy and danger as art. This whole theme of catharsis still needs more study, and it would be especially worthwhile to seek to interrelate the historical interest in catharsis with the insights of contemporary psychology. But, in any case, catharsis is clearly another instance of art's ability to communicate meaning in more than a discursive fashion.

If we consider even these brief sketches, it can be seen that, across history, aesthetic experience has been related to universal human insight, mystical intuition, transcendental metaphysics, inductive learning, and emotional growth. Our analysis of these categories is hardly complete, but one basic conclusion seems justified. Probably more than in any other area of human experience, the historical philosophies of artistic experience show that we learn in many ways other than rational deduction. Art has and needs its formalists, but there is much more to the human experience of art than form alone. The goal of the present book is to show that the many forms of insight available through aesthetics may be effectively used in moral theology.

We have reviewed these meaning-centered approaches to the arts in a somewhat scatter-shot fashion so as to show the wide range of ways in which scholars have seen the arts as helping us to form deeper insights into the meaning of life. To pull the material together a bit more tightly, it can be stated that the meaning approaches to the arts fall into three main families. No one of the eight approaches we just summarized fits purely into only one of the three families, but the three families will help us organize the approaches.

First, some of the theories we summarized held that aesthetic experience gives us a direct intuition into the meaning of life. Following in the spirit of Kant, Croce and Collingwood have an intuitive approach, i.e., that art gives us a direct insight into meaning, completely apart from logic or from our inductive experiences. The illuminationist outlook of Plato and Augustine stems from this same intuitive viewpoint, as does that part of Aquinas' work which concentrates on the transcendental attributes of being. The romanticists such as Wordsworth and Coleridge also have an intuitionist approach to aesthetics.[43]

Second, some of the meaning theories hold that art educates us by moving our emotions. The recurring interest in the issue of catharsis has an emotivist character to it. So do many of the theories of moral sense or moral taste (such as the approach of Shaftesbury whom we will consider in the next section).

Third, some of the theories hold that aesthetic experience is an intellectual, rational learning experience, although not of a discursive/deductive sort. In this approach, artistic experience is more natural to us humans; it is part of our day to day comtemplative learning processes, rather than being a separate sort of intuition or emotion. Aristotle's thinking on art as an imitation of life falls into this category. So does much of Aquinas' thought related to art, including his insight that we can know by "connaturality" or "at oneness" with reality. So too does the more contemporary thinking of John Dewey.[44]

As the book proceeds, we will see that each of these three basic approaches—that we can learn aesthetically through intuition, through emotion, and through non-discursive but still rational and natural learning experience—has its place in a theory of moral theology and imagination.[45] We will also see that the third of these approaches has the most to offer. Because the third of these approaches sees imaginative aesthetic experience as a form of reflective human learning, it will be especially helpful in relating aesthetics and moral discourse. It should also be noted that the third approach rather closely parallels the epistemological outlook of Aristotle, Aquinas, and Newman. Earlier, we saw that the epistemology of these authors offered special promise for a more imagination-oriented moral theology.

The Aesthetic as Moral Teacher

Besides these more general theories of art and meaning, the history of aesthetics offers another theme of special importance for the present book. In the past many of those who ascribed special human learning qualities to art forms have asserted that art's human learning qualities make art a very helpful direct teacher of moral values. Some of the scholars who have sought to connect art and morality have wanted to use art in a crass and moralizing fashion, but many theorists of the arts as a teacher of morality have been quite sophisticated. Plato, his worries over art not withstanding, saw that art at its best could teach character and make people virtuous.[46] Plotinus was aware that one of the stages of beauty is moral beauty.[47] Lord Shaftesbury in the eighteenth century connected beauty and virtue and spoke of one's "inward eye" or "moral sense"[48] which operates on both ethical and aesthetic questions. Percy Shelley described imagination as "the great instrument of moral good."[49] John Dewey's approach clearly makes artistic experience an important moral teacher. We must allow for some over-statement, and for the fact that great artists have not always been great moral personalities. But as we construct an approach to imagination and moral theology, it is well to note that the theme of aesthetics and the teaching of morals has a long history.

The Developing Concept of Imagination

When we last spoke about imagination as it was treated by Thomas, we were dealing clearly with a sense faculty, lower than intelligence, and related to three other internal senses. Since that time a good deal has happened to the concept of imagination so that now most people think of it as a mental faculty which contains a sense component or referent. Thomas, with his concepts of agent intellect and *excessus*, may well have understood the same reality as later imagination theorists, but he did not describe the reality under the term imagination.

The trend to make imagination an intellectual or mental activity can be seen in Baumgarten who, while not writing explicitly on imagination, did speak of the need to work out a theory of some type of sense-based intellectual knowledge as a basis for aesthetics.[50] Francis Bacon spoke more clearly about imagination as a faculty on the same level as memory and reason.[51] Both Hobbes and Kant distinguished two types of imagination (Hobbes' simple and compound imagination; Kant's reproductive and productive imagination) so as to highlight what they saw as a higher and more intellectual activity of imagination (i.e., the production of new images from existing images, instead of simply representing existing images).[52] These early efforts to articulate a more comprehensive theory of imagination ran into opposition from scholars such as Hume, who tended to think of imagination as flights of fancy which distract us from the truth.[53]

Probably the most significant impetus to the modern thinking about imagination came from the Romantic movement in literature in the late eighteenth and early nineteenth centuries. Previously, we noted that the Romantics considered imagination to be a form of immediate intuitive insight into truth, probably higher than reason. Samuel Taylor Coleridge was the most important Romantic writer on imagination.[54] To get at the problems raised by Locke, Coleridge distinguished imagination from fancy. In this scheme, fancy became a form of memory, whereas genuine rearrangement of sense data into new images was the work of the imagination, which Coleridge called an "esemplastic power." Coleridge also distinguished Kant's higher level of imagination (the productive imagination) into two levels, the primary imagination which everyone possesses, and the secondary imagination, i.e., the special artistic insight found in poets, artists, etc. Much subsequent thinking on imagination followed the approach of Coleridge, including the earlier twentieth century work of Croce and Collingwood.

Other twentieth century research on imagination criticized the Romantic approach. For example, the Meyers-Briggs personality inventory holds that an overly Romantic approach to imagination often hinders effective practical accomplishment. This book's thinking on imagination will differ from Romanticism, in that it will approach imagination more experientially and less intuitively, but the importance of Romanticism for the historical development of imagination cannot be ignored.

Earlier, I asserted that while Aquinas limits the term imagination strictly to sense operations, his overall view of human mental activity (particularly as understood by scholars such as Rahner) may not be dramatically different from much of the contemporary thought which includes the whole area of mental creativity in its approach to imagination. In this light, the work of Gilbert Ryle in the middle of our century is quite interesting.[55] Ryle argues that modern notions of imagination have become too diffuse and refer to too many diverse learning activities. Ryle would not want to go back to the Thomistic notion of imagination as a mere presentation of sense images, but his position would seem to call for a further analysis of some of the more precise categorizations of mental activity which existed before the Romantic period. In the present book we will use the modern notion of imagination as having a sense component but as also including a range of human creative mental activities. But the values in the Thomistic distinctions will be kept in mind for whatever assistance they can give our inquiry.

Before leaving this historical overview of aesthetics, it should be said that this last theme, creative or productive imagination, parallels the other aesthetic themes in reminding us that in the search for moral truth we might do well to travel other roads as well as the road of discursive reason.

SACRAMENTAL AND MYSTERY THEOLOGY

One of the first things which strikes many of us in our early religious experience as children is an awareness that Christianity is a religion of mystery, ultimately a religion of the mystery of God. Our early notions of Christianity as mystery often have a crypto-Cartesian character, e.g., we tend to think that religious mystery is somehow inferior to fact, we look on religious mystery as a temporary problem which will be solved once we get to heaven, and we focus on a whole series of mysteries so as to make our approach to mystery seem more systematic and logical.

Deeper reflection however shows us that the Christian approach to mystery is very profound and transcends clear and logical Cartesian explanations. God is described as radically mysterious in the Scriptures. Cf. Romans 11:33–34 ("How deep are the riches and the wisdom and the knowledge of God! How inscrutable his judgments, how unsearchable his ways! For who has known the mind of the Lord? Who has been his counselor?") and many other passages. Theology has continually used this theme of mystery across the centuries. In the virtually unending discussions about why the incarnation took place, one enduring common thread is that God had to express himself in a form in which the mystery of who God is could be communicated to human persons (communication here does not mean mathematical understanding).

Roman Catholic teaching makes it clear that the nature of God as mystery does not mean that we are completely unable to come to any objectively true understanding of God. But it is also clear that our objective understanding of God does not now and never will exhaust the mystery of God.[56] From this viewpoint, the Roman Catholic approach to the mystery of God is quite closely parallel to what I have previously suggested about moral principles, namely that we need moral principles but that principles do not exhaust the whole of moral experience and the moral life.

If we reflect further on why it is that God is mystery, we can say that our embodied, finite spirituality is by its very nature incapable of an exhaustive understanding of the infinity of God. Traditionally we have held that we humans have a materiality about us as well as a spirituality, whereas God is pure spirituality, even more so than the angels. To borrow the ancient philosophical notion of *analogia entis*, we share with God a spiritual nature which gives us a basis for communication with God. But our spirituality is limited by matter and thus not fully communicable with the divine spirituality.

Proceeding from these thoughts, we can say that for communication between God and humanity to take place, God must somehow express himself in matter. Such expression of God in material form will not take away the elements of ambiguity and mystery which we experience in God, but it will open up the possibility of communication between God and humanity. Once we speak of God's self-expression in matter, we have begun to articulate another ancient theological notion, the theology of symbol.[57] Symbols are not artificial signs of the realities they present to us; rather symbols are intrinsically apt to express the realities they present. Indeed for embodied spiritual persons such as human beings, symbols are one of our most important ways to come to knowledge and understanding which is not possible through discursive processes. To put this in another way, symbols are an anthropological necessity for human beings. Over the course of Christian history there have been more and less satisfactory theological uses of symbols, but in the main Christian thought systems have held to the concept of *analogia entis* and thereby to the importance of the symbolic in human life.

In the previous section on aesthetics, I made the case that aesthetics has pointed to the validity of forms of human learning and experience which go beyond the discursive, and I mentioned briefly the connections between artistic experience and symbolism. If we stop to consider that the arts always are expressed in material forms such as words (mental images), sight images, or sound images, the importance of symbolism in art becomes all the greater. As symbolic, the arts relate profoundly to a basic insight of the Christian tradition, i.e., that God must express himself symbolically in matter in order for humans to begin to communicate with the mystery of God. From this perspective Dewey may be very much on target with his suggestion that artistic experience is paradigmatic for all of human experience.[58]

These insights about mystery and symbol are part of our common Christian heritage and thus belong to all the Churches. However, in Roman Catholicism the theme of God's self-communication in symbolic expression has been especially prominent because of the strong sacramental-liturgical tradition which has been so much a part of Roman Catholic history. Of course it is true that not all Roman Catholic theologizing about the sacraments has been completely adequate. Sometimes there have been excessively mechanical and magical approaches to the sacraments. There have been formalists in sacramental theology just as in aesthetics (with both kinds of formalists being more concerned with the correct structure of symbolic elements than with the human meaning of symbols). But in spite of these difficulties, Roman Catholic sacramental theology and practice has contributed an enormously important insight into the nature of humanity and the nature of religious experience. In its sacramental and liturgical practice, Roman Catholicism has highlighted, perhaps more than any other branch of the Western Christian tradition, the human need for symbolic, non-discursive forms of insight into the mystery of God. Orthodox Christianity has also given very great emphasis to these themes.

The historical import of sacramental theology for Roman Catholics raises the following question in our present context: If in sacramental theology Roman Catholicism clearly recognizes the human need for symbols as well as for theoretical statements, could not the same thing be said about moral theology? Could not moral theology and the moral lives and education of believers also benefit from symbolic approaches to moral truth, as well as from logical deductive approaches? Traditionally, we have called our dogmatic theological statements symbols, so as to suggest that these statements include more than what they actually and correctly state. Could it not be that our moral principles might also be construed as symbols which suggest deeper insights into the moral life than what they explicitly and correctly state? Later on we will probe these questions. The point for now is simply that historical reflection upon the Christian and especially the Roman Catholic approach to mystery, symbols, and sacraments ought to challenge us to ask some crucial questions about the nature of Christian ethics or moral theology.

CHRISTIAN SPIRITUALITY

It would be possible to cite a whole host of ways in which the history of Christian spirituality has suggested non-discursive ways of knowing the mystery of God. Since moral and spiritual theology were very much one in the early centuries (before the development of private penance stimulated the creation of a separate and sometimes overly act-centered moral theology), spirituality's approaches to knowing God can be seen as especially important for moral theology. We will not attempt a complete historical overview of how spirituality has sought to enter into the truth of God. Our considerations will be limited to three key themes: discernment of spirits, mysticism, and the ways of knowing God.

Discernment of Spirits

Discernment of spirits is a process of making life decisions in which the decision maker (or makers), while not ignoring objective data, concentrates especially upon the various stirrings, impulses, and movements which are taking place inside his or her subjectivity. The word ''spirits'' in the term discernment of spirits refers precisely to the internal movements or reactions which a person experiences when considering various alternative courses of action. The fundamental notion underlying discernment of spirits is that the mystery of God is truly present in the inner stirrings of human persons so that these stirrings, as well as objective data, can be a genuine source of human experience of truth. The point of discernment is not to ignore objective data or logically reasoned conclusions, but to assert that there is more than objective data in the human approach to meaning and life.

What discernment basically wants is for the human person to get in touch with the deepest core level of his or her being and to act out of this core level awareness. Or, to say this in another way, what discernment wants is for the human person to reach that level of awareness in which the divine and the human come together as a basis for decisions, so that the person's genuine autonomy and freedom will be a God-rooted autonomy and freedom. Discernment does recognize that the human person will never fully catch up with himself or herself at this core level, but it holds that we can get closer to that level, and thus act with a different kind of human knowing and experience.

Discernment of spirits has a long history in the Christian tradition. Discernment of spirits is explicitly mentioned twice in the New Testament, and it was a subject of much writing in the Patristic period. Medieval mystics such as Bernard of Clairvaux and, later, John of Ruysbroeck were much concerned with discernment. Ignatius of Loyola made discernment a major focus of his classic work, the *Spiritual Exercises*, and Jesuit spirituality in recent centuries has made discernment an important factor in modern Catholicism, a factor which has had a notable resurgence in recent decades. Protestantism has also been concerned with discernment over the last few centuries. Sometimes the Protestant concern has stressed the reality of discernment while using other terms (cf. the Wesleys' emphasis on religious experience), but in other cases Protestants have explicitly written on discernment.

There is one interesting parallel between the history of discernment and the history of aesthetics. In both cases there have been ongoing debates about the nature of valid criteria for testing whether artistic expressions or discernments are of genuine value. Many different sets of criteria have been proposed, both for testing works of art and for testing discernments. Most would seem to agree that the experience of great art and the experience of discernment go beyond what we are able to describe in logical terms, but there is no uniform approach to the criteria question.

A great deal more could be said about the history and methods of discernment and about discernment's impact on the contemporary Church.[59] Our purpose, however, is simply to point out that the discernment tradition, with its emphasis on the truth to be found within the human subject, stands as a very important instance of the Christian tradition's moving beyond logic and discursive methodologies in its approach to meaning and life. Especially since discernment relates to decision making, and therefore to moral thinking, the history of discernment seems to have much to offer for an inquiry into the role of imagination and creativity in moral theology. Some scholars would argue that every moral decision is at least partly an exercise of discernment and thus a creative or imaginative endeavor.[60]

Mysticism

While the discernment of spirits tradition concentrates mostly upon the stirrings, impulses, etc., which humans experience when considering various alternatives for action, mysticism seeks to penetrate even more deeply into the roots of human consciousness and experience so as to come into union with the very center from which human existence springs. Mysticism thus stands as an especially clear claim to human understanding which goes beyond the discursive.[61]

A remarkable fact about mysticism is its widespread occurrence in so many different historical and cultural situations. Claims for mystical experience can be found in most of the world's great religions.[62] Mystical experience even occurs in groups which are not theistic, but only religious in the broader sense of seeing a deeper transcendent meaning in life. Almost all forms of mysticism speak of mysticism as involving a profound experience of unity with reality, but there is much variety as to what this experience of unity involves. Some forms of mysticism tend to be pantheistic, identifying God with the entirety of creation, while other forms are more monotheistic, seeing God as the transcendent source of all creation. Some mystics are more unworldly, seeing their experience as something of an escape from the surrounding world. These mystics tend to describe mystical experience as a direct intuition of God, separate from all other human experience. But other mystics are much more worldly in their approach, i.e., they see mystical experience as integrated with their concrete day to day experience here on earth.

Three major points about mysticism's history ought to be noted in the context of this book. The first is that, among many scholars and religious leaders, there has been an ongoing historical nervousness about mystical experience and its genuineness. Mystical experiences have sometimes been claimed by persons who are mentally disturbed or by those on drugs. Some mystical experiences have diverged very far from what humanity has learned through reason. Some mysticism seems to have come from an escapist approach to life. Both churches and scholarship have found it necessary at times in history to reject a given form of mysticism as unacceptable. Usually these rejections have been of a specific approach, with most scholars and Church leaders considering mysticism itself to be a genuine human experience. When mysticism has been accepted as a true possibility by philosophy and theology, it has been accepted partly because its approaches and more discursive approaches were seen to be compatible, with each supporting the other. This point is instructive for a moral theology of imagination; it too will need to dialogue with principles. The dialogue will be necessary because in a unified humanity, the several forms of knowing (principles, mystical insights, experiential learning, etc.) ought to be fundamentally coherent with each other.

The second point is that when mystical experience has been accepted as genuine, it has been seen as an experience closely related to artistic experience.[63] Thus many of the major insights about an aesthetic vision of reality can be applied to mysticism as well. Indeed the existence of aesthetic experience is a key factor which has prompted many thinkers to take mystical experience seriously.

The third point is that, while some approaches to mysticism have been quite esoteric and considered mystical experience as only for the few, a fair analysis would suggest that at least some elements in mystical experience are widely available in human experience.

Recent studies on mysticism and holiness have especially emphasized this theme.[64] Admittedly there may only be few great artists and few great mystics. But just as many can be moved humanly through the experience of great art, so too many persons would seem to be able to respond in some way to mystical experience. Mysticism, like art, raises many possibilities for an imaginative interpretation of reality. These possibilities help open the issue of a more imaginative moral theology. They are possibilities for the many, not simply for the few.

Ways of Knowing God

To expand on the issues just discussed, brief notice can be taken of the medieval mystics' approach to knowing God. An important insight of the medieval mystics was that there are three ways of coming to a knowledge of God.[65] The first of these ways was called the *via affirmativa* (the affirmative way). This approach held that we could affirm certain truths about God, that we could make true statements about who God is. The *via affirmativa* thus opened the possibility for rational or logical statements about God. The medievals were clear, however, that the *via affirmativa* was not the only way to speak about God. They went on to speak of a *via negativa* (the negative way) in which we could move toward understanding of God by denying finite realities of God. Thus God became infinite, incomprehensible, immovable, etc. This second way to know God already began the move beyond the discursive, but it only prepared the ground for the medieval mystics' third and most significant way of knowing God. This was the *via eminentiae seu transcendentiae* (the way of eminence or transcendence). This third way suggests a transcendent knowledge of God which goes beyond all categorical approaches. If moral theology seeks to discover the "God dimension" in our moral choices, it would seem appropriate for moral theology to follow medieval mysticism in seeking transcendent and mystical ways of knowing God.

Along with other issues which could be cited, the issues of discernment, mysticism, and transcending knowledge of God all serve to show that the history of spirituality offers many insights into the possible nature of a moral theology which makes use of imagination and creativity. In what follows we will have much use for the insights available from the history of spirituality.

THE HISTORY OF MORAL THEOLOGY

The previous sections of this chapter have surveyed the history of several key disciplines which can assist our project of articulating a moral theology of imagination. Besides these disciplines, the history of moral theology itself offers much that will help us as this book unfolds. Even though ethics and moral theology have clearly stressed moral principles, they have also raised many other issues about the nature of our moral knowing. Here three of the key issues from the history of moral thinking will be reviewed: practical reason, probabilism, and conscience.

Practical Reason

If we look at the major historical thinkers who wrote on ethics, we very often find that these thinkers used care in distinguishing the type of reasoning used in abstract logic from the type of reasoning used in ethics. Great thinkers recognized that since ethics dealt with concrete matters, its thought patterns could not be quite the same as the patterns found in logic. Aristotle, as we have seen, spoke of *phronesis* which is the mental operation used in moral judgment.[66] He distinguished *phronesis* from theoretical knowledge, and also from poetic or productive knowledge. It is well known that Immanuel Kant saw it necessary to follow his *Critique of Pure Reason* with a second critique, the *Critique of Practical Reason*. Daniel Maguire has recently shown how Thomas Aquinas also made a significant use of practical reason in his approach to moral matters.[67]

Our purpose here is not to go into a detailed analysis and critique of how practical reason functioned in Aristotle, Aquinas, Kant, and others. Our point is simply to argue that the historical prominence of notions such as practical reason shows that geniuses of the past recognized that moral reasoning was not the same as abstract logic. Efforts to work out a theology of imagination and ethics today will differ from the *ratio practica* approaches of the past, but they will build on these approaches. Especially in Chapter 4 we will develop the implications of the traditional insight that moral reasoning is different from other forms of reasoning.

Probabilism

An investigation of Roman Catholic moral theology in and around the eighteenth century shows an interesting further example of the kind of thinking just discussed in terms of practical reason. The problem which confronted Catholic moralists in the eighteenth century was that very often there was no simple deductive way to exclude all doubt about which course of action to take on a given moral issue. The very fact that there were so many concrete possibilities for action tended to bring about instances in which moral decision making could not be a closed system such as logic. Several options emerged in the debate over what one should decide when one was in moral doubt. Some thought that the safest course should always be followed. Some thought that any course whatever could be followed when there was doubt. The more commonly accepted opinion, however, was that, when there was doubt, one could resolve the doubt by following any opinion which was reasonably or, as was usually said, solidly probable.

Various problems can be raised about the tradition of probabilism. One difficulty was that solid probability was usually assessed by checking whether or not several theologians agreed with an opinion, so that the criterion for probability was quite external. This external orientation might be called the "counting noses" approach to probabilism, and it is to be hoped that a contemporary and imaginative moral theology might come up with something more than a counting of noses. A second difficulty was that in the probabilist tradition doubt about an issue could always be removed by a clear statement on the part of the appropriate law maker. This notion about clear law always solving moral dilemmas creates a high confidence in law's ability to address all concrete cases, a confidence which many metaphysicians and moralists would not hold today.

But even granting these problems, the probabilist tradition is a very clear historical instance of moral theology's not being an exact science, but quite often an effort on the part of decision makers to do the best they could with the resources at hand.[68] It is hard to read the historical material pertinent to probabilism without getting the impression that the probabilist authors understood moral theology to be at least partly a matter of following one's best hunch. To put this in another more sophisticated way, the probabilist tradition has always suggested that the making of moral decisions is an art as well as a science.[69] To the extent that it is an art, moral theology stands to be enriched by a stress on imaginative creativity.

Conscience

Traditional moral thinking about conscience also fits in with our considerations about moral thinking being more than logic. If we look to the long history of thinking about conscience,[70] one important note emerges, namely that, in terms of a person's moral worth and dignity, it is more important that a person be sure of his or her choices than that he or she be correct. Of course the person has to do everything possible to assure that a moral decision made in conscience is the correct decision. But if the person has done everything possible to be correct, the person remains a good moral person even if he or she makes an incorrect decision. In this case the person is clearly acting in good faith and is therefore a morally good person. Acting out of honest conviction is thus the most central measure of a person's moral worth in traditional moral theology.

Surely, such an understanding of conscience suggests that the criteria for making moral choices are not quite the same as the criteria for logical deductions, and that moral choices are very often not closed logical entities. In articulating this perspective on conscience, traditional metaphysics and moral theology explicitly recognized that moral certainty did not have the same open and shut character as metaphysical or mathematical certainty. All this leads us to an important conclusion, namely that in building a whole moral theology for persons of conscience, we need more than mathematical or metaphysical perspectives.

Perhaps the best way to summarize this chapter is to call it a chapter of "historical building blocks." While we have not described or evaluated each building block in detail, we have cited an impressive number of them. They will help us construct a moral theology of creativity and imagination. There are also numerous contemporary building blocks to which we will turn in the next chapter.

3

Some Contemporary Insights Supporting a Moral Theology of Imagination

The focus of this chapter will be quite similar to the preceding chapter, except that this chapter will deal with contemporary insights which give foundation to a moral theology of imagination. The chapter will deal with four major areas: first, related developments in contemporary philosophy, fundamental theology, and aesthetics; second, developments in psychology; third, developments in moral theology itself; fourth, current developments in biblical interpretation. The first and third of these four areas will be dealt with at much more length than the other two. We will not, however, undertake a complete or full length examination of any of the areas. Rather our purpose will be to briefly review these major areas so that we can draw upon them in the next chapter which will attempt to construct a moral theology of imagination.

At first I had considered giving this chapter five sections, with the fifth section dealing with the pertinent insights of feminist theologies. Without doubt feminist approaches have helped us break out of past overly rational stereotypes and toward a more imaginative and creative process of philosophizing and theologizing. On reflection it seems to me that feminist perspectives have influenced each of the four areas we will take up, in various ways and to various degrees. Thus rather than a separate section, it seems best to keep in mind the importance of feminist thinking as we go through each of the four sections of this chapter, and as we move into the remaining chapters. If we are less exclusively preoccupied with one-sidedly rational approaches in contemporary philosophy, theology, Scripture, and ethics, we should not forget that we owe that less exclusive preoccupation at least partly to the women's movement.[1]

CONTEMPORARY PHILOSOPHY AND FUNDAMENTAL THEOLOGY

Transcendental Thomism

In the last few centuries, Thomistic philosophy came to be more and more under the influence of the modern scientific idea of certain objective knowledge of the truth, with this knowledge being very much separated from the real and vital mental life of the knower who knows truth. Modern science has been very preoccupied with physical facts and very suspicious of our knowing processes which are thought to somehow distort the facts, and some forms of Thomism picked up much of this one-sided scientific outlook. Late in the last century Pope Leo XIII issued his great encyclical *Aeterni Patris* which began a revitalization process in Thomistic thought. The renewal of Thomism continued into our own century with the neo-Thomist scholarship of authors such as Jacques Maritain and Etienne Gilson. These authors began to open up some of the dynamism in Thomas' thought, with Maritain's treatment of poetic and mystical intuition in his book *Creative Intuition in Art and Poetry* being a major example.[2]

An even deeper renewal of Thomism came about beginning in the early 1900's with the work of Joseph Maréchal and Pierre Rousselot and continuing in our own era with the scholarship of Karl Rahner, Bernard Lonergan, and their followers.[3] This renewal of Thomism is known as Transcendental Thomism, and it has had an enormous impact on the Catholic Church in the Vatican II period. Even the critics of Transcendental Thomism concede its remarkable importance in stimulating the theological advances which emerged during the Vatican II period.[4]

Transcendental Thomism of course accepts the position of most Thomists that, as human beings, we truly know reality. But it also thinks that Kant's question (i.e., the question of the conditions within us which make it possible for us to know) is deeply significant. Kant's inquiry into these ''conditions of possibility'' within us is a transcendental inquiry precisely because the conditions it searches for are what make us transcend other kinds of beings who cannot know as we humans know. Kant's difficulty was that he never really succeeded in linking the transcendental conditions of human knowing with real actual knowing. His philosophy remained on an ideal level.

The Transcendental Thomists' goal is to bring together Thomas' realism and Kant's transcendentalism. They link the two not by positing any sort of *post factum* bridge or connecting link between knowing persons and the things which persons know. Such a bridge would never work anyway. Instead, the Transcendental Thomists insist that in the very act of knowing both the human subject's conditions for knowing and the objects known are immediately present. Maréchal speaks of an immediate and dynamic union of the knower and the known.[5] Rahner, borrowing from Martin Heidegger, uses the notion of *Vollzug* (performance) to insist that we really accomplish or perform actual knowing instead of only theorizing about how we are equipped to accomplish knowing.[6] Heidegger's approach to the metaphysics of knowing will recur as an important theme in the next few sections of this chapter when we consider contemporary philosophies of hermeneutics and language.

The Transcendental Thomists all begin with this basic step of fusing the realistic metaphysics of Thomas with the transcendental inquiry of Kant. But different Transcendental Thomists elaborate their common insight in different ways. Bernard Lonergan has a deep interest in Newman, and, like Newman, an orientation toward dialoguing with the British empirical tradition. Rahner, in addition to his direct studies under Heidegger, has roots in the debates over German idealism and he is very familiar with existential phenomenology. Rahner's doctoral dissertation was a brilliant retrieval of a more whole vision of Thomas' metaphysics and epistemology. Much that we saw in the last chapter about Thomas' approach to the agent intellect and to our knowing on the basis of an *excessus* or excess toward being is better understood today because of Rahner's work on Thomas.[7] Rahner's position that we know out of a pre-apprehension (*Vorgriff*, a term with a Heideggerian background) of reality shows the transcendental turn which he has integrated into his fundamentally Thomist approach.[8]

The importance of Transcendental Thomism for our project of a moral theology of imagination is this: once we begin to look at how we know as well as at what we know, we can no longer propound approaches to moral theology which uncritically adopt the scientific ideal and ignore the issue of how we humans come to moral truth. Moral theology will no longer be a search for some pre-existing "out-there-now-real";[9] rather, the real moral truth will unfold itself as we appropriate it in a learning dialogue. This does not mean that a moral theology working out of Transcendental Thomism will turn to relativism, but such a moral theology will explore most seriously the question of how moral learning takes place.

For instance, themes such as story and the practice of virtue will emerge as very important when we look, transcendentally, into the necessary conditions which make moral learning possible. Most especially, the question of a moral imagining will emerge as a crucial aspect of the process of coming to moral insight. If, as Transcendental Thomism says, our thought processes are truly dynamic, creative imagination seems a major way to make moral theology more dynamic. Rahner himself titled the last chapter of his dissertation "The Possibility of Metaphysics on the Basis of the Imagination."[10] A moral theology springing from Transcendental Thomism will follow this in looking at the possibility of moral theology on the basis of the imagination.

The Emergence of the Hermeneutic Question

Like Transcendental Thomism, contemporary hermeneutic philosophy has had a major impact on all human thought, including theology. To explain the importance of hermeneutics for theology, we will summarize hermeneutical thinking from Schleiermacher and his predecessors up to the current work of Paul Ricoeur.[11] At the end of the summary, we will look at the specific importance of hermeneutic philosophy for moral theology, especially for a moral theology of imagination.

The hermeneutic question, i.e., the question of how we interpret texts, has existed throughout human history. We saw earlier that a central preoccupation of medieval aesthetics was the issue of how to interpret Scripture. Before modern times, however, it was thought that all interpretations could ultimately be corrected so as to fit into some kind of overarching synthesis. There were no ultimate problems in interpreting texts. In modern times, with the development of the critical philosophies of Descartes and Kant, the problem of interpreting texts and avoiding misunderstandings became a more central issue in human thought.

Early in modern times, the concern about textual hermeneutics had two main features. First, such hermeneutics tended to be regional, i.e., to deal with individual interpretation problems (in Scripture, science, etc.).[12] No major effort was made to develop any universal metaphysical approach to the problem of interpretation. Second, following the tenor of the times, early modern hermeneutics tended to be highly polarized. Working from one pole, some hermeneutical theories tended to be highly positivistic. These theories insisted on our ability to come to pure objective interpretations, e.g., to reconstruct history exactly as it occurred, free of any prejudice. Such positivistic theories moved toward what later writers would call a "hermeneutics of suspicion,"[13] seeking to remove all false accretions from texts, and rejecting as invalid all understandings of texts that developed in ages subsequent to the writing of the text. Much of the earlier modern biblical criticism moved in the direction of this positivist hermeneutics.

Other hermeneutical theories rejected the notion of a positivist recovery of the scientific meaning of the text. These theories were much more concerned with the inner mental state of the author of the text. Recovering the author's genius and intention was the proper goal of textual interpretation. Both Kant and Coleridge's notions of imagination went in this more subjective direction, as did romantic poetry and literature in general. Croce's intuitionist aesthetics worked along these same lines. Romanticist aesthetics became very much separated from science and from objective truth, so that aesthetics became marginalized in the minds of many.[14] The decline of the liberal arts which we have seen in our own century no doubt stems at least partially from this marginalization of aesthetics.

In the early part of the nineteenth century, Friedrich Schleiermacher moved the hermeneutic question from a regional question (usually about Scriptures or about classical antiquity) to a universal question about how we interpret all texts, a universal question about how we interpret all reality. While Schleiermacher's question was of decisive importance, he never really succeeded in answering it. Schleiermacher realized that both technical inquiries about the exact meaning of a text and more psychological inquiries into the mind of the author were important in hermeneutics, but he was not able to integrate these two forms of inquiry. Like the Kantian and romanticist which he was, Schleiermacher inclined to favor the psychological side of interpretation theory. This of course was unacceptable to many scientific positivist thinkers who saw Schleiermacher as being involved in a hermeneutic circle from which he could never break out toward real truth. This critique of Schleiermacher should not, however, obscure the fact that he may well have been the first person to ask the right hermeneutical question, i.e., the critical question of a universal approach to hermeneutics.[15]

In the mid and late nineteenth century, a major intellectual event was the development of modern scientific approaches to history in the scholarship of authors such as von Ranke and Droysen. At the same time the other human sciences were beginning to make their impact felt. All these developing human sciences lacked the kind of hard data which is the ideal in the physical sciences. Thus, the issue of the truth status of the human sciences, especially of history, became an increasingly crucial project for hermeneutics or interpretation theory. This was especially so for Wilhelm Dilthey whose work at the end of the nineteenth and the beginning of the twentieth century made the interpretation of history the basic issue in hermeneutics. Dilthey realized that history should no longer be understood as a series of discrete, fully measurable events, but that rather we will understand history by understanding the interconnection of historical events. But Dilthey also held on to the need to explain history and the other human sciences in a positivist, natural science oriented manner. Dilthey was not able to overcome the tension in his thought between understanding history psychologically and explaining it scientifically. Like Schleiermacher, Dilthey, with his historical emphasis, had moved the hermeneutic problem even further onto the central stage of modern thought. But also like Schleiermacher, he leaned enough toward the Kantian idea of getting into the mind of past historical figures that he was unable to break out of the hermeneutic circle.[16]

Advances in Twentieth Century Hermeneutics:
Phenomenology and Ontology

The last few paragraphs have sought to set the stage for the growth of twentieth century hermeneutic philosophy which, as we shall see, proves to be crucially important for today's approach to imagination. Early in our century two major developments occurred in the hermeneutic debate: the phenomenology of scholars such as Husserl, Scheler, and Merleau-Ponty, and the ontological approach of Martin Heidegger and, more recently, of Hans-Georg Gadamer.

Husserl's phenomenology stressed the importance of our conscious experience of things. Scientific thought was so concerned with the goal of getting at things as they are in themselves that human experience was often not dealt with. Husserl sought to bracket human experience, to describe things from the point of view of our consciousness of them, rather than from the point of view of scientific or metaphysical reality. Human beings, for instance, experience sunrises, even if there is no such thing as a sunrise from the point of view of Copernican astronomy.[17]

Husserl's phenomenology is most helpful to us as we wrestle with our experiences of language, art, historical events, etc. Phenomenology can help rescue us from one-sidedly scientific approaches to reality. Important contemporary philosophers of the hermeneutic question such as Paul Ricoeur have called for a grafting of phenomenology into contemporary hermeneutics.[18] Phenomenological descriptions would also seem to be an aid to us as we strive to make moral choices. Knowing how something is experienced in a person's consciousness could well be an important help in the moral evaluation of that which is experienced.

At the same time it must be acknowledged that Husserl's bracketing or reduction of all things to our conscious experience of them is a method which is ultimately too much cut off from the metaphysical question about what things mean at the level of essence. To put this in another way, Husserl's phenomenology ultimately retreats into a Kantian idealism. Thus while phenomenology can greatly aid the hermeneutical quest, it is not an adequate hermeneutics in and of itself.

Perhaps the most decisive advance in the entire history of hermeneutics is found in the shift to ontology in the work of Martin Heidegger. In general, earlier hermeneutics had started out by assuming that scientific explanation of an action and interior psychological interpretation of the mind of the person doing the action were two separate realities. Then earlier hermeneutics sought to develop an epistemology which would reunite these two realities. Heidegger, in his famous analytic of *Dasein* (There-being), argued that the very act of finite historical knowing about events is essentially a true metaphysical reality.[19] Thus there is no longer any need to find any epistemological bridge to put psychological interpretation and scientific explanation together. They are together in the very essence of the human person's finite knowing of historical truth. Past approaches had tended to set our finite historical interpreting power aside and to search for some absolute or God-like epistemology, which would never be found. After Heidegger there would be less fear that limited human understanding was not true understanding, and less fear that science would be defective if it were tainted with human interpretation. A true hermeneutics was now possible. As Paul Ricoeur would later put it, after Heidegger's ontology, it became possible to speak of a hermeneutic arc, rather than a hermeneutic circle.[20]

Heidegger's ontological approach to hermeneutics has been most notably developed and articulated by Hans-Georg Gadamer in his brilliant work *Truth and Method*. Gadamer begins with an inquiry into aesthetics in which he de-Kantianizes the prejudices of many moderns who hold that aesthetics takes us into subjectivity but not into truth. Gadamer's notion of play is an especially significant element in his notion of aesthetics. When we play, we suspend some of our inhibitions or prejudices so as to truly enter into the game. The result is that in many respects, the game plays us more than we play the game. The game's playing us makes true and very often new understanding possible in the dialogue between the game and ourselves.[21] Similarly in art, it is not so much a question of our penetrating into the mind of the artist to understand the work of art. The art work too plays us and understanding ensues.

Gadamer moves on in the second and third parts of his book to deal with history and the human sciences, and then with an ontology of human language. He sees the human person's ongoing appropriation of meaning, as meaning represents itself in language, to be paradigmatic of all true human understanding. As historical finite beings with our prejudices (which are not necessarily bad for Gadamer),[22] we understand in interaction with texts whose presented meaning we interpret as we move through the context of history. From this perspective, both works of history and works of fiction are equally able to convey reality to us.[23]

The Work of Paul Ricoeur

In my judgment, in the latter part of the twentieth century, the most significant research on hermeneutics (and also on philosophy in general) is to be found in the writings of the French philosopher Paul Ricoeur. Ricoeur shows himself to be very much in sympathy with the historical perspectives which Gadamer offers on the hermeneutic problem. He also agrees with the ontological turn in hermeneutics to be found in both Heidegger and Gadamer. The one place where he disagrees with Gadamer (and at times he calls it a small disagreement) is that he does not believe that Gadamer, with his high ontological emphasis, has sufficiently developed the methodological aspects of textual interpretation.[24] Ricoeur, while holding to the ontology of hermeneutics, has very much developed the methodology of language interpretation, both in his work on the nature of text and in his highly important writings on metaphor.[25] In dealing with metaphor, he has also touched most helpfully, though less extensively, on the subject of imagination.[26] We will briefly review all three of these themes—text, metaphor, and imagination—as they occur in Ricoeur's works.

Text

Among Ricoeur's many rich insights on written texts,[27] the following three points can be noted. First, because texts are written, they acquire a life and status of their own, independently of the authors who write them. Texts in other words get "distantiated"[28] from their authors. Thus it is possible for us to truly interpret and understand texts without having to understand the intentions of the original authors or the first readers of the texts. Nineteenth century scholars constantly got hung up on the problem of how to get behind texts. Ricoeur, in a manner which echoes Gadamer's notion of play, sees texts as opening up a world "in front of"[29] them where true interaction with the reader and true appropriation by the reader is possible. Such an approach to traditional texts in moral theology would seem to offer a much revitalized method of understanding moral texts, a method which might help moral principles (which can be seen as texts) to come alive again.

Second, Ricoeur insists that, in addition to texts making sense which can be understood through the rules of structural linguistics or semiotics, texts also have reference, i.e., texts point toward meanings.[30] To put this in another way, Ricoeur states that texts are discourse about something. Ricoeur does not object to the structural analysis of texts but he does reject the one-sided outlook of French structuralism.[31] This structuralism, in a manner reminiscent of older approaches to pure scientific knowledge and to formal aesthetics, limits linguistic studies only to the immediate sense of the text which is worked out on the basis of precise and exact rules. For Ricoeur, the world that the text opens out in front of us is more than the world of scientific logic; it is a world of meaning mediated through texts. Moral principles interpreted through this kind of approach to texts would be principles which give us genuine meaning and truth. Such moral principles would surely not lead us into relativism.

Third, Ricoeur points out that a major characteristic of texts is that they contain words which are polysemic, i.e., capable of having many meanings.[32] This is why human interpretation of texts which truly bear meaning is a recurrent necessity. The truth of texts emerges as the texts are interpreted by the readers whose very essence, ontologically, is to be finite historical knowers. This is how human understanding takes place: in creative appropriation of the meaning of texts rather than through positivistic science or idealist epistemology. This suggests that both Ricoeur and Gadamer have a considerable affinity with the work of Aquinas, especially as Aquinas is understood by the Transcendental Thomists. Gadamer shows this affinity by his explicit reference to Thomas' notion of agent intellect.[33]

Ricoeur goes on to apply this notion of texts to a wide variety of fields, arguing, for example, that the insights of the human sciences are basically texts to be interpreted hermeneutically. Citing all of Ricoeur's applications of his text model would take us too far afield, though we have already noted that moral principles might well be approached through Ricoeur's notion of textual interpretation.

Metaphor

While Ricoeur deals with a wide variety of texts and other realities which he interprets as texts, there is one particular textual reality whose interpretation Ricoeur sees as paradigmatic for all other texts.[34] This paradigmatic textual reality is metaphor. Ricoeur quickly rejects an ornamental theory of metaphor which holds that metaphor's purpose is simply to decorate a work or to add in a dash of colorful variation.[35] Rather, Ricoeur holds that metaphor confronts the reader with something which is logically absurd, something which the reader must strive to assimilate and relate to meanings which the reader already possesses. To construct the meaning of the metaphor the reader must in one sense let go of his or her pre-conceived notions, but at the same time the reader cannot construe metaphor to mean anything he or she wishes; rather the reader must find something which is familiar in the strange.[36] Understood in this way the metaphoric process calls for genuine creativity on the part of the interpreter (as well as on the part of the originator of the metaphor).

Ricoeur would argue that this process of being confronted with the unfamiliar, and being creatively stretched to find new meanings, is actually what happens in all our efforts to understand texts. The predication of any notion about the subject of a sentence is analogous to a metaphorical statement about the subject. At least pre-consciously, the person articulating the sentence is always reaching out and seeking after deeper meaning. With this in mind it may prove very helpful to attend to the metaphorical aspects of our texts in moral theology.

Ricoeur sees the metaphorical process as running in two directions.[37] To get at the sense of a text, we must begin by constructing the meaning of the individual metaphors. But to get at the deeper meaning of the individual metaphors we must understand them in light of the text as a whole. In all metaphors what we are doing is redescribing reality and thus extending the battlefront of what we can express.[38] Hence metaphor opens up for us the possibility of a textual hermeneutics which restores and recollects reality in a constructive fashion. Such an approach takes us far beyond the hermeneutics of suspicion.

Imagination

In commenting on his own interpreters, Ricoeur has suggested that metaphorical process might be seen as the epistemological process of interpreting texts.[39] But, in Ricoeur's perspective, what is happening ontologically when we exercise linguistic creativity through the metaphoric process? What is happening ontologically is that we are exercising imagination. Ricoeur has not written on imagination nearly as much as on metaphor, but he does not disagree with those scholars who see imagination as a central though somewhat implicit theme in his thought.[40]

In general Ricoeur's writings on imagination are more concerned with how imagination functions than with a metaphysical description of imagination. Ricoeur tends to follow Kant's schematization of productive imagination, and from this schematization he sees imagination as giving foundation to the metaphoric process in three ways. First, imagination enables us to form vision, to see reality as a whole on a conceptual level. Second, and on a more sense-oriented level, imagination helps us to form pictures or figures (recall that metaphor is a figure of speech) out of which our vision can spring. Ricoeur rejects Hume's notion that imagination is only weakened sense impressions in the mind, but he does see a concrete picturing function as well as an overall vision function in the imagination.

Third, and perhaps most importantly, Ricoeur holds that it is through imagination that we are able to suspend judgment in conflictual situations wherein a metaphor's image does not square with our previous conception of reality. It is precisely through this imaginative suspension of judgment that we are able to resolve metaphorical conflicts and find new meanings in reality.[41] Mary Schaldenbrand, in an excellent article on Ricoeur and imagination, summarizes all of this by stating that Ricoeur's approach to imagination is best understood as the achievement of kinship through conflict.[42] If we can dare to imagine when we face conflicts, perhaps we can find the common roots which underlie our conflicts and then move ahead—together—on the basis of the common or kinship forming roots which metaphorical imagination has opened up for us.

As of now we are only beginning to scratch the surface as regards the implications in moral theology of Ricoeur's notions of text, metaphor, and imagination. But even on the basis of our surface scratching, the possibilities of Ricoeur's hermeneutical approach seem very great in the area of moral theology. So often we find ourself in highly controversial moral situations. With imagination, perhaps both traditionalist and antinomian groups can learn to let go of their prejudices long enough to come to moral interpretations based on deeply creative imagination, moral interpretations which truly capture the heart of our moral texts as these texts must be read and interpreted at this time in history. Such fresh and imaginatively skillful approaches to moral issues will not be easy to work out, but they are much needed in our times.

To close these remarks on Ricoeur and the hermeneutic tradition in philosophy, it should again be noted that our purpose is not a complete philosophical evaluation even though we have seen much that will be very useful in the rest of this book. One small point of criticism relates to something we noted in the last chapter, namely that theories of morality tend to base themselves on three themes: intuition, experiential evidence, and emotion or feeling. Ricoeur's notions of metaphor and imagination seem to relate to two of these themes, intuition and experience, very well. The feeling issue is surely implied in Ricoeur's approach to imagination, but it is a point which needs more development.[43]

Insights from Fundamental Theology

So far we have seen important bases for a moral theology of imagination in two major philosophical systems, Transcendental Thomism and contemporary hermeneutics. We should also note that these philosophies have entered very directly into fundamental theology in the works of David Tracy and others, with Tracy's book *The Analogical Imagination* being especially significant in our context. If we take the position that moral theology can well be understood as a branch of systematic theology, systematic theological approaches to imagination are *ipso facto* moral theological approaches to imagination.

Early in *The Analogical Imagination* Tracy explains and develops Gadamer's notion of the classic.[44] Classics in literature and the arts endure and achieve permanent relevance because, as classics, they contain a "surplus of meaning" which can always address people, which always needs to be interpreted afresh. Tracy then argues that the great documents of the Christian tradition are religious classics, and that the proper function of theologians is to be interpreters of religious classics.[45] For Tracy, the theologian cannot simply be a repeater of what was said in the past. As a repeater he or she would merely pass on *tradita* rather than being an interpreter of a living *traditio*.[46] Nor can the theologian be a totally autonomous generator of new ideas. He or she must let himself or herself be played by the tradition in the spirit of contemporary hermeneutics. In this context Tracy praises the work of Rahner (and later that of others such as Barth and Reinhold Niebuhr)[47] as genuine interpreters, i.e., as persons who retrieved our Christian classics rather than merely repeating them.

Tracy also states that in addition to interpreting the Christian classics, systematic theologians also seek to determine how the various classic texts fit into an overview. But establishing this overview is still a task of interpretation, in which different theologians might stress one of the three themes of manifestation of God's presence, proclamation of the Word, and action for social change.[48]

On the specific theme of imagination in theology, Tracy makes use of one of the major traditional approaches to God and to the infinite, namely that we know God's being and infinity by analogy.[49] God is partly like us and partly not like us so that to move toward a transcendental notion of God we must both affirm and deny things of God. In other words, we must find our likenesses to God in our differences from God. This process is clearly an analogical process. It is very much like the process of imagining that we find in Ricoeur, much like the theme of finding kinship in conflict. If the fundamental theologian's epistemological task is to interpret the classics of our religious tradition, the theologian (and here I would include the moral theologian) does this by exercising a creative imagination, a creative analogical imagination which finds infinite meaning in finite texts.[50]

Other theologians have also taken up the question of the place of imagination in the more fundamental areas of theology.[51] But Tracy's work is most useful for us because of its comprehensiveness, and because of its affinity to the major philosophical trends we have reviewed.

Continuing Work in Aesthetics

In the last chapter we noted the history of aesthetics and saw how philosophers from various traditions sought to find truth in aesthetic works and experiences. We have already seen in this chapter that aesthetics has continued to be a major concern in contemporary philosophy so that current as well as historical aesthetics offers important help in the construction of a moral theology of imagination.

We have quite explicitly cited the aesthetic contributions of Gadamer, including his notions of play, of classics, and of fiction truly mediating truth. Gadamer has other contributions to aesthetics, including a notion of beauty which, although Gadamer does not note it, strikes me as somewhat similar to Aquinas' (or Albert's) notion of splendor of form.[52] Some of the other thinkers we have mentioned in the present chapter have also seen aesthetics as a key element in their imaginative interpretation of reality. Rahner and Heidegger both deal at length with the importance of poetry, with Rahner seeing the poetic word as a way of speaking which is especially apt to express the word of God.[53] Ricoeur's stress on creativity and metaphor clearly has aesthetic overtones.

Other philosophical systems have also been at work on aesthetics. From the point of view of phenomenology, Mikel Dufrenne's *The Phenomenology of Aesthetic Experience*[54] is probably the most important work. Without getting into the metaphysical questions about phenomenology at this point, we can surely state that the descriptions of aesthetic objects and aesthetic experiences which are offered by Dufrenne and other phenomenologists have been a key source for both transcendental and hermeneutic philosophers. Dufrenne's closeness to the work of hermeneutic thinkers is underlined by the fact that he and Ricoeur once wrote jointly in Ricoeur's early and more directly phenomenological years.[55]

Another important contribution to aesthetics has been made by Roger Scruton, writing out of the British analytical-empirical tradition.[56] Like the hermeneutic philosophers, Scruton wishes to get through to what he sees as the genuine truth in aesthetic experience. Thus he has difficulties with the overly intuitive approaches of Kant, Croce, and Collingwood, all of whom end up getting aesthetics and science too far separated from one another. It seems regrettable that Scruton's work does not interact with the hermeneutic or transcendental thinkers discussed above. Nor do authors such as Gadamer and Ricoeur deal very much with the linguistic and aesthetic thinking to be found in contemporary British philosophy (although Ricoeur's criticism of French structuralism would apply to some aspects of British linguistic philosophy). Some worthwhile interconnections and criticisms might emerge from an interfacing of the two systems of thought. Such interconnections and criticisms would further amplify one of the major judgments of this book, the major judgment that aesthetics, with its stress on beauty and form, opens up one of the most central areas for the exercise of human creativity and imagination. In our times, as in any times, the aesthetically sensitive person will be more free to imagine. In particular, he or she will be more free to exercise moral imagination.

After reading these comments about aesthetics and morality, some readers might be inclined to reply that in a number of cases, persons with high aesthetic abilities have not been particularly moral persons. This regrettable fact should remind us that aesthetics and imagination of themselves will never be a completely adequate source for moral theology. At the same time one might also argue that those aesthetically capable persons who lacked moral character may not have had as complete an aesthetic vision of life as appeared to be the case at first glance. A more complete aesthetics might have helped them be more moral persons.

INSIGHTS FROM MEDICINE AND PSYCHOLOGY

Our attention now makes a brief shift to a very different area of human thought: medicine and psychology, disciplines which have made significant modern discoveries about the functioning of the human brain. In 1836 a little known French physician by the name of Marc Dax delivered a paper dealing with *aphasia* (the loss of the power to speak). Dax reported that patients with *aphasia* generally had injuries to the left side of the brain while patients with injuries to the right side of the brain did not lose the power to speak. Previous to Dax's time everyone had assumed that the two hemispheres of the brain were identical mirrors of one another. Even Dax's work was largely ignored until a generation later when another French physician, Paul Broca, began to perform autopsies on patients with speech loss. By the mid 1860's Broca had located a specific area on the left side of the brain where lesions resulted in speech loss. At first this led to many theories about the dominance of the left side of the brain, a dominance which was tied in with the fact that right handedness was controlled by the left side of the brain.

For some time the right side of the brain was ignored in the face of the supposed dominance of the left. By the 1930's, however, medical studies of injuries to the right side of the brain began to show that visual, musical, and spatial abilities were controlled by the right side of the brain. This led to the development of an overall picture in which the right side of the brain was seen as more imaginative and intuitive, while the left side was seen as more logical and rational. Medical researchers today caution against an undue dichotomizing of our brains, and some philosophers still will not relate their theories of human thought to the medical research about the brain. On the whole, however, there seems to be no denying that certain of our mental operations are correlated to certain parts of our brains, even though we do not fully understand all of the correlations.[57]

The early chapters of this book have been arguing that the entire scope of human mental activities ought to be part of a systematic approach to moral theology. In particular we have argued that, while logically derived moral principles are not to be ignored, creative imagination ought to enter into moral theology. Relating this to the modern medical/psychological research, the argument could be restated by saying that we need a moral theology for the right side of the brain (visual imagination) as well as for the left side of the brain (logical principles). More exactly we need a moral theology for the whole person with all pertinent mental activities involved. In the early days of brain research, science downplayed right side brain activities. Moral theology, under the force of the scientist ideal, may have done the same.

Medical research is not of itself a sufficient basis for moral theology or any philosophical discipline. But the insights of medicine about the range of our brain activities do seem to offer an important confirmation of the more philosophical and theological considerations we have made about needing both discursive and non-discursive approaches to meaning. Ricoeur's position that we need to get not only at the logical sense of language (*à la* the French structuralists), but also at the deeper meaning of language (which is discourse drawing on a creative metaphorical process)[58] seems to relate quite well to both sides of the brain. So does much else we have seen.

CONTEMPORARY INSIGHTS IN MORAL THEOLOGY ITSELF

In the previous sections of this chapter, we have looked at a number of current fields of study which offer insights pertinent to the development of a moral theology of imagination. The writings of important contemporary ethicists and moral theologians also offer some highly significant insights which can help in the construction of a moral theology of imagination. Our purpose in this section will be to offer a summary report of these contemporary moral insights, and we shall leave some of the critical and evaluative reflections on them for the next chapter. The summary report will have five sections: vision and Christian vision, themes which enhance vision, liturgy and ethics, virtue and character, and Christian imagination.

Vision and Christian Vision

In the earlier sections of this book, I have argued strongly for the existence of forms of moral knowing other than rational discursive knowing. Many moral theologians today argue in favor of such broader forms of moral knowing. James Gustafson's well-known four "base points" for Christian ethics include not only principles and situational analyses (which are two more logical base points). Gustafson's base points also include a sense of the meaning of human personhood and a sense of the meaning of God, two points which broaden the base of Christian ethics.[59] Charles Curran has recently written a good deal about the "stance" of moral theology, a stance which is based on the paschal mystery as it is experienced in the five dimensions of creation, sin, incarnation, redemption and resurrection.[60]

While various terms might be used to capture this broader basis for Christian moral knowing, the idea that this broader basis is a "seeing," or, more precisely, a form of vision, strikes me as most helpful. Stanley Hauerwas of Notre Dame has articulated this theme of vision most fully,[61] but the theme has also been made quite central by other authors such as Bernard Häring whose major recent work on moral theology begins with the notion of a vision of the whole.[62]

Hauerwas works out of a deep conviction that moral choices are much more than isolated moments of decision.[63] Instead our moral choices say something about us who decide. Even more so, our moral choices are not isolated incidents because they come from our history and from our roots in community. Precisely here vision assumes primary importance for Hauerwas. With vision we can see community shared values. With vision we can be in touch with the historical roots which engender our values. Morally speaking, vision is not just a vision of anything we wish. It is a vision of the good. In this respect, Hauerwas closely follows the insights of the novelist/ philosopher Iris Murdoch.

In our context, it is important to note that Hauerwas specifically connects his notion of moral vision with aesthetics, even tying the two themes together in an article title.[64] Good art for Hauerwas makes a claim on us; it makes us look at realities we otherwise might not see. He quotes Murdoch on the artist's need to let himself or herself be tested by the art work which has its own autonomy, and holds that moral judgment must follow a similar pattern. All this has similarities to the notion of Gadamer and Ricoeur that we are played by the texts we interpret.

The comments so far made about vision could be applied to any sound moral vision, no matter what sources shape the vision. But Christian moral theologians are not just writing about any moral vision. They are writing about Christian vision. Thus, the more-than-rational vision which shapes Christian morality is specifically Christian and especially biblical. Häring's vision of the whole is so rich in its scriptural bases that some students, so much used to the scientific in ethics, find his writing coming from a very different world. Curran's fivefold paschal mystery stance seeks to root moral theology in a Christian context. James Gustafson's major new work *Ethics from a Theocentric Perspective*[65] does very much the same thing. We will see more of Hauerwas' thinking on this point when we consider current moral writing on the imagination, but he too opts for a Christian vision.

The comments above do not deal with the exact question of how Christian vision shapes our approach to morality or how this vision interrelates with other elements in our moral experience. Such questions will be looked at in the next chapter and later. For now the point is simple: Christian vision is a key notion for many of today's moral thinkers. It is a notion which ties in strongly with this book's basic theme of moral theology and imagination. Our vision, our seeing life as it is, involves more than logic. Our vision is a creative, integrating, imaginative grasp of the meaning of life.

Themes Which Enhance Our Vision

Ethicists such as those mentioned above do not limit themselves simply to general statements about vision. These authors also turn to various vision builders, i.e., to specific types of human experience and activity which can enhance our Christian vision. One of the most important and commonly discussed of these "vision enhancers" is narrative or story. Through narrative and story we are able to get in touch with the roots out of which our vision is formed. Thus in stories a type of learning is possible which we cannot achieve through discursive processes.

The contemporary concern for story goes far beyond the realm of moral theology. The great success of the book and TV series *Roots* and the ever increasing popularity of genealogical research show the concern for story in society at large. The interest in journal workshops and the keeping of journals suggests the same thing. In theology, some scholars are exploring a theology by autobiography, e.g., Gregory Baum with his collection of theological autobiographies in the book *Journeys*. Even more significant is the work of John Shea who has devoted several highly creative books to the theme of putting us in touch with our faith by means of stories.[66]

In the field of ethics, two authors who have especially stressed the theme of narrative or story are Stanley Hauerwas and Alasdair MacIntyre. Hauerwas' most succinct statement on the importance of narrative is found in his commentary on Richard Adams' *Watership Down*, the story of a rabbit community.[67] In the ten theses which begin his commentary, Hauerwas makes several key points. He states that the secular liberal community thinks that we can get along perfectly well without any common story and that such liberalism thinks we can always find scientific answers to all our problems. A story-formed community, on the other hand, will not be so sure that it has all the answers. Such a community will listen for surprises, for strangers, and for imaginative new ideas which it cannot control. The members of such a community with their common story will also have a real caring for one another, a caring which will manifest itself in acts of kindness, trust, etc. Much that Hauerwas says here seems right on target in our present context. As a society we very much need to let go of our excessive confidence in science so as to be truly imaginative about our future, e.g., about our future approach to the nuclear weapons issue. Perhaps we can do some of this moral imagining if we are a community with a vision formed in a common story.

Alasdair MacIntyre states that we live our lives in narrative form even before any artist or poet writes narrative accounts of our lives.[68] It is thus impossible for anyone to morally evaluate any individual action when the action is taken from its narrative context. Only when we look at a human action as part of a narrative does that action have intelligibility or moral meaning. We act out of a larger wholeness which narrative enables us to envision. MacIntyre, like Daniel Callahan and Edward Shils, also lays great stress on the importance of tradition as a source of objective moral wisdom. Tradition heightens narrative's importance because narrative serves to bear tradition to us.[69]

Besides narrative, some of today's moralists mention another pair of vision enhancers which are often found within the fabric of narratives. This pair is the comic and the tragic. We have seen that since ancient times, the comic and the tragic have been thought to mediate the meaning of life to us. Daniel Maguire is one of the current moralists to write on the importance of the comic or humorous.[70] Humor for Maguire gives us a vision into the meaning of our humanity, especially into our finitude. Humor is one of the best ways to help us get past the human tendency to absolutize the relative, to help us remember that only God is God (here there are echoes of H. Richard Niebuhr's notion of radical monotheism).[71] Humor confronts us with the incongruous in our lives. Through dealing with incongruity, humor reminds us that, as finite beings, we do not have logical answers to all the problems we face. Maguire's insights on humor remind one of Rahner's notion that in laughter we let ourselves go, we give up the effort to always be in control.[72] Bernard Häring also sees humor as quite important in the moral life. Many of Häring insights on humor parallel those of Maguire. Häring adds the very significant note that there are close links between humor and the ability to love humanly.[73]

Humor can of course be abused. All we need do to see this is to consider the persistence of sexist, ethnic, and racist jokes which use humor to dehumanize rather than to humanize. But in general, laughter does connect us with life. It does so by getting beyond the discursive, by getting us to the level of creative imagination.

Humor is very often interconnected with tragedy, with groups that have suffered much tragedy often being possessed of great humor as well. A number of moralists are clear that moral learning and growth can take place through the experience of suffering and tragedy. Hauerwas develops his approach to tragedy by critiquing the view of suffering to be found in modern science and in some segments of the natural law tradition. Science and natural law can tend to think that all human problems can be solved by principles. When everything is seen as solvable by principles, the sense of tragedy can disappear. Life's sufferings become problems to be solved rather than mysteries to be contemplated. Hauerwas does not disagree with the conclusions to be made from the double effect principle, e.g., that surgical procedures such as amputations and sterilizations can sometimes be permitted, that some medical treatments need not be offered to dying patients. But the legitimacy of these double effect conclusions does not take away the tragic aspects of sickness and dying, even though some double effect thinking can be so convinced it has the answer that it can forget the tragic.[74]

Once he has asserted the place of the tragic, Hauerwas makes many moving applications of the tragic to ethics. He works out the implications of MacIntyre's notion that medicine is a tragic profession, and he is especially eloquent on the implications of a sense of tragedy for our society's approach to retarded children. A look at the health care field suggests that many doctors and other health professionals can be so imbued with the scientific worldview that they have a hard time dealing with death. A sense of the tragic could surely enhance the human practice of medicine and deepen our understanding of many other life areas as well.[75]

Hauerwas is not alone in calling for a more adequate sense of the tragic in ethics. He is joined by authors such as Maguire and MacIntyre.[76]

Another theme which helps us work out a sense of moral vision is beauty. The traditional aesthetic conviction about the importance of beauty is seen as crucially significant by a number of today's best moralists. We saw earlier that some ancient and medieval scholars held that there was a transcendental or overarching unity between the good, the true, the one, and the beautiful. Thus, if we can truly appreciate beauty (an imaginative process), we have made a good step toward understanding truth and goodness, including moral truth and moral goodness.

Bernard Häring works on this theme of beauty in a key section of his new three volume work. The section is entitled "A Morality of Beauty and Glory."[77] Häring acknowledges that beauty would have little or no meaning in a morality which was only interested in individual actions or individual moral decisions. However, as soon as we say that morality must look at the whole person, beauty becomes a key source of deeper insight into the meaning of the human. True to his method, Häring quickly moves from his reflections on beauty to the specifically Christian experience of the beautiful in our liturgies, Scriptures, and tradition. Of special interest is the fact that Häring ties beauty in with glory or doxology, which, as we shall quickly note, is a key theme in systematic and liturgical theology today.

Liturgy and Ethics

Celebration in general and liturgical celebration in particular could well have been included in the last section with vision enhancers such as narrative, tradition, comedy, tragedy, and beauty. However the interest in liturgy and ethics has been quite high of late; thus, a separate and more emphatic section seems in order. The notion that celebration is an important human event and source of learning is a long-standing notion. We have already seen Gadamer take up this notion in his work on play. Books such as Josef Pieper's *In Tune with the Word: A Theory of Festivity*, Hugo Rahner's *Man at Play*, and Harvey Cox's *The Feast of Fools*[78] all describe the basic human importance of celebration, an importance which excessively logical approaches to life can sometimes forget.

In the field of liturgical studies, scholars have been striving for a deeper and more integrated approach to liturgical worship, an approach which does not see liturgy as a separate compartment, but as integral to life and to theology. The most significant liturgical work taking this approach is Geoffrey Wainwright's *Doxology: The Praise of God in Worship, Doctrine and Life*.[79] Wainwright's title echoes both the concern for a morality of glory which we saw in Häring, and the concerns of Paul Ramsey which we will see shortly.

In the field of Christian ethics, some of the most important work on the theme of liturgy and ethics was done for the 1979 convention of the Society of Christian Ethics and for the follow-up issue of the *Journal of Religious Ethics* which appeared later that year. The *Journal* articles show a general agreement that there is an important relationship between liturgy and Christian ethics, but there are some differences in tone or nuance. Ramsey wishes to interrelate not just liturgical studies and ethics, but liturgical studies, theology, and ethics, i.e., he uses three categories in a manner similar to Wainwright. Ramsey also argues for multidirectional influences between these disciplines so that, for example, ethics can both enrich and be enriched by liturgical experience.[80] Donald Saliers agrees on the importance of the link between liturgy and ethics, but he tends to argue more for liturgy's influencing ethics instead of the other way around.[81] Later on we will need to have a similar discussion about moral principles and imagination. Do moral principles beget imagination? Or vice versa? Or both?

Regardless of how it is articulated, the interplay of liturgy and ethics makes a fundamental point in our context. If ethics and liturgical worship are intertwined, ethics is clearly more than a discursive learning from principles. We are principled people in our morality, but we are praying people too, with our prayer and worship experience being a school of moral insight.

The Virtues and Character

So far our review of contemporary moral thinking has mentioned many valuable sources of moral insight: vision, narrative, tradition, tragedy, comedy, beauty, liturgy. If, in addition to principles, we need these rich sources of moral insight, how do we attain or appropriate them? In my opinion, one of the most exciting and refreshing developments in moral theology today has been the recovery of the ancient notion of virtue as the crucial means of appropriating the communal wisdom found in narratives, etc.

We have traditionally understood that the virtues are good dispositions or good habits, habits we develop by doing good actions again and again. As people of virtue we live out our common vision by practicing it, by doing it, most of all by being it. Logical deductions alone will not be enough for us. The heritage we envision in narrative calls us to live a style of life, to be a certain kind of people. If we do in fact become people of virtue or character, we should be able to make good moral choices, even if we are not always clear on the logical bases of our choices.

If we study the revival of interest in virtue which is taking place in some moral circles today, we can find two main strains to the revival, strains which might be called a weak revival and a strong revival. In the weaker revival, which can be seen in the works of William Frankena, rationally deduced obligation of a Kantian sort is still the most crucial factor in ethics. Virtue is more of an individual reality, helping the person dispose himself or herself to come to terms with the basic rational obligation.[82]

The stronger revival of virtue is most eloquently and articulately present in Alasdair MacIntyre's *After Virtue*.[83] In MacIntyre's view, communally based tradition has developed certain essential practices which we must acquire so as to live a moral life. The acquiring of these practices is virtue, and virtue is the heart of our moral growth. Great writers may produce brilliant new novels or histories, but they cannot do so without first being able to write in a known human language, or no one will understand them. They must have the practice (or virtue) of language. Similarly the great moral hero or heroine may take himself, herself, or society to whole new levels of moral accomplishment, but he or she will do so on the basis of being a virtuous person, a person who has acquired the human moral practices we find embodied in narrative, comedy, tragedy, beauty, etc.

From this perspective, the most important and basic reality or end in ethics is for persons to be virtuous. Indeed to be virtuous is to be ethical. Out of lives of virtuous practice, people will of course look at specific actions and people will try to work out rationally coherent accounts of their actions. But they will deal with actions and reasons precisely as virtuous people. Their reasoning will never be pure in the sense that mathematical and metaphysical reasoning are pure. Their moral reasoning will be built on their experience of living out and developing the practices or virtues which they have acquired from their communities.

Understood in this sense, virtue has undergone a strong revival because it is the means to moral reasoning, not simply an aid to moral reasoning which already exists on some other independent basis. We saw earlier that the great traditional thinkers such as Aristotle and Aquinas were clearly aware that moral reasoning was not the same as mathematical or metaphysical reasoning. Moral reasoning was practical reasoning, i.e., reasoning coming out of practical lived experience. It is thus no surprise that today's revival of the notion of virtue has included a revival of the notion of practical reason in authors like Maguire.[84] MacIntyre himself defines virtues in relation to practices.[85] From practice comes practical reason. And practical reason, both to revitalize tradition and to move to the future, will often need to be imagining and affective reason.

MacIntyre's notable philosophical revival of the concept of virtue is supported by some leading Christian theologians and ethicists. James Gustafson's continuing interest in the dispositions and sentiments which accompany our moral actions closely relates to a virtue ethic.[86] The reunion of spiritual and moral theology in contemporary Roman Catholicism argues to a virtue ethic, i.e., to a concern with who we are as a basis of what we do. We noted this spiritual/moral reunion in Chapter 1. It is especially well exemplified in the writings of Bernard Häring.[87] More conservative Roman Catholic ethicists such as William E. May find the concerns of a virtue ethic to be very congenial. May appreciates the stress on who we are as well as on what we do.

Stanley Hauerwas is the Christian thinker who has most explicitly adopted the approach to virtue found in MacIntyre. Much of Hauerwas' thinking is implicit in the comments on MacIntyre made above. In a review of *After Virtue* (written jointly with Paul Wadell), Hauerwas appears to accept the majority of MacIntyre's insights, especially MacIntyre's historical critique of what has happened to ethics since the enlightenment. Hauerwas' main criticism is that he finds MacIntyre's concept of the virtues as ''practices'' to be vague.[88] Hauerwas holds that MacIntyre would have been clearer on this point if he had grounded his notions in a specific context such as a Christian understanding of life.

The revival of a virtue ethic (which used to be so significant in Catholic moral thought) is surely one of the most major indicators of the growing awareness that there is more to ethics than discursive reasoning. But still there is the issue of how virtue ethics appropriates themes such as narrative and beauty and then leads us forth to creative judgments in the sphere of action, i.e., there is the issue of virtue calling for an imaginative appropriation of themes such as narrative and beauty. As we shall see in the next section, ethicists have already begun to raise this issue.

Moral Theology and Imagination

Many items in the previous sections on contemporary moral theology have important implications for a moral theology of imagination. But in addition to these implications, the issue of moral theology and imagination has been explicitly addressed by ethicists such as Daniel Maguire, Rubem Alves, Stanley Hauerwas, and Philip Rossi.[89] Maguire's treatment is fairly complete. He devotes an entire chapter of his book *The Moral Choice* to creative imagination. In the chapter Maguire develops five main conditions which he sees as necessary for the morally creative imagination: excitement, quiet, work, malleability, and *kairos* (the right moment).[90] Ronald Knox's *Enthusiasm* and Josef Pieper's *Leisure: The Basis of Culture*[91] are among the key works Maguire uses to explain his first two conditions: excitement and quiet or passivity. Maguire's third condition, work, is echoed in Hauerwas' notion (this time writing with James Foubert) that imagination is a disciplined seeing.[92] This theme of imagination and work ties in strongly with one of my own concerns, namely that many of our young people do not have good literary skills or a disciplined appreciation of the arts. Will imagination be possible without work to acquire these skills?

Maguire's fourth condition, malleability or openness to new currents and ideas, recalls many examples such as the story of Willis Carrier, the father of modern air conditioning. In the early 1900's Carrier had perfected the techniques necessary for air conditioning but he could not interest his employers in going into the air conditioning business. Carrier had a malleable imagination and his employers did not. With the help of others he decided to start his own company which went on to become highly successful. This malleability theme (which does not mean that we abandon moral norms) would seem to be a main element in the practical moral reasoning which scholars have been calling for since the days of Aristotle.

Maguire's last condition that there is a *kairos* or right moment for imaginative discovery reminded me immediately of the famous image with which Bernard Lonergan begins his classic work *In-*

sight.[93] This is the image of Archimedes running naked through the streets of Syracuse shouting *Eureka*! after he had discovered the principle of specific gravity while plopping himself down in the baths of Syracuse. Archimedes (who may have been the original streaker) no doubt had Maguire's other four conditions (enthusiasm, quiet study, hard work, openness), but he surely personifies the notion that there is a right moment for imaginative discoveries to be made.

While many of Maguire's insights on imagination would be agreed on by other authors such as Hauerwas, there are also some significant differences in the approaches of Maguire and Hauerwas. For the purposes of the next chapter, which will present my own approach to moral theology and imagination, it will be helpful to note the points of difference. Two main differences can be cited.

First, Maguire lays a great stress on the interrelationship between imagination and affectivity or emotion.[94] Hauerwas tends to follow the anti-emotivism which is very strong in MacIntyre and also present in Ricoeur.[95] Thus his approach is more intellectual (but still with an awareness of emotion and without an overly one-sided Kantian rationalism). Hauerwas' idea of imagination as disciplined seeing clearly shows the intellectual bent of his thought on imagination. My own instinct on this point tends to favor Maguire, i.e., to recognize that imagination is an intellectual function but at the same time to work an affective element into the moral theology of imagination. We have seen, however, that in both the history of aesthetics and the history of ethics, there has been an ongoing struggle to adequately interrelate the three elements of intuition, experiential reflection, and emotion. Maguire and Hauerwas both argue for important values in their respective positions on the emotional and intellectual aspects of imagination. Our next chapter will need to wrestle further with this point.

The second difference between Maguire and Hauerwas can be described as a difference of tense. Hauerwas wishes to use imagination to get us back to basics, to get us more in touch with the roots from which Christian civilization has sprung. For Hauerwas imagination will articulate our traditional moral commitments (e.g., to the weaker members of society) in a fresh and vital fashion.[96] Maguire on the other hand (and here he is supported by Alves)[97] wants to use imagination to move us forward into the future, to help us form new insights and even new moral principles.

In the last analysis the tradition-seeking and future-seeking aspects of imagination need not be opposed to one another. Both can be seen as important elements in a moral theology of imagination. But they are different elements, and the interrelationship of them will be an important project for the next chapter.

There is one note to be made in closing this section on contemporary moral theology. The impressive work which is now being done on the less discursive aspects of moral theology in no way implies that serious work of a more rational or discursive sort has ceased or become unimportant. We have already noted, for instance, the current research into the double effect principle. The point is not to eliminate discursive research in ethics. The point is to use imagination to integrate the discursive and the non-discursive.

An Illustrative Parallel:
Contemporary Biblical Study

Everything which we have so far considered in this chapter has either given foundation to a more creative and imaginative moral theology, or it has been a direct part of today's more creative moral theology. The last section of this chapter will have a somewhat different focus. It will explore another field of current Christian study which offers some notable and close parallels to the current developments in moral theology. The study field with close parallels is contemporary biblical interpretation. We will not forget that biblical studies can be and are a source for moral theology. But for our purposes it will be most helpful to see how biblical scholarship parallels moral scholarship in its use of imagination.

Biblical interpretation in the last century worked largely off of the concept of history found in von Ranke, and others, i.e., biblical interpretation looked for an exact historical reconstruction. Early in our own century biblical scholarship did begin to recognize the problems of nineteenth century historicism. Under the leadership of Hermann Gunkel and others, a new school of biblical interpretation developed, the school of form criticism.[98] Form criticism, with its effort to explain the Scriptures in terms of the basic literary genres or forms to be found in the Scriptures, was an improvement over historical criticism. But form criticism still involved a quite scientific and deductive outlook on the part of biblical scholars, an outlook in which biblical texts were generally interpreted in terms of pre-existing forms or patterns into which the texts were fit. Very little attention was paid to the uniqueness or beauty of an individual biblical text. Nor was much attention paid to the overall meaning of the biblical canon as a whole.

Beginning in the 1960's, Scripture scholars, without rejecting the validity of historical and form criticism, began to develop new methods of biblical criticism, methods which are more interested in the uniqueness, beauty, and overall meaning of biblical texts. James Muilenberg, in a highly seminal work, called for the development of a rhetorical criticism, a criticism based on close attention to the literary quality and impact of individual biblical pericopes.[99] Scholars such as James Sanders and Walter Brueggemann have proposed a school of interpretation known as canonical criticism.[100] This approach tries to assess how the canon of Scripture was arrived at (why were some books included and others not?), and what the canon means as a whole.

John Dominic Crossan and others have developed a structural school of biblical interpretation.[101] The structuralists' approach does not look for literary forms in the classical biblical sense. Rather, the structuralists concentrate on the basic linguistic elements which make up the various biblical texts. Contemporary biblical structuralism is a lot like the French structuralism which we earlier discussed. With Ricoeur, I would have difficulty in making structuralism an exclusive method of biblical interpretation. But if biblical structuralism is joined to the more meaning-centered approaches of contemporary rhetorical and canonical criticism, it can be a legitimate part of the effort to come to a more whole approach to biblical interpretation.

From what has been said so far, it can be clearly seen that the efforts to look at the Bible as rhetoric and as integrally developing canon are very similar in a general sense to the efforts of moral theology to become less exclusively rational and scientific. Both moral and biblical theology are looking for more broadly human ways of interpreting the texts they exegete. However, the parallels between biblical and scriptural study are much more than broad and general.

In very concrete and specific ways, contemporary moral and biblical approaches can be said to parallel one another. Four of the important specific parallels will be cited here.

First, important major figures from the newer schools of biblical interpretation are drawing on the same contemporary philosophers we saw as central in the background of a moral theology of imagination. Sandra Schneiders, a most articulate Catholic spokesperson for less exclusively scientific approaches to biblical study, relies heavily on both Gadamer and Ricoeur in working out her approach to biblical interpretation.[102] Walter Brueggemann's more recent writing illustrates how he has found Ricoeur's insights to be most helpful.[103] Crossan, while a structuralist, also makes some use of Ricoeur.

Second, contemporary biblical and moral studies are very interested in similar vision enhancing sources. We earlier saw moral theology's concern with narrative, tragedy, comedy, and beauty. These same notions come up in biblical scholarship, e.g., in Brueggemann's interest in narrative and in grief, in Crossan's comments on narrative, comedy, and tragedy, and in Muilenberg's appeal to the Bible as great literature and therefore as having aesthetic significance.[104]

Third, contemporary biblical scholarship struggles with the two values of stability or conserving the past on the one hand as opposed to creativity or prophetic movement into the future on the other hand. This tension is clearly shown in Brueggemann's recent book on canonical criticism.[105] Earlier we saw tensions between Hauerwas and Maguire on whether imagination is a stable conserving force or a creative liberating force. The struggles of biblical criticism show the same kind of tension.

Fourth, and most importantly, contemporary approaches to biblical criticism parallel moral theology in stressing the importance of imagination as a key to interpretation or understanding. Brueggemann, in seeking to articulate the meaning of the prophetic tradition which is at the heart of the Old Testament, entitles his book on the subject *The Prophetic Imagination*. One of Crossan's major articles on structuralism has the subtitle "Biblical Hermeneutics and Literary Imagination." Sandra Schneiders, in explaining how newer biblical scholarship seeks to unite objective and subjective elements, describes today's efforts at biblical interpretation as a "Paschal

Imagination.''[106] It is not our purpose here to go into any discussion of these biblical approaches to imagination. But imagination's strong presence in current biblical scholarship is a very clear parallel argument which supports the main project of this book, the development of a moral theology of imagination. The other specific parallels between biblical and moral scholarship add even more credibility to the type of effort being made in moral theology to deal with imagination and related themes.

Besides these four comparisons, it might be helpful to note some of the ways in which biblical studies have been and can be a direct source for moral theology, as well as a parallel discipline. Early in this century, both biblical and moral studies were very fundamentalistic. As the century passed, biblical studies moved away from fundamentalism. Eventually, the move from biblical fundamentalism began to have an important impact in moral theology, helping moral theology move to a less fundamentalist and less legalist approach. At the present time, biblical studies are moving to become less rational, moving to become more interested in themes such as the benevolence and abundant love of God in whom we can place radical hope. If the past developments in biblical studies had their subsequent impact on moral theology, might it not be argued that these newer and more imaginative biblical themes such as benevolence and hope will also come to have great impact on moral theology?

The principal purpose of this chapter has been to show that there is an impressive amount of contemporary research which helps provide a foundation and support for a moral theology of imagination. In the light of our brief review of that research, and in the light of the historical material from the last chapter, we are now ready to move to this book's central project: a comprehensive statement of a moral theology of imagination.

4

The Meaning and Purpose of Moral Imagination

To this point we have looked at some of the contemporary factors which appear to call for a moral theology of imagination. We have also reviewed some aspects of historical and current philosophy and theology which are pertinent to a moral theology of imagination. The goal of the present chapter is to make a comprehensive and integrated statement of what moral imagination is and why it is so important.[1] The chapter will be divided into four main sections based on the following four questions: What is moral imagination? What are some of the key issues to be raised in the discussion of moral imagination? Why is moral imagination so significant, both for moral decisions and for us as moral persons? How does moral imagination function in our lives?

WHAT IS MORAL IMAGINATION?

In any human learning experience there are two main movements to what takes place. On the one hand when we learn we always get in touch with some specific concrete data. Even in our most abstract and theoretical learning experiences, we, as incarnate embodied human persons, never achieve a form of learning which is totally detached from concrete and particular sense experience. Thomas Aquinas recognized this centuries ago when he propounded the Aristotelian dictum that all knowledge begins with sense knowledge. Thomas made the same point in another way when he asserted that all our knowledge involves conversion to the phantasm, i.e., attention to the concrete sense level of experience.

But we humans would never know as we know if we were only

capable of conversion to the phantasm or attention to the concrete. Instead we turn to our phantasms or images as persons with a whole wealth and depth of understanding. We turn to our concrete experiences as persons who are open to a profound horizon of meaning. Ultimately we turn to the concrete as persons who are open to the holy and awesome mystery of God. Thus there is another level to all human learning experience: the level of the transcendent, the level of the universal, the level where we move beyond the concrete and move to efforts to state the deepest meaning of life. To return again to Aquinas' language, not only do we convert to our phantasms; we also abstract from them to come to more universal forms of knowing. For Aquinas therefore, the two main movements in human knowing are called conversion and abstraction.

At this point a very natural question arises: Which comes first, conversion or abstraction? Do we first turn to concrete data and then abstract more theoretical and universal insights from the concrete? Or do we begin our knowing with our abstract insights already in place, at least intuitively, so that we fit the concrete data into an already existing pattern? While history has seen many conflicting viewpoints on this matter, in the final analysis, the "which comes first" question is truly a chicken or the egg question. We cannot convert to phantasms or images without at the same time abstracting to universal insights, and we cannot form more universal insights without at the same time attending to concrete data. The two movements in our knowing are always reciprocal. One does not exist without the other. Some styles of knowing may give greater emphasis to the concrete, while other styles emphasize the abstract. But no knowing can be truly human unless it is based on a truly adequate relationship between concrete knowing and abstract universal knowing.

It is precisely this issue—the perennial need for an adequate relationship between the concrete and the universal—which makes imagination such a crucially vital theme for all human knowing, including moral knowing. If the universal in our knowing is stressed to the exclusion of the concrete, we will fail to really look at the data on a given subject. We will quickly put the data into a pre-conceived category, a category in which the data may not necessarily belong. On the other hand, if we simply stress the concrete factors in our knowing, we may very well fail to see the real meaning of the data in a deeper human sense.[2]

Working from this context, imagination can be described as the basic process by which we draw together the concrete and the universal elements of our human experience. With imagination we let go of any inadequately pre-conceived notions of how the abstract and the concrete relate to one another. We suspend judgment about how to unite the concrete and the abstract. We let the two sides of our knowing play with one another. By allowing this interplay between the two aspects of our knowing, we get a much deeper chance to look at what we know, to form a vision of it.[3] With this deeper, imagining vision of reality we are able to make a more appropriate connection between conversion and abstraction.

Several comments are necessary to fill out this basic description of imagination as a playful suspension of judgment leading us toward a more appropriate grasp of reality. First, both our concrete knowing and our more abstract knowing offer us images which can be played with. If the more abstract side of our knowing were purely abstract we could never play with it, we could never form an image in light of which we could playfully suspend judgment. At its deepest roots, abstract thinking is pre-reflexive and beyond our ability to grasp. God who is the root of our pre-reflexive knowing can never be fully symbolized in human thought. However, throughout history, humans have found ways to concretize their abstract thoughts so as to form images of life's deepest mysteries including the mystery of God. These images will always limp a little. (God, for example, can never be fully described as male or as female.) But they are genuine images, which both give us truth and can be played with so as to help us get at deeper truth. In other words, there is an imaginative world both in the new insights we form every day and in our long-standing traditional insights. Thus we can look at our long-standing insights with what Ricoeur calls a "second naïveté."[4] We can suspend judgment and play with our long-standing insights.

Second, because there are imaginative worlds both to our traditional insights and to ongoing learning, the suspension and playfulness involved in imagination seem to run in two directions. In one direction we suspend our traditional insights and let our new insights and images play upon our traditional views. Perhaps our standard mode of concretizing a traditional insight has not adequately captured the insight. Perhaps our playing with the standard mode in the light of new experience will enable us to come to a better grasp of what we have been trying to understand all along. In the other direction, we let our traditional images and wisdom play our new experience, or, as Ricoeur would say, we let the text play us.[5] When we form a new insight, we have a great tendency to say something like "Here it is, I've got it." We have to refine our new images and insights in the light of our horizons of past experience. In imagination there is thus a twofold play, an interplay of our learning experiences.

Third, our description of imagination as suspension and play underscores the crucial nature of themes like story and metaphor to the whole process of imagining. If imagination calls on us to playfully suspend judgment, stories clearly will help us to make this suspension and to play with our ideas. Stories are inherently more playful than many other forms of thinking. As soon as we hear opening words from a story (words such as "Once upon a time"), we know that we have a freedom to suspend technical judgment and to play with the story. Many of the elements in stories (comedy, tragedy, tradition, etc.) also help shift our thinking into the playful mode. As for metaphor, the very essence of metaphor seems to be that our thinking, learning process is stopped or suspended by the metaphor which challenges us to look at reality in a different way. Recall Ricoeur's suggestion that, metaphysically, the metaphoric process is a process of imagination.[6]

Fourth, it should be clearly noted that the purpose of the suspension and play which are the core of imagination is not to lead us to bad judgments or to no judgments. Rather the purpose of imagination is to lead us to better, more sound judgments. The process of getting conversion and abstraction together is not always a simple process. Non-imaginative theories of knowing are so anxious to get to judgments that they can short-circuit the work of in-depth imagining which is essential to good judgments. But the great thinkers of all eras and in all fields have always been highly imaginative persons. They judged better because they could imagine.

I write these lines near the time of the centennial of the opening of one of America's all time great engineering feats, the Brooklyn Bridge. Without doubt the Roeblings, father and son, had tremendous technical knowledge as engineers of the bridge. But they had a sense of the human spirit too, and of the human future. They had an ability to play with their ideas, an ability to plumb the depths of the human heart as well as the depths of the East River. For this reason their bridge, with its gothic towers and elevated walking promenade, has had a special hold on the American imagination.[7]

It is of course true that one could play with suspended images indefinitely or associate them in all sorts of inappropriate ways. This approach is often called fancy and it had been much criticized across the ages by scholars such as David Hume.[8] Genuine imagination, even when it deals with fiction, clearly surpasses idle fancy. It seeks to be productive (as Kant put it);[9] it seeks to open us to the truth. Even when it works with strange, never-to-be-real images, genuine imagination leads to truth. Up to now we have spoken of true imagination as a suspension of judgment and a playing of different levels of our experience against each other. But imagination does more than this. In its play, imagination looks for deeper and more appropriate unities in our experience, unities and insights into truth which we might easily miss without imagination.

The experience of metaphor helps clarify the difference between true imagination and mere fancy. Metaphors strike us as incongruous at first. We have to give up our usual patterns of thought to wrestle with a metaphor. But in the end, our ability to imagine enables the metaphor to open up fresh and more adequate insights into truth. Mere fancy, on the other hand, does not unify our experience or lead us toward truth.

So far our description of imagination has applied to all types of imagination, and indeed there is no area of human life in which we do not need to be imaginative. But in our context it should be especially noted that we need imagination in moral matters. While the basic dynamics of imagination are the same in moral theology as in any other sphere of imaginative activity, some brief comments can be made on the agenda for imagination as it operates in the moral sphere.

Moral theology presents us with the two basic levels which we find in all human knowing. We have our very precious moral tradition, but our forms of expressing that tradition never fully capture all of it. We need therefore to imaginatively grasp our moral tradition ever more deeply. Similarly we have a constant flow of new moral experiences, but we need our imagination to help us integrate our new moral experiences, to help us avoid one-sided descriptions which distort our current moral experiences. To say this in another way, in moral theology we need to let our ongoing moral experiences play with our moral tradition, and we need to let our tradition play with our current moral experience. Thus when we consider how it is that we come to true and objective moral judgments, moral imagination can be seen as a most important factor in our arrival at such true moral judgments. While other factors also enter in, we come to moral judgments at least partly through an exercise of moral imagination.[10]

KEY ISSUES CONCERNING MORAL IMAGINATION

In the last two chapters, our literature review raised several major issues about imagination and moral imagination, issues which were noted but not really discussed. To complement the basic description of moral imagination just presented, four of these major issues will now be considered. Is imagination a sense or intellectual function? Do we imagine experientially, intuitively, or emotionally? How does imagination relate to principles, especially moral principles? Do we imagine to move out to our future or to get in touch with our past?

Imagination: Sense or Intelligence?

Earlier we saw that for Thomas Aquinas imagination, while a high sense faculty and close to the spiritual realm, was strictly a sense faculty. We also saw that in the last few centuries, many scholars have laid increasing stress on imagination as an intellectual process. Something similar has happened to one of Thomas' other high, but still sensual faculties, common sense. Today when we say that someone had common sense, we are thinking of an intellectual attribute, probably of an intuitive intellectual attribute.[11]

To the basic question of whether imagination is sense or intelligence, the best answer is not an either-or answer, but a both-and answer. Aquinas is clearly right in arguing for a sense dimension in our imagining. Across the centuries, questions of form, shape, visual and audio effect have been major factors in our appreciation of art and beauty.[12] If the Brooklyn Bridge did impress itself on the

American imagination, its impression, as it raised the human spirit, was a visual, sensual impression. Even in our more abstract and conceptual thinking, there is a sense dimension which impacts us and influences how we view reality.[13] Our abstract ideas please us if they fit together nicely, and this fitting together is at least partly a sense experience. To speak out our moral principles, we have to give these principles a form or a shape. Then we can imagine our moral principles in a way which will always be partly a sensing way.

At the same time, a careful consideration of the process of imagination shows that there are other elements in imagining besides sense impressions. For one thing we can control many aspects of imagination, by making a deliberate effort to suspend judgment and to take up the play which is crucial to imagination. Second, there is a comparing, contrasting, and sometimes a joining of our sense impressions. This activity of comparing, contrasting, and uniting images is very close to the heart of human imagination in my opinion.[14] Third, there are judgments about the appropriateness and inappropriateness of our imaginative comparisons and contrasts. It seems soundest to consider all three of these activities as part of our imagining. If these activities are part of our imagining, imagining is an intellectual process as well as a sense process.

This section began with the question of whether imagination is a sense activity or an intellectual activity. My position is that it is both, but in answering, I have actually suggested that imagination involves even more. While we are never in full control of how various images will strike us, our capacity to compare and unify images and our capacity to take the time we need for imaginative play with ideas are both capacities over which we can exercise some control. Thus human imagination, in addition to its sense and intellectualist elements, involves the human will and discipline as well.[15] Later on, when we move to the theme of imagination and moral education, we will need to look at will and discipline issues as well as sense and intelligence issues which relate to imagination. For now we can conclude that imagination is a broadly based human capacity, involving sense, intelligence and will. It also involves human emotion as we shall see in the next section.

The traditional position that imagination is solely a sense operation and thus in many ways beyond our ability to control may help explain why imagination has often been feared, especially in the moral area. Careful scholarship has pointed out that our capacity to fantasize is a great and good gift from God, a gift without which we could not function.[16] But the sensual power of fantasies, especially of sexual fantasies, had led to a popular tendency to think of our fantasies as essentially bad, rather than as essential goods which call for discipline and control. In saying this I am not suggesting that all of the past concerns about imagination were totally misplaced. But if we conceive of imagination as a more broadly based human operation involving intelligence and will as well as sense, imagination in itself can be seen as containing principles of association, judgment, and discipline which are called to regulate the play of impressions in a productive fashion. There can be immoral uses of imagination, but such uses are not the purpose or thrust of imagination.

Aquinas surely recognized the importance of the several elements of imagination we have just reviewed, but he would not have named anything but the sense data as imagination strictly speaking. My view, shared by many today, is that Aquinas, for all his genius, was a little too anxious to divide everything into neat categories. We need a more integrated view of human psychology and human learning, a view which is able to combine sense, intelligence, will, and emotion, and see their interrelationships in human learning and decision making. In particular, we need an integrated view of imagination.

Imagination: Intuition, Emotion, or Experience?

Earlier, when we were considering the history of aesthetics and moral theory, we saw three main families of approaches to the question of how we know in aesthetics and morals: intuitional theories, emotivist theories, and experiential theories. Thus it seems fair to ask how imagination relates to the triad of intuition, emotion, and experience. In some respects this question overlaps with the preceding comments on sense and intelligence. But there are still some other points to explore. If we grant that imagination involves intelligence, what sort of intelligent operation is it? Is imagination a more intuitive or a more reflective form of knowing? If we grant that imagination is partly a sense activity, what about imagination's impact on our emotions? How strongly does emotion influence the judgments of appropriateness we make in the imaginative process? These are the questions we will now explore.

To begin with, and following the drift of the last section, our clear need for a whole view of imagination suggests that intuition, emotion, and experiential learning are all a part of the imaginative process. To make this point we will comment briefly on the importance of each of three issues: intuition, emotion, and experiential learning. Then we shall turn to the question about how these three themes relate.

The association of imaginative themes surely rests at least partly in intuition. So does the judgment that an imaginative connection is appropriate. In a significant degree, great artists, great poets, and charismatic moral leaders are great because of their intuitive insights. To say that imagination is at least partly intuitive does not mean that we possess a clear and distinct idea or a clear set of rules which give us advance knowledge of how to make imaginative associations. Nor does the role of the intuitive in imagination mean that we can imagine without any concrete and experiential learning. Intuition in our imagination is probably best understood along the lines of Karl Rahner's well known theme of pre-apprehension (German: *Vorgriff*),[17] i.e., we have a pre-reflective openness to meaning which does not have any objective content and is only actuated in the actual context of an imaginative experience. We can never know or imagine without this pre-apprehension, but at the same time this pre-apprehension can only operate in the presence of concrete human experience.

Some modern scholars such as Gadamer have sought to revive an earlier and more positive meaning of the term prejudice (pre-judgment) to get at the intuitive side of imagination. Gadamer argues that prejudice used to have a favorable sense: not that we have our mind made up, but that we learn in view of an openness to transcendence.[18] In many ways the character of our intuitive openness to transcendence is gift, with this gift being a major factor in why some people are more imaginative than others. I believe, however, that the intuitive side of imagination can be developed and shaped. We will return to this point shortly.

Imagination also has a clear emotional element. The sense elements in our imaginative experiences impress themselves on our emotions as well as on our intelligence. Though we humans do not all react in the very same ways, we respond emotively to beauty. We are moved by symbols. An important aspect of our awareness that imaginative ideas are either appropriate or inappropriate comes from our emotions. Of course our emotions are not an infallible guide to productive imagining. Emotions must be evaluated critically and refined and developed to the extent possible. But the element of taste (which stems from both intuition as well as from emotion) will always be an inherent and not fully controllable part of the imaginative process, so that imagination will always be associated with spontaneous emotive reactions of attraction and/or repulsion.

Finally, imagination stems very much from our human learning experiences.[19] The poems we read, the art we like, the languages we learn, the sciences we study, the people we meet all have a profound impact on our ability to imagine. Throughout this book, one of our central theses has been that experiential learning is much more than logical learning, though logic we need. We have a whole variety of concrete learning experiences. On the one hand these experiences are real and specific. They cannot simply be reduced to intuition or emotion. We can teach people language, music, science, sport, etc. (admittedly with varying degrees of success). But on the other hand the reality of these concrete learning experiences cannot be explained in cold logic either. Language, music, science, and sport all have their rules which we can learn. But great use of language, great music, etc. cannot be defined in terms of rules alone.

If we accept the argument of the past few paragraphs, human productive imagination is based on intuition, emotion, and learned experience. But is there a priority among these categories? Is one of these three categories more central to the development of imagination? Without trying to solve all of the historic philosophical debates, my position is that, on the practical level, our third category, learned experience, is the most important category.

There are several reasons for my position. First, of the three categories, learned experience is the one we can most readily shape, both in our own lives and in the lives of those around us. The whole premise of liberal education is that we can help others see the rules of language, music, art, etc. and that we can share with others specific concrete examples of great literature, music, and art. Sadly, this premise seems to decline as unreflective technology waxes more and more strongly in much modern education. The whole idea of cultural and athletic exchanges between East and West, North and South is that, while we cannot immediately and directly share our intuitions and emotions, we can share some of the concrete and classical output of various cultures. Our literature review in the last chapter saw a great interest in stories, narratives, and traditions as a means to moral development and education. We can share the classics of our moral experience in a way which will enhance moral growth and development.

Second, concrete learning experiences offer more to imagination than their direct impact on the experiential learning dimension of imagination. In an indirect manner, concrete learning influences the intuitive and emotive dimensions of imagining. We saw earlier that intuitive dimensions and concrete specific dimensions always pre-suppose and interpenetrate each other in human learning. Thus classics of literature, art, etc. call forth the intuitive dimension of human learning. These classics give those who read, see, or hear them an opportunity to develop and cultivate the intuitive dimensions of human living. Thus our classics shape at least partially the manner in which the intuitive dimension works. From this perspective, there is a legitimate human concern for the quality of the classics and classical learning experiences which we share with our young people. These experiences will affect them at a depth we can never fully describe. At the same time an excessive narrowing of what we make available to the young (or to any of us) reduces learning to a dehumanizing censorship and propaganda. Efforts to positively enhance the quality of art, music, literature, etc. available in education always seem desirable. But excessive efforts to restrict what is available are clearly problematic.

Similar thoughts apply to emotion. Our emotional responses can be refined and developed through our concrete learning experiences. There will always be the phenomenon of taste, and no two of us will ever imagine or emote in exactly the same way. But some education of emotion is possible through learning.

Finally, giving priority to concrete learning in the make-up of imagination is coherent and necessary in order to develop a theory of imagination which is based on an Aristotelian and realistic view of the world.[20] Epistemologies whose essence is either intuition or emotion ultimately cannot account for the real character of human learning as a genuine experience of truth. Particularly in moral theology, I do not think an approach which is based on intuition or feeling can ever be completely adequate. Early in this century G.E. Moore in his famous *Principia Ethica* did reduce ethics to feelings and intuitions.[21] He rejected any explanation of morality which was based on a true understanding of our nature. My position is that imagination really does help us understand our nature, does help us find objective or human moral truth. Surely imagination draws on intuition and emotion but it draws on them in conjunction with a concrete learning experience which moves to truth. Not only that, imagination is an essential step in the human move toward moral truth. It joins the abstract and the concrete and thus opens levels of experience which we would never achieve through principles alone without an imaginative context.

Imagination and Moral Principles

I have mentioned several times that, while imagination does not replace moral principles, it offers moral perspectives not available in principles alone. This raises a major question: What exactly is the nature of the relationship between imagination and moral principles?

To begin with, to make our way through any area of life, we very much need principles. This is true in science, in literature and art, and of course in morality. We need to make abstractions from our concrete experiences, to encapsulate our concrete experiences in principles. In every area of life, the sum total of human imaginative experience is so large that we cannot possibly walk through all of our experience each time we have a decision to make. Thus, through the human capacity for abstract thinking, we discern principles in our experiences. These principles stand as a sort of short-hand summary for the meanings which are inherent in human existence. For a religious believer these principles seek to give expression to the mystery of God who is at the root of all human experience.

While principled thinking is needed in all areas of human life, it is especially needed in moral life. None of us has time to be in total touch with all dimensions of the human moral project in each moral decision we make. Life is too short. We need the systematized moral insights available in principles. Young people in particular need to learn to rely on principles because their life experience is limited.

However, even though we must grant all this value to principles, both in life in general and in moral life in particular, there are three major reasons why principles alone are not enough for us in human and moral life, three major reasons why principles must be interrelated with the imaginative process.

Imaginative Learning of Principles

First, for the human person to truly own his or her principles, it is essential that he or she actually walk through the imaginative process of discerning principles, at least in some cases. The human person must learn to suspend judgments, to play with ideas, to make appropriate connections and on this basis to understand principles in a human way. With this kind of approach principles will make the deepest possible human sense. With this kind of approach humans can truly own their principles. Even principles which the individual has not walked through imaginatively can be more deeply owned if the individual has at least some direct experience in the imaginative human process out of which our principles are learned.

Recently, for the first time in my life, I had the experience of taking a high quality lock apart. I had always believed that most locks were well designed and reliable. But as I played with the numerous tumblers and springs (which I did successfully reassemble), I acquired a whole new understanding of locks. I found out that the inventor of the tumbler lock had a rich imagination, and I acquired an ownership of the imaginative processes out of which locks are designed. Doubtless, I could have lived the rest of my years without this particular understanding, but still each of us does need some concrete experience of how ideas are imaginatively developed. Otherwise our ideas, in whatever sphere of life, will seem too sterile and fixed, and we will not get in touch with the imaginative life which is at the root of all ideas. This fact has many implications for educational programs in general and for moral education in particular. It is not enough simply to teach moral principles. We have to create an imaginative context out of which moral principles can be deeply owned.[22]

Imaginative Deepening of Principles

Second, the nature of principles is that while they are genuinely true, they never express the full depth of the truth. We come to our principles in light of our deepest openness to meaning, to God. But our principles never fully capture that deepest openness. Our principles are always subject to further refinement. When we articulate our principles, we necessarily do so in words. The words we use will necessarily have a multiplicity of meanings or, as Ricoeur would say, a polysemy.[23] We must therefore keep studying our principles to more fully discern their meaning. Our grasp of principles is always true but limited.

Thus, the great scientist needs to know the limitations of scientific principles. He or she needs to have a sense for the "more" toward which principles point. The dogmatic theologian needs to know that a faith principle such as the divinity of Christ in no way closes off contemplative reflection on the divinity of Christ. The faith principle channels the contemplative reflection in a proper direction, but it does not stop the reflection or foresee all the fruits of this reflection.[24] The faith principle is the minimum of what needs to be said to understand the Christ, but not the maximum of what can be experienced in the understanding of Christ.

Similarly, moral theology presents us with a constant need to search for deeper meanings in our principles. One might very credibly argue for instance that the just war theory has been an historically adequate moral principle (or set of principles), but that in the nuclear age we need to come to a new and deeper understanding of the just war tradition.

Up to this point, we have generally spoken of imagination as a major means of working with and through our moral principles so that we can genuinely own them. But these latest thoughts are speaking about going beyond principles, about getting deeper into the meaning of our principles. This too is an imaginative process, a process in which we play with our principles (or contemplate them, which can be a form of play). At this level, principles themselves become images, images which we sharpen by associating them with other images.[25]

In moral theology, this refinement of principles needs to continue in every age. A major reason why we need to lead people to an imaginative grasp of moral principles in the first place (instead of using an uncritical handout method of teaching moral principles) is that an imaginative learning of moral principles will greatly assist the imaginative process of deepening our moral principles.

Imaginatively Applying Moral Principles

Third, no matter how well and creatively we have learned principles, and no matter how deep and adequate is our understanding of principles, we still have the human task of applying principles to specific cases or issues. This is especially true concerning moral principles. If we grant that human history is real, no moral case is ever totally and exactly the same as a previous moral case. Thus there is always a need to verify the relationship between the principle and the specific case, to be sure that a given case is covered by a given principle and that the principle ought to be applied to the case in a specific way. It is of course true that in many instances the application will be easy and the application process fairly automatic. Only in more complex circumstances will we typically be aware of the challenge involved in applying moral principles. But in no case can we completely escape the human task of assessing whether we are applying a moral principle in an appropriate manner. Or, to say it in another way, in no case can we totally avoid using imagination as we apply our moral principles.

It is in this context of applying moral principles that Ricoeur's notions of metaphor and textual interpretation seem most directly applicable. Our moral principles can be understood as texts. We, as moral actors, need to let the texts interpret or play us and our behaviors. We need to let the texts open up for us the world of moral reflection. But at the same time, we need to play the texts or principles. We need to appropriately interpret the texts so as to apply them to current moral cases.

The three points just discussed—learning moral principles, deepening moral principles, and applying moral principles—all suggest a common theme: we very much need both moral principles and moral imagination. More specifically our moral principles, valuable as they are, cannot accomplish their purpose unless they spring from and move us toward a continuous process of moral imagination. Thus, the question about principles vs. imagination in moral theology is not an either-or question. It is a both-and question. In every moral decision we need both moral principles and moral imagination.

Another question rises in this context: Since believing Christians can find much moral wisdom in the Scriptures and in the teachings of the Church, can believing Christians give a greater autonomy to moral principles, and rely less on the conjunction of imaginative skills and moral principles? Especially for Catholics this is a key question, because of the strong presence of moral teaching in the Roman Catholic tradition.[26]

Without doubt, Roman Catholicism renders its believers great service through its clear teaching of moral principles. This clear teaching has made and can make moral living sounder for many persons. Some of the other Churches have recognized this in recent decades and have looked for ways of exercising a ministry of moral teaching.[27]

Nonetheless, imagination remains very necessary to the full life of the well-taught believer. The believer still needs to have the human imaginative experience of learning, at least for some of his or her moral principles. Catholicism has always strongly emphasized that grace builds upon nature. Imagining is our natural way of coming to moral principles, and faith should build on this foundation. Simply telling people the Church's moral principles without appealing to imagination will not facilitate a sufficiently human grasp of these principles. In its liturgical celebrations, Roman Catholicism, with its high sacramental tradition, has always made a strong appeal to the imaginative dimension as a means of communicating our faith experience of the passion, death, and resurrection of Christ. In liturgy we use story and symbol, tragedy and tradition. We need to do much of the same in the teaching of moral values.

Like individual believers, the Church, in its role as moral teacher, also has an ongoing need to deepen its understanding of moral principles and to creatively and imaginatively apply its moral principles to developing human problems. Thus it seems to me that the magisterium should understand the exercise of moral imagination to be one of its most important ongoing functions, as it seeks to come to judgments on difficult moral issues.[28]

Individual believers can be very much helped by the magisterium's effort to exercise imagination in moral matters. But the nature of moral matters is such that the creative imagining of the magisterium cannot take away the need of the individual person to be imaginative in the moral area. There is so much going on in the total moral life of the whole human community that no institution, no matter how benevolent, can ever do all the imagining necessary in the lives of individual believers. For this reason, a large part of the Church's role as moral teacher will be to go beyond the clear teaching of moral principles and to help and encourage believers in the exercise of appropriate moral imagination. The Roman Church with its liturgical tradition has many rich resources for sensitive education of the human moral imagination. These resources need a vigorous and vital development in our times.

The comments just made are based on a positive and harmonious relationship between moral principles and moral imagination. This of course is the way things should be and it is what we must strive for. There will, however, be times when either moral principles or moral imagination will get out of hand, in the moral thinking of an individual or a community. Moral principles will sometimes be claimed to be so exhaustive that there will be no further need to ponder their meaning. Or moral imagination will slip into proposing viewpoints which do seem to be pure fancy with no regard for the truth to be found in moral principles. In these cases, confrontation between imagination and principles will be necessary so as to achieve a proper balance. Not only will principles need to discipline imagination; imagination will need to revitalize principles.

Imagination: For the Past or the Future?

In the last chapter we saw two distinct language patterns in common use vis-à-vis moral imagination.[29] Some scholars see moral imagination as a means of reconnecting us with our past by the creative use of stories, symbols, traditions, etc. These authors correctly sense a high degree of moral breakdown in our society and hope that an imaginative recovery of the past will help overcome this breakdown. These authors will often lay strong stress on imagination as a way to virtue, with virtue springing from an established social framework which we have largely lost in our society.

But other scholars are much more future oriented in their language about moral imagination. These authors hold that as a people we simply must find ways to move into the future. They see moral imagination as a means to the discovery of new and different ideas, a means, for instance, by which we can work out a new international socio-economic order which will be much more just than is the present order. This latter group of scholars sees themes such as dreaming and hoping as the more proper activities of imagination.

In my conversations with other theologians and with friends since I began working on this book, I have run into the curious phenomenon that the subject of moral imagination seems equally attractive to persons of a more conservative bent and to those of a more progressive bent. Moral imagination's call for a revival of the liberal arts and a revival of the classics of our culture is very attractive to those who are frustrated with our overly technical world, and who wish to deal with their frustrations by retrieving the best of our past. Likewise, moral imagination's call to creativity and new vision is very attractive to those whose main concern is about where we should go in the human future. It seems hard to get anyone too mad about the notion of moral imagination because almost everyone finds something likable about moral imagination.

In the final analysis, the past oriented and the future oriented approaches to imagination may not be that far apart. It would of course be naïve to think that all tensions between past oriented and future oriented persons can easily be set aside. But at the same time both past and future oriented persons share some important common concerns: both groups are quite discontented about the present, and both of them see imagination as one key to needed changes in the present shape of the world around us. As I see it, both the past and the future are very much needed to help us address the difficulties of the present. It is often remarked that the most ultra-reactionary members of one generation are usually the most ultra-liberal members of the previous generation, who got so stuck in the present (when they were in the previous generation) that they became totally unable to move anywhere else, totally unable to deal with either the past or the future.

To spell this out a bit further, genuine movement into the future very much needs to be energized by the symbols, traditions, and stories of the past. Such past stories, symbols, and traditions can be life-giving. They offer us structures such as language out of which it is possible to build as we move into the future. Very often when we develop an approach to a problem which we find to be highly creative and liberating, we will discover on subsequent reflection that this liberating approach has a great deal of the past as part of it. Seminarians, for example, will complain about their community prayer life and state that they can design a prayer form which will foster better community prayer. When such seminarians are allowed to implement their new prayer designs, it can be amazing how often they reinvent the Liturgy of the Hours.

Of course the future may modify and develop some of the insights from the past as it moves forward. Many creative efforts are much more than simple reinventions of the past. Nonetheless, without the plateau of insight which the past offers, many future accomplishments, both in moral life and in life in general, would not be possible. The old adage about those not knowing the past being doomed to repeat it applies to moral theology as much as to anything else.

Thus we need the past to help energize our moral imagination. But this does not mean that we should simply give ourselves over to a vain nostalgia, which overly romanticizes the past and closes out all real openness to change. In general, the moral writing today about stories and symbols has a vital and energetic approach to the past, though I do think that the moral imaginers who stress the past could try to dialogue more fully with the moral imaginers who stress the future.

A point of special importance about moral imagination and the past is that, as we recapture the vitality of the past through moral imagination, what we recapture is a *socially shared past*, a past which sprang out of commonly held social and moral values. The very reason why some things from the past became classics to be saved for the future was that they were socially appreciated. In our era of sometimes extreme individualism, many efforts to move to the future can become overly individualistic. Imaginative attention to our moral past can therefore help us in dealing with the modern tendency to forget the social dimensions of moral issues. This point is especially well made by MacIntyre with his insistence on the social nature of virtue.[30]

As far as moral imagination and the future is concerned, I believe that we very much need a future thrust in our approach to moral imagination. If our past insights are to avoid becoming stale and fixed, these insights must be challenged by a sense of dream, a sense of new possibility. To get to the future, we need the traditions of the past, but without the pull or challenge of the future, the living *trad-*

itio can deteriorate into lifeless *tradita*. For example if today's Christian thinkers on the war and peace issue were not open to the new problems which humanity is likely to face in future generations, their repetition of the Church's past teachings on war might serve little useful purpose. However, with a real sense of the future, it may be possible for Christian thinkers to articulate an approach to war which will be of great value for the next few generations. Such an approach to the ethics of war will not abandon our tradition, but it will revitalize that tradition because of the pull of the future.

One benefit of an imaginative concern for the future is that such a concern will help us avoid an attitude toward the present which is critical, but which offers very little that is constructive. It can be relatively easy (if one has courage, which is not always so easy) to point out what is wrong with the present.[31] The harder task is to offer viable alternatives for the future. This is where a future oriented, creative imagination comes to the fore. Recovering the best of the past, it leads us into our future and toward God.

I have argued for a synthesis of past and present in a moral theology of imagination. Granting the importance of the synthesis, can one of these two imaginative movements (to the past or to the future) be said to be more definitive of moral imagination? Our analysis so far seems to suggest that movement to the future is the more definitive category. Our definition of imagination spoke of suspending judgment (second naïveté) and of playing with our images, so as to come to new images which we can then judge as appropriate for action. New appropriate images which help us journey into the future are thus the end-point of the effort of moral imagination. Even in common language when we speak of imagination we think of creativity and newness, i.e., we think of moving to a new future. The Jesuit William Lynch's 1965 book *Images of Hope*[32] preceded much of the current theologizing about imagination and about hope, but it remains a classic statement of the interconnection between our ability to imagine and our capacity to hope in our future.

None of this in any way undercuts the importance of traditions, symbols, and stories, all of which are crucial to the imaginative process. The past and the future are synthesized in moral imagination, but the creative move to the future is the more genuinely synthetic aspect of moral imagination.

At the Second Vatican Council, the image of the Church as a

pilgrim Church became very popular.[33] Pilgrimage suggests that we are on a journey, that we are headed toward our future. Since the Council, some very significant theologians have used the notion of future in their description of God. In this vein, scholars have described God as the absolute future, the power of the future, the future of man, etc.[34] Teilhard's notion of Christ as Omega Point has this same future echo, as do many of the insights to be found in contemporary political and liberation theologies.

Our point here is not to offer a detailed or critical evaluation of any of these modern theologies. Our point is simply that a lean toward the future, in an approach to imagination which stresses both past and future, is very consistent with a great deal of contemporary theology.

WHY IS IMAGINATION SO IMPORTANT FOR US?

This chapter has sought to define moral imagination and to answer some key questions about it. But why is imagination so important in moral theology? Why does it merit the emphasis which it is getting in this book? While many perspectives might be offered on the significance of imagination for moral theology, four major perspectives will be presented here: imagination and the natural law, imagination and poetic vision, imagination and spiritual-biblical insights, and imagination for persons and communities as well as for individual decisions.

Imagination and the Natural Law

First, and perhaps most importantly, there is the connection between moral imagination and the crucially central insight of Roman Catholic moral theology on the subject of natural law. For many centuries, Roman Catholicism has held that we are able to know the moral order naturally, i.e., that we can come to a true and objective moral knowledge based on our human capacity to know and even apart from revelation. The whole of the Catholic interest in science, scholarship, art, and politics comes out of this natural law tradition.

A great deal of the traditional writing on the natural law emphasizes a theme which we might call the "what" question about the natural law, i.e., the question of the natural law's content, the question of what moral principles we humans know through the natural law. This "what" question is highly important. But at the same time there is another highly important natural law question. This is the "how" question, the question of how our humanity enables us to know natural moral principles. In the final analysis natural law has more that just a human content. It is also a human way of knowing morality.[35]

Based on this last point, that natural law is a human way of knowing the moral order, I would assert that imagination is a very large factor in the human or natural way of knowing morality. As incarnate beings who begin with sense knowledge, our way of coming to truth, in moral matters or any other area, is very much an imaginative way. The very nature of our humanness calls on us to form images (which we will often describe in language), to associatively play with these images, and through this play, to come to judgments of truth. It seems very difficult if not impossible to hold to the essence of the natural law tradition, without acknowledging the human imaginative process in and through which we are able to form natural law judgments. We simply would not know the natural law in a human way without participating in such a process.

Earlier in this chapter, we saw the broad-ranging character of human imagination. Imagination has strong ties with our senses, our emotions, our will, and our social context, as well as with several different levels in our intelligence. This wide ranging character of imagination shows the broad humanness of the concept of imagination. If natural law calls us to a human way of knowing in ethics, natural law *ipso facto* calls on us to exercise the full range of our imaginative capacity as we go about moral knowing.

Imagination and Poetic Vision

In this context, the contemporary emphasis on vision in ethical scholarship begins to take on its full meaning. Ethics, especially Christian ethics, is a discipline of vision, of seeing life as it really is. This vision, this "seeing as" is very much an exercise of imagination. Vision involves looking deeply at reality to see it as it really is. Vision involves using all of our human imaginative capacity. To form vision, we often have to let go of our pre-conceived notions, suspending these notions so as to come to a deeper seeing and a deeper truth. Metaphor very often enters into the development of vision, enabling us to see something to be other than we had thought it to be. Using a term which comes from Wittgenstein, Ricoeur emphasizes that the metaphorical or imaginative vision of reality is an operation of "seeing as."[36]

In this context also, we can see the import of the idea that Christian ethics is an art as much as a science.[37] The process of forming vision, of associating our various images of life, so as to come to a whole view, is very much an artistic process. We have always tended to think of truly great artists, musicians, and poets as persons gifted with a special vision into life, as persons richly gifted with imagination. The works of such artists, even when fictional, can contain as much or more insight into truth as can accounts of real events. Moreover, the great scientists have been able to serve humanity partly because their thinking has made visionary and artistic leaps to new insights. In the final analysis, the need for artistic insight crosses the whole of life, including the moral life.

Obviously, not all of us are called to be great artists. Obviously, too, even the great artist, who makes a moral gift of self to humanity through works of art, does not always satisfactorily express his or her artistic/moral insight in other areas of life. But the fact remains that all of us are called to be moral persons. The kind of imaginative insight we need to live as moral persons belongs in the same family as the insight exercised by artists and poets.[38] It is surely legitimate to think of moral theology at least partly as an art.

Imagination, Spirituality, and Scripture

These thoughts about why moral imagination is so important tie in with a theme cited in Chapter 1, the revival of the discernment of spirits tradition as a means to decision making. For a large part of the history of the Church, moral decisions were closely related to the spiritual life. It was thought that holiness was a major factor in helping us make moral choices. In particular, in the methodology of discernment, it was thought that the impulses, drives, and stirrings of the human spirit were an important locus for making moral decisions. It was thought that we could find God's will by looking within the human spirit. Discernment's relationship with moral theology went into eclipse in recent centuries, as persons were swayed by the modern scientific view to see ethics as exclusively a science, as devoid of all artistic insight.

Recent years have seen a great revival of interest in discernment. People again realize that moral principles, valuable though they be, are often not enough for us as we face our most difficult life choices. Many people today want to make moral decisions based on their holiness and sense of God's presence.

In very many ways, discernment can be understood as an exercise of moral imagination. Like imagination, discernment wants to get beyond the shallow and the obvious. It wants to get at the deepest human meanings. It wants to keep wrestling with the mystery of God whom we can never fully express in principles. It wants to stretch human imagining so as to make an integral connection between our deepest self-direction (''autonomy'') and God's will as expressed by the Spirit (''theonomy''). With this type of imaginative discernment, the religious or theological dimension of morality will no longer be extrinsic to morality, as it has been in some past moral systems. From such a faith-oriented perspective, all of our efforts to foster moral imagination (through creative education, etc.) can be seen as efforts to foster discernment of spirits.

Along similar lines, one of the growing concerns in moral theology today is to find ways to help moral theology become more biblically based. If there was one drawback to the natural law tradition, the drawback was that natural law insisted on the autonomy of the natural moral order so strongly that it was hard to find a place for biblical insights in the Catholic natural law system.[39]

Today, in the wake of Vatican II, nearly all Catholic scholars want to do better at incorporating biblical insights into moral theology. But how do we go about this? If we limit ourselves to moral principles alone, or to logical deductions from principles to cases, we will find some use for biblical insights, but our use of these insights will be fairly restricted. However, if we see moral theology as involving a richly imaginative process of understanding, reunderstanding, and creatively applying moral principles, biblical insights can serve to fire our imaginative insights throughout the entire process of moral discernment. We saw earlier that biblical scholars themselves have been moving toward more imaginative study of Scripture as a much needed supplement to scientific exegesis. Moral theology can and should join biblical scholarship in a more imaginative use of Scripture.

For some years now, there has been a debate, especially among Catholic scholars, about whether or not there is such a thing as a distinctively Christian ethic.[40] Those Catholic scholars who limit themselves to moral principles alone have tended to deny the existence of a distinctively Christian ethic. If we move beyond principles to the level of moral imagination, biblical symbols and stories would indeed seem to create the possibility of a Christian moral imagination. While Christians may not come up with formally different moral principles, Christians can articulate their principles through Christian symbols and stories. These symbols and stories can give Christians an ongoing imaginative way of developing their insights into and applications of moral principles, even though Christians hold these principles in common with other persons.

Imagination: For Persons and Groups as Well as Decisions

Finally, in terms of moral imagination's importance, once we admit that moral decisions are not always simple deductions from principles, moral theology becomes much more than a theology of moral decisions alone. Moral theology becomes a theology of developing moral persons who have the resources to make good decisions, even when the circumstances are not that clear. The overly scientific bent of some recent moral theology was so decision-oriented that the need to move beyond decisions to the development of moral persons was sometimes overlooked. Today we are again much concerned about the development of moral persons, with the revival of a philosophy and theology of virtue especially emphasizing this concern. To state this in another way, today's moral theology is much interested in developing persons of character.[41]

In this framework, moral imagination seems especially apt in helping people grow and develop as strong moral persons, i.e., as persons of good character. Imagination within a person is a vital force, a sign of life. With moral imagination, the person is truly and constantly alive to the world around him or her. With imagination, the person develops habits of creativity and insight. The person who imagines celebrates life. He or she is in tune with the deepest meaning of the world. Such a person brings very good resources to decisions, even when facing problems no one has ever faced previously in exactly the same way. We need to teach people moral principles, but to enhance their growth as moral persons, we need to help them also to be creative imaginers.

In moving beyond a one-sided emphasis on decision making in moral theology, we should also note that not only individuals but groups or communities are called upon to exercise imagination in the moral sphere. Much of the language I have used in this chapter has been about the individual person exercising moral imagination, but in the final analysis communities as well as persons need to develop moral character and exercise moral imagination as they seek to address the great issues of our times. We have noted that story and virtue spring from a socially shared context. Moral imagination extends the socially shared moral context of the past into the present and the future.[42]

While the notion of sharing moral vision and imagination applies to any human community, we might note that the Church especially seems called to be a community where moral imagination is exercised. Earlier we spoke of the magisterium's need to be morally imaginative, but in a larger sense, all levels of the Church community need to exercise moral imagination. The nuclear arms issue has become central in so many Christian communities in the United States largely because these communities have learned to exercise moral and pastoral imagination on the nuclear arms issue. Following from this, a key agenda item for many Catholic groups in the United States (parishes, dioceses, schools, etc.) will be the finding of truly imaginative ways of communicating the full meaning of the U.S. bishops' recent nuclear arms pastoral.

The mention of the community's role in exercising moral imagination leads to another important observation: moral imagination will be an extraordinarily difficult project at times. It will not always work. It will sometimes fail, due to our human limitations. When moral imagination does fail, we will sometimes make it through by leaning on our principles. But sometimes we will have to wait patiently until imagination does come.[43] This line of thought is perhaps best summarized by the words of Habakkuk: "For still the vision awaits its time; it hastens to the end—it will not lie. If it seem slow, wait for it; it will surely come, it will not delay" (Hb 2:3).

How Moral Imagination Functions

Based on our description of moral imagination so far, the functioning of moral imagination can be said to have three main phases: the forming of images, the associating of images, and the judgment of appropriateness. Much has been said already about each of these phases, but some further reflections will be helpful, especially in terms of how to avoid pitfalls in the functioning of each phase. We shall comment on each of the three in turn.

Forming Images

The first phase is the forming of images, both of the actions being considered and of the pertinent moral principles. A person's cultural and educational experience concerning language, art, science, etc. will have a great deal of impact on just how the person forms his or her images, just how the person renders images (which will always have a sense component) intelligible. The more cultural background a person achieves, the more readily he or she will be able to form images, and thus move to moral goals for the future.

The connection of this first phase of moral imagination with education and culture raises an important question. Is moral imagination only for the well educated and highly cultured, and would this in turn mean that moral imagination is principally for the economically advantaged? Two lines of response ought to be made to this question. First, in point of fact, all of the world's cultures have developed symbols and art forms. Imagining is a fundamental quality of being human, engaged in by all people everywhere. Thus, imaginative interpretations of reality are available to persons in a whole variety of social and economic situations. Sometimes persons from Western countries fall into the error of thinking that only they have culture. This can lead to a failure to recognize or even an effort to repress other cultures with their symbols and images. The dealing of whites with black cultures, both in the United States and Africa, is one prominent example of the Western failure to appreciate other cultures.

Second, it should be noted that education into classical symbols and art forms can assist the development of imagination. Thus, without one's culture's propagandizing itself against others, there is an important social and moral responsibility to assist the imaginative development of all people. The Church especially should seek to help people develop a Christian imagination out of which a moral life can be more readily lived.

Comments such as these raise the issue of how we go about sharing of the fruits of human imaginative creativity. An important point in terms of such sharing is that those cultural accomplishments which are most able to help persons form creative images are also the most sharable cultural accomplishments. If a person builds a house, there is some reasonable limit to the number of people who can live in the house. But if a person writes a great novel, there is in principle no limit to the number of people who can read the novel, assuming that we do not limit the number of books printed or people taught to read. The same is true for great works of music and art. Thus it is in the public interest for governments and individuals to work for the educational and cross-cultural sharing of classical images.

In addition to the theme of major cross-cultural sharing of classical works, we should think too about ways to foster more sharing of the less classical but still deeply human images which all of us form from day to day. Even these less classical images merit appropriate recognition, so that the wealth of human imagination becomes more well known and more able to serve as an inspiration for new imaginative creativity and for moral living. Children love to share their attempts at art; in parallel ways, we might all learn to do more of the same.

Associating Images

Once we have formed images of our options for moral action and of the pertinent moral principles, the next step is to let these images have their impact on one another. We reflect on our moral images, seeking to get further and further into the real depth of what they mean, seeking to fit the images together in a way which will lead to a genuinely good moral choice.

Several times I have described this reflection on our moral images as play, as suspension of judgment. To reflect on our moral images, to really think about them, we do need to let go, to open ourselves up to the full power and meaning of the images. Religious contemplation, when properly understood, is a leisurely or playful action.[44] Moral contemplation must have the same play aspect.

A number of factors can hinder persons from being genuinely reflective and playful in their moral thinking. Power or force is one such factor. If moral choice is conceived of primarily as response to alien or outside power, there will be very little room for reflective moral thinking. In a natural law worldview, God does communicate his will to us, but he communicates in a manner which accords with our intelligent and image making nature, rather than in an alien or authoritarian fashion. Thus, excessively authoritarian persons seek to play God in a way which God himself does not choose to employ in communicating with us.

In the end both persons who are uncritically committed to the status quo and persons who are uncritically opposed to the status quo can operate out of a very similar tendency to be authoritarian and to base their ethics on the principle of who can exercise the most power. Both groups have little interest in the reflective imaginative consideration of moral options and principles. These groups' concentration on power seems to go against the heart of the natural law tradition. Their concentration is a refusal to let themselves be played or changed by the truth to be found in moral cases and moral principles.

None of these denies in any way that we can make good moral decisions to exercise authority, to obey authority, or to resist authority. The institutional Church may also decide to act in these same ways. But these decisions themselves are reflective, rather than uncritical uses of power. These decisions come out of playful, human reflection on our moral images.

Fear of power also keeps us from playful and reflective consideration of our moral images. Fairly often I run into persons whose image of God is that God is out to get us. Such persons want to be told what to do, and they are afraid of using their moral imaginations. Their religious or prayer lives will often be quite limited because their fear keeps them from really being open to the power of the Gospel stories. In moral matters, these persons will often find decisions related to sexuality to be especially difficult, as their excessive fears often come to the surface in the area of sexuality.

In a social context, the power persons and the fear persons often interact with one another in such a way as to make it more difficult for either group to imagine reflectively on moral issues. Sometimes the whole social policy of a nation or other group can become distorted, because the power-fear dialectic cuts off all truly imaginative reflection on what our social actions mean. For instance, recent historical studies have quite clearly shown that the Western countries' attitude toward China in the nineteenth and early twentieth centuries was a failure in social imagination. The West at that time lacked all capacity to playfully associate images so as to develop a vision of who the Chinese were. All that was left were static and ultimately unimaginative stereotypes.[45]

Judgments of Appropriateness

After developing our rich moral images and then playfully letting these images interact, we need to make moral judgments about how we should act. Sometimes these judgments will be quite simple. But other times they will be more complex, perhaps involving a deeper interpretation of one or another moral principle, perhaps involving a new insight into the nature of the action we are considering. A moral imaginer in the early twentieth century might have come to see, for example, that an action he had thought was liberating the Chinese people was in fact exploiting them.

But just how does this judgment happen? How does the moral judgment take place? The judgment may involve logic, but it is never simply logic. The judgment may involve reliance on authority, but as a human moral judgment it is never simply based on authority. Is there a way we can go deeper and come up with a better description of what a moral judgment is?

If we consider that human imagination always involves a sense element, the themes of figure and form might help us get a clue to imaginative judgment. Imaginative judgments, even when very abstract, involve matter and space; they involve the way in which things are arranged or fit together. Imaginative moral judgments thus concern how our actions and our principles fit together; they are judgments of the fitting or of the coherent.

These notions of fittingness and coherence seem to me to be closely related to what traditional Roman Catholic philosophy had in mind when it spoke about moral certainty.[46] These notions also seem to relate closely to Aristotle's concept of practical reason. Practical reason cannot accomplish an exhaustive analysis of all pertinent data. But it can reflect on the data as imaginatively as possible, and it can fit the data together into a reasonably coherent pattern. A person who acts on the basis of this sort of practical reason or moral certainty knows that all the complexity and difficulty of life have not been eliminated. But he or she has creatively and humanly achieved sufficient conviction so as to act with true confidence.

Throughout this chapter I have several times used the word appropriate when discussing the criteria for practical moral judgment. From our practical, playful, imagining reason we discern what is most fitting and judge that to be the appropriate course of action. In so doing, we are following a method much the same as the discernment method as it has developed across the centuries.

Two scholars, one from the nineteenth and one from the twentieth century, have especially influenced my notion of imaginative moral judgment as judgment of the fitting or appropriate. Cardinal Newman's concept (in *The Grammar of Assent*) of knowledge as developing through converging probabilities seems very much to support the concept of practical reason arriving at the fitting through a truthful reflection upon our images of reality.[47] H. Richard Niebuhr (in *The Responsible Self*) explicitly moves beyond a deontological ethic (based on rules from authority) and a teleological ethic (based on logical derivation from moral principles). Niebuhr calls for an ethics of responsibility which he explicitly describes as an ethics which seeks after the fitting.[48] To that I would only add that we get to judgments about the fitting, first by forming (out of our history and life experience) moral images, and then by playfully reflecting upon them.

5

Some Examples of Moral Imagination

The last chapter developed a theory on the meaning and function of moral imagination. The present chapter will seek to flesh that theory out by presenting some examples to help show how moral imagination works. As we begin considering the examples, two cautions must be noted. First, it will not be our purpose to achieve a detailed examination and discussion of any of the examples to be presented. The purpose will be narrower: to show us how moral imagination might be of use in approaching the examples. Second, our main purpose will not be to give specific answers to the moral dilemmas raised in the examples. We noted above that clear answers will not always be available either through moral principles, or through moral imagination, or even through a junction of principles and imagination. Thus, there will be times when moral imagination calls on us to wait and hope rather than to come up with an overly facile answer. In some of the examples I will suggest a possible answer, but in other cases I will not propose answers. Whether or not an answer is proposed, the main purpose will be to see how moral imagination can help us in dealing with moral dilemmas.

The examples to be considered will be drawn from three major areas: biomedical ethics, sexual ethics, and the ethics of peace and justice. There are of course other key ethical areas such as law and ethics, but the three areas we shall draw from are, in my judgment, the areas which have stimulated the widest range of interest in moral theology today. We will by no means cover every issue to be found in each of these three areas, and the issues which are of most concern to some readers will surely be omitted. The purpose is not to be exhaustive, but simply to give a sense of how imagination might work in some of the major branches of ethics.

As the examples unfold, imagination will be seen as working in different ways in different examples, but always in accord with the threefold scheme of forming images, associating images, and making appropriate moral judgments. In some examples (e.g., care for the dying, the meaning of women, attitudes toward socialist economics), the task will be to form new images to replace inadequate ones. In other examples (e.g., sexuality and the retarded, world hunger) the task will be to form images where we seem to have none. In still other cases (e.g., artificial birth control) the task will be a more genuine association of existing images. In many cases, the need for appropriately imaginative judgments will be present. In some of the cases (e.g., casual sex), strengthened moral imagination will support the traditional understanding and application or moral principles, but in other cases (e.g., the nuclear arms issue) moral imagination will call us to new understandings and different applications of basic moral principles. In most of the examples, several different functions of imagination will overlap, but the reader will probably see each case as especially illustrating one or two key functions of moral imagination.

EXAMPLES FROM BIOMEDICAL ETHICS

Care for the Dying

In my own experience in serving as an ethical advisor for a number of Catholic hospitals in several cities, care for dying patients strikes me as the biggest single issue which patients, doctors, nurses, pastoral care ministers, families, and others face on a daily basis. While my personal experience is not as extensive in other health care settings, I believe that the issue of care for the dying is a major issue in all health care settings.

We should note at the outset that there are two types of problems related to care for the dying—the problem of dying patients being undertreated (not given enough care), and the problem of dying patients being overtreated (having too many medical technologies applied to them). Both of these problems are important, but the second of them, overtreatment, is the more common and thus will be our point of focus.

The problem of overtreatment is that too many patients are given therapies which add little significant time to their lives, therapies which are often quite expensive and which sometimes increase the pain of patients' dying days and hours. Such therapies can also tend at times to hamper human communication between the dying patient and his or her family and loved ones. Very often such therapies are administered because no one wants to talk about not administering them. This is especially true concerning the use of CPR (cardio-pulmonary resuscitation).

The complexity of the problem of care for the dying is heightened by the fact that Roman Catholic medical ethics has for many generations had clear, logical, and quite acceptable moral principles designed to address the issue of care for the dying.[1] Based on these Catholic principles, there is no need to use therapies which do not offer the dying patient any reasonable benefit. But still such therapies are used, both in Catholic and in secular health care settings. The case seems to be a clear issue of a situation in which sound moral principles are not enough.

Surely, there are many reasons why contemporary society has difficulty in caring for the dying in a suitable manner. With so many new medical technologies, there are naturally questions about when—and when not—to use them. The fear of medical malpractice suits makes many physicians think they should always use available therapies, regardless of the circumstances of the patient. Guilts that many family members feel about their dealings with one another in life can create a false sense of obligation to use all possible therapies at the time of death.[2]

Deeper than all of these matters, however, lies another reason why we often fail to care well for the dying, a reason which is especially important in terms of moral imagination. This reason is the fear of death, the sense that death is an absolute enemy to be fought off at all costs. Fear of death is profoundly present in our contemporary culture. Advertising, for instance, all seems to be designed to emphasize youth, beauty, thinness, etc. and to deny the reality of death. The marginalization of older persons in our culture is in many respects an effort to put older people out of the mainstream of life so that they won't remind us of our common mortality. Doctors in particular can develop an imposing fear of death. So much of their professional training deals with conquering diseases that when they fail to conquer death they think they have failed completely. In this context, death becomes the ultimate enemy, which must always be acted against.

Coupled with the fear of death comes an exaggerated emphasis on the physical aspects of life, so that we can tend to forget about many of the deeper meanings of life and thus equate life with physical life. The disproportionate concern with physical sexual activities which exists in some quarters and the very excessive salaries paid to many professional athletes are but two examples of the overstress on the physical side of life.

If sound moral principles are not enough to work out an adequate approach to death and to care for the dying, I think our deepest need is for a renewed understanding of death, an understanding in which death no longer need be understood as the ultimate human catastrophe. Moreover, I think that such a renewed understanding is most readily available through an exercise of imagination. Particularly for Christians who celebrate in an ongoing way the passion, death, and resurrection of Jesus, I think a new imagination about death is possible.[3]

In this new imagination, death does not cease to be death; its agony and passion do not disappear. But in the Christian story there is more to life than physical death. In this story, we can be filled with a hope that goes beyond death, and we can be able to let go when death cannot be avoided. With our imaginations filled with the Christian story, we can play with our image of death, and we can let this story-formed image lead us to more appropriate decisions in caring for the dying, decisions which will involve not rendering certain forms of treatment when such treatments are not indicated for those who are surely dying.

Such a deepened, story-formed image of the meaning of death can also help lead us to a deeper image of the meaning of life, an image which prizes physical life, but also an image which is clear that there are many human life values which go beyond the physical. Many of our great heroes and heroines of the past have risked or sacrificed physical life for the sake of deeper life-oriented values. We can think, for instance, of the courage of Thomas More as he stood for religious liberty, or the bravery of American pioneers such as the Donner party whose search for a better life led them to undertake very risky and for some even fatal wagon journeys across the American West. These people clearly knew that there was more to life than physical survival at any cost, and for this reason they have become our heroes and heroines. Stories of such heroes and heroines fire our imagination. They call us to a different appreciation of life than that which exists in much modern culture, an appreciation which will let go of physical life in favor of death when the circumstances warrant. This was surely the approach of Jesus who for Christians is the greatest of heroes.

Such an image-formed approach to death and life might also help us come to a more satisfactory understanding of the purpose and responsibility of medicine in relation to dying patients. A one-sidedly scientific outlook creates the notion that the purpose of medicine is always to cure persons. A more human and Christian notion of death recognizes that life is not always something to be clung to and that for this reason we need not do everything possible to stave off death when cure of the dying is no longer possible.

Instead of the "curing" image, we need a new image of our responsibility to the dying, an image which stresses our covenant (another biblical theme) to be with the dying, to keep them company, above all to care for the dying when we cannot cure them.[4] In this context some of the older medical codes with their stress on bedside manners for physicians, on how to talk to families, etc., might be instructive. There was much paternalism in older codes to which we should never return.[5] But in former eras curing was not nearly so possible, and medicine may have been more ready to discuss what we must humanly do when we cannot prevent death.

Here again, we could arrive at a care theory on the basis of logical principles. But our imaginations, drawing on powerful stories of human care, might well be more able to foster an ethic of true care for dying than are our principles alone. In so many cultures, there are stories of great heroism on the part of those caring for the dying. Nathaniel Hawthorne's daughter Rose is but one example from the American past. Her work with incurable cancer patients still stands as a remarkable testimony to what can be accomplished when we genuinely and humanly seek to keep company with the dying.[6] The religious community which she founded, the Sisters of the Sick Poor, still continue her heroic work of care for the sick and dying.

True care for the dying is not something anyone can do alone. It is a human task which we do together. Too often in an overly cure centered approach, doctors can feel that they are totally responsible for dying patients since only they have the means to cure. When death is unreasonably feared and curing is not possible, doctors (and all the rest of us too) can find communication about dying patients very hard. If we can use our imagination to arrive at a more care centered ethic, perhaps all of us—doctors, nurses, ministers, family, and most importantly the patient himself or herself—can join together in the process of care for the dying. The patient may not always be competent, but when competent, he or she ought to be the primary decision maker in decisions about the care to be rendered when death is expected.

In my remarks so far I have especially commented on Christian symbols or images such as resurrection and covenant. I have sought to show that prayerful play with these images can lead us to new insights and actions concerning, death, life, and care.[7] But more imaginative approaches to the meaning of death and the value of life are by no means limited to Christians alone. Stories of heroism in care for the dying, stories of deeper insights into the value of life, and stories of bravery when facing death abound in many religions and cultures. For Christians, the symbolism of the resurrection will be paramount in all imagination about death and after life. But rich human imagination on this theme is possible in many contexts.

I introduced this section on dying by speaking on our difficulties in caring well for the dying in spite of our clear moral principles on the subject. The difficulties are surely there and they can be helped by imaginative, story-formed insight. For the record it should be noted that there has also been significant progress on this issue in recent years. Some doctors care very deeply about this issue. Some hospitals have issued helpful new protocols on the subject. The U.S. Veterans Administration has recently adopted helpful new guidelines. One of the Vatican's best recent statements has been on this issue. New approaches such as hospice care are emerging which help make it possible for persons to die in their homes or in other appropriate non-hospital settings such as care centers established specifically for the dying.[8]

Much therefore has already been accomplished in the quest for a more human approach to care for the dying. Or to say it in another way, imagination has already been at work on the theme of death and dying. Hospices with their new settings for death especially represent an exercise of creative imagination. But more needs to be done, and this too will call for imagination.

The Cost of Health Care

Over the course of the twentieth century, ethical literature has gradually developed the concept that a reasonable level of health care is a human right.[9] The literature holds that health is so basic to other human goods that all persons deserve adequate care of their health. Diseases can strike all persons, regardless of social or economic status, so that it does not seem just to base access to reasonable health care on criteria such as economic status or social worth. There are of course arguments as to how much health care persons can expect as a right. What aspects of health care are basic and therefore to be understood as a right? And what aspects of health care can be seen as frills and thus not as a matter of right?[10] Debate about these issues does not, however, deny the growing consensus that health care is a right. Pope John Paul II spoke about this right in his recent encyclical *Laborem Exercens*.[11]

The sad fact is, however, that, in spite of the building ethical consensus, relatively little is being done to enhance the health care rights of many persons in the United States. As I write these lines, it seems that the inflationary spiral which has marked our economy since the Vietnam era is coming toward an end. Prices for many items are not increasing nearly as fast as they did a few years ago. Careful study of recent cost of living figures shows, however, that health care is one major area where prices are continuing to rise at a high rate. The good news about inflation has not yet been good news on the health care front.

In addition, so much of the emphasis on health care in our culture still focuses on caring for persons only after they have become seriously ill. Though some good steps have been taken, relatively little is being done to promote preventive health care.[12] Such care, while it is less financially remunerative for doctors and other health professionals, is also less costly and easier to distribute to more people. All in all, the emerging theories about the human right to health care have had only a limited practical effect in the United States.

Obviously the skyrocketing costs of health care are a tragedy for the poor. Some of the poor fall through the cracks of programs such as Medicare and Medicaid, and very often these programs are not adequate for the poor who do qualify for them, but who have no other health insurance. Perhaps less obvious is the impact of high health care costs on middle class people. They too will often avoid seeing doctors because of fear of the medical bills. As a result, both poor and middle class persons often end up attending to their health only when major crises develop. In the long run, all of this serves to make health care even more costly. Economic pressures in the health care system can also make it less attractive financially for doctors to practice in areas other than affluent suburbs. Inner city people and rural people can find it very difficult to see a doctor, even if they have enough money to pay the bills.

We have therefore a genuine crisis in achieving a just delivery of health care. But where does imagination fit in? How might imagination help us address this crisis? The key, as I see it, is that imagination can help us form a new vision of the doctor's role in society and a new vision of how doctors might appropriately be compensated for their services.

For many centuries we have held doctors and their services in great esteem, and, as part of that esteem, we have assumed that the proper way to compensate doctors was to pay them directly for their services. Historically such an approach worked very well. One thinks of stories of doctors traveling great distances to see their patients, often traveling in cold and snow, in the middle of the night, usually in simple, horse-drawn carriages. Patients who lacked cash could often pay the doctor in sacks of potatoes, or other bartered goods, and when patients could not pay at all, doctors were very often able to run their own charity or welfare systems. I spent much of my youth in a small town where it was not unusual for the doctor to sit up all night with a dying patient (at the patient's home), so I have personally experienced the classic tradition of the good doctor in our culture.

The power of this classical view of the doctor in our culture is so strong that it is very hard for many of us to let go of this view. In particular, it is hard for us to entertain as realistic any notion other than the idea that patients should directly pay doctors for services rendered. Even in the tremendously complex context of modern medicine, where family doctors are much less common than in the past, and where the classical model of the country doctor neither can nor should be fully recovered, we still find it hard to consider anything but traditional economics in the field of medicine.

But this is exactly where moral imagination can be of such help to us. One of the main functions of moral imagination is to help us suspend our standard moral judgments so that we can entertain and play with new images which might be more appropriate in a changed social context. Specifically, with moral imagination we might be able to let go of our traditional approach to financing medical care so as to consider freely and without fear what other options there might be in a world in which the cost of health care has become such a pressing problem for so many.

If we could learn to let go and play with new options in health care financing, we would see that there are already many imaginative options which we could play over and try to interrelate. Health maintenance organizations (HMO's) where one pays a fixed annual fee for all needed care are one such option. Cut-rate approaches to simpler health care needs may be a viable option in some contexts. (Some people are calling these cut-rate schemes the McDonald's and Burger King approach to health care.) The nationalized health care systems of countries such as Canada and Great Britain also deserve very serious consideration.[13] These national systems have surely not been the medical and moral disasters which some conservative groups predicted they would be. The system proposed by Senator Edward Kennedy also deserves consideration. Kennedy's system would insure the health care needs of every American but it would keep the private interests (doctors, insurance companies, hospitals, drug companies) in place as part of the system.

No doubt objections could be raised to every one of these newer initiatives in the financing of health care. Moral imagination will grant the possible objections, but it will keep on playing with these and other alternatives. Moreover moral imagination will have the openness needed to implement one or some combination of the newer alternatives, even if that alternative is not perfect. Moral imagination will look for and try to preserve what was best in the traditional doctor/patient relationship, but it will not be so wedded to that relationship that it is unable to really entertain new options.

Again we might stress the crucial importance of moral imagination's freedom to shed old images (e.g., of the doctor as always to receive a direct fee for service) and to genuinely play with new options. Principled ethical discourse has generated the several financing options for health care which we have just mentioned. But relatively little has happened in the United States, precisely because of our inability to exercise a collective moral imagination in the area of health care. Thus we know the scholarly options, but as a people we cannot really let ourselves pursue them. Even the initiatives of countries which are ideologically close to the United States (Canada, Great Britain) have not been sufficient to overcome our lack of imagination, our lack of an ability to suspend judgment, and truly play with new options for health care financing.

Besides the fundamental question of how we should finance the cost of health care, moral imagination might also help us in several other areas which are related to the cost of health care. Two such areas will be mentioned here. First, when discussing death and dying we spoke of the image of medicine as caring for patients rather than always curing them. We also noted that steps to prevent health crises ought to be an important part of an overall health care program. These themes of care and preventive care can be imaginatively developed so as to lay a greater stress on themes such as nutrition, exercise, sleep, clean water, good sanitation, etc. Creative and imaginative work on these themes has already taken place in public service ads, educational programs for children, etc. The challenge is to stretch our imaginations even further along these lines.

I once heard a little girl tell her mother that she never needed to worry about getting lost when she went shopping with her mother. All she would need to do, even in a big department store, would be to listen for a husky smoker's cough and she could find her mother immediately. I doubt very much that the child could have given a logical argument against smoking, but on the imaginative level probably no one could have more effectively helped convince the mother to stop smoking.

Second, one of the most agonizing questions in medicine today has to do with where we should channel our resources in medical research. Granted the tremendous costs of medical research (a major factor in the cost of medicine as a whole), we cannot do every medical research project which is technically feasible. We have to make decisions about which research ought to be done and which research must be foregone, at least at the present time. Principled discussion is surely needed in this area.[14] But at the same time, an imaginative grasp of what our humanity means, an imaginative grasp of the covenant loyalty we owe to one another, might help us make these difficult decisions. An imaginative grasp of our humanity might suggest, for example, that we are more obligated to research ways of developing clean water and increased crop yield in poor countries than we are obligated to research relatively rare diseases which affect only relatively small numbers of people.

There are no easy answers to this question, or to any question related to the just delivery of health care. True moral imagination can help to make the difficult answers at least a little more accessible.

EXAMPLES FROM SEXUAL ETHICS

Casual Pre-Marital Intercourse

Of the many stances taken in traditional sexual morality, the traditional stance against casual pre-marital sexual intercourse may well be the single most coherent and well supported position.[15] In terms of the meaning of our humanity, there are and continue to be very strong arguments against casual pre-marital sex. Sexual intercourse by its nature calls for human commitment between the parties sharing the intercourse. It is not simply a physical action which can be meaningfully done only for pleasure, for experimentation, etc.

However, as our first chapter noted, for all the logic and clarity of the traditional opposition to casual pre-marital sex, the traditional view seems to be observed in our times as much in the breach as in actual observation. Those involved in the pastoral ministry can testify from experience that clear principles are not enough on this issue. We need, therefore, to find a new way of speaking about casual pre-marital intercourse, a way of speaking which will make abstention from such intercourse attractive, a way which will make young people want to abstain from casual intercourse and want to wait for marriage.

As I see it, an imaginative appeal to our young people, an appeal which holds up to them the beauty, wonder, and grandeur of marriage and family life, may be much more effective than an appeal to principles alone. If we can fire our young people's imaginations with a sense of the greatness of marriage, the chances of their seeing sexual intercourse and marriage as inherently joined will be much better. In an era such as ours when many marriages fail, no approach to teaching the ethics of casual pre-marital sex will be perfectly successful, but a more imaginative approach holds promise for significant success.

Two main emphases can be employed in an imaginative appeal to the goodness of marriage as the motivation to avoid casual pre-marital sex. First, an appeal can be made to concrete instances of deep and loving marriages, an appeal which points out all the good these marriages have brought to the partners, their children, their relatives and friends, and, indeed, to all society. Fortunately many people have examples of such marriages available to them in their own families, so that the appeal can be quite personal and reach levels of awareness which go beyond the level of logic. Some people will not have as much direct experience of good marriages, but in these cases literature, music, art, poetry, and history might all be brought into use as means of evoking the greatness of marriage.[16]

As part of this process of highlighting the success of specific marriages, churches might do more to celebrate the long-term anniversaries of parishioners. Also, in the tradition of recalling the lives of the saints, married saints could be given more stress. A difficulty here is that the past fears of marriage have led to a disproportionately low number of canonizations for married saints. But whether canonized or not, great examples of married love can be recalled and celebrated by the community.

The second main emphasis deals with a theme we have already raised several times, the theme of covenant.[17] A major focus of the Old Testament is that God reaches out to us with a faithful and steadfast love. This is God's covenant with us: God loves us with an everlasting love. The Old Testament covenant is perhaps best summed up in Yahweh's words "I will be their God and they will be my people." These words come up again and again in the Old Testament.

In the New Testament, Jesus understands his love for us as very much a continuation of the covenant love of the Old Testament. The whole thrust of the paschal mystery, i.e., of Jesus' passion, death, and resurrection, is that Jesus loves us with a faithful and lasting love. Different traditions of spirituality have approached devotion to

Jesus differently. But the covenant theme—that Jesus loves us faithfully and that we can count on him as we await his return—is fundamental to all forms of spiritual devotion to Jesus.

From this context of covenant love, Christian marriage takes on an even deeper meaning so as to invite people even more to avoid casual pre-marital sex in favor of the marriage commitment. While Christ's love covenant with us is expressed in many ways, Christian marriage, from biblical times, has been understood as a very special or privileged expression of covenant love. The married couple, in their faithful love, are expressing Christ's love for all of us. They are making this love real in the world. From a faith perspective, our counting on married love and our counting on Christ's love are very much intertwined. To keep Christ's love real in this world, all of us, no matter what our states in life might be, are in need of the witness of married love.

When a marriage is reasonably happy and successful over the years, the married couple will often develop a concrete sense that there is more to their success in marriage than they can explain on the basis of their own efforts or other natural causes. This "more" is, from a faith perspective, the presence of Christ's covenant love, the presence of a God-dimension. At the bottom line, it is the couple themselves who must discover that God is a covenant partner with them as they live out their marriage. But all of us need to do what we can to make this faith covenant aspect of marriage stand out more clearly.

Every aspect of the married life of the couple shares in their covenant mission of witnessing to the love of Christ for the world. But for our purposes we should especially note that sexual communion witnesses to Christ's covenant love. Sexual communion involves the deepest reaches of our humanity and is thus especially apt to proclaim Christ's love. In particular, the faithful expression of sexual communion over many years mirrors the fidelity of Christ's love. This does not mean that intercourse must always be so serious that it can never be fun, but it does mean that to be genuine fun, intercourse must occur in an adequately human context.

Some may find this sort of talk naïve and idealistic, and from the point of view of mere logic perhaps it is. My whole point is that to articulate a viable stance against casual sex we have to get beyond the level of logic. Whether we appeal to the human imagination in a

secular sense (by the heroic examples of great marriages), or in a religious sense (by evoking Christ's covenant love), or both, we simply must give our young people rich symbols which can play on their
imaginations and lead them to a new level of judgment about casual
sex. I have stated the imaginative argument against casual pre-marital sex, but this argument ultimately applies to casual sex in any
form.

The Debate over Birth Control

In the Roman Catholic context, contraception is one of the most
intractable problems in sexual ethics today. The official position of
the Roman Church opposes artificial contraception in all cases. This
position, which has been clearly reaffirmed by Pope John Paul II in
speeches in various parts of the world,[18] is based on the teaching of
the Church that the procreation of children and the unity of the couple are so inextricably intertwined as purposes of marriage that the
couple in its conjugal love can never act directly against either of
these purposes. On the other hand, assuming that the statistical researchers are correct, millions of Catholics around the world, especially in the developed countries, believe that artificial contraception
is morally good in some cases. These persons base their position on
the tremendous importance of covenanted sexual love in marriage.
They hold that, in some cases, the avoidance of artifically contraceptive measures unreasonably prejudices their right to and need for
conjugal sexual love.

The focus in what follows here is not to achieve a definitive answer to the contraception dispute. Rather, the focus is to ask whether
there is some way in which moral imagination might help the two
groups in this dispute talk to and listen to one another so that the dispute ends up not being quite so intractable.

I think an important advance in the contraception debate might
be possible if the two groups could learn to share and play with one
another's images, if the two groups could temporarily suspend judgment in the classic imaginative style, so that the symbols, metaphors, and images of both groups might be given room to operate.
While not wishing to predict the outcome at this point, I believe that
such imaginative sharing might do a great deal of good.[19]

As I see it, the dominant image underlying the opposition to artificial birth control is the image of children as gift, mystery, and wonder, the image of sexual intercourse as an act of openness to the gift, mystery, and wonder of children. We very much need this image of the child as gift in our times. Modern technology has fostered a thought world in which children can all too easily be thought of as technical products to be planned rather than as gifts to be beheld in wonder and mystery. The technological attitude toward children is significant for many issues besides contraception. The openness to abortion and *in vitro* fertilization and the tendency not to perform life saving operations on humanly savable handicapped newborn children stem, to a significant degree, from this same view—that children are products to be planned instead of gifts to be accepted.[20]

This does not mean that all parental planning in regard to children is wrong. Parents can and should plan to give their children opportunities in life, and even official Catholic teaching respects as fully legitimate a couple's concern about the number of children they have.[21] It remains true, however, that the planning angle can be overdone, with the child's whole life being orchestrated to fulfill the parents' desires. Little League baseball often strikes me as an example of parents, especially fathers, arranging their children's lives to achieve the parents' unfulfilled desires.

Surely significant numbers of couples who favor contraception have thought about and believe in the giftedness of children. But this theme is often absent in pro-contraception rhetoric and in the general mentality of our society. Thus, those persons who have this giftedness as their dominant image find themselves unable to relate to the imaginative thought world of those favoring birth control. The image of child as hope-filled gift is crucially important and needs to be owned by all parties in the debate over birth control. The move toward birth control, especially in the permanent form of sterilization, of its nature involves an element of abandoning hope for the future. In any ethical position this abandonment must be taken into account.[22]

In my reading of Pope John Paul II's remarks on sexual matters, particularly those made while he was in the United States, I think his biggest criticism is a criticism of an underlying selfishness which marks the sexual outlook of many persons, especially in the developed countries.[23] I think this basic criticism of John Paul II is very legitimate, and that the child as gift theme is one of the keys which people must come to terms with in order to respond to the concern of John Paul II.

It might also be noted that the theme of child as gift is a richly imaginative theme both in the secular world and in the religious world. There are few, if any, events in life which raise more hope and call for more celebration than the birth of a child. Catholics are always taught that Easter is the most important feast in their liturgical calendar, and we have already seen the importance of Easter's theme of resurrection in shaping an imaginative approach to death and dying issues. But the fact is that, no matter what they are taught, Catholics (and all Christians) like Christmas better and celebrate Christmas more fully. The powerful image of the newborn child stamps Christmas and fills our imaginations with new hope, care for one another, and a desire to express our care with gifts. The child as gift image is thus a basic image which must be played with in all imaginative reflection on birth control.

To move to the other side, the dominant image of those who see artificial birth control as moral in some cases is the image of the sexual union as good, as strengthening the covenant of married love. From this viewpoint, to make it impossible or nearly impossible for a married couple to have intercourse becomes clearly wrong. Thus if another pregnancy would subject the spouses to death or severe health problems, to psychiatric or economic collapse, the love covenant image is used to argue in favor of artificial birth control as a reluctant but moral necessity.

In the previous section, when trying to work out a more imaginative approach to communicating the wrong in casual pre-marital sex, I described the power of the theme of marriage covenant especially in its biblical roots. In that context I stated that sexual union was an integral part of the meaning of marriage as the symbol or image of God's covenant love. Abstention from intercourse can and should have its place at times in any marriage, but in our era the importance of ongoing sexual communion is clearly and incontrovertibly recognized. Marriage is less well socially supported today than it was in the past. This makes the covenant image and its implications for sexual sharing all the more significant.

Without doubt the Catholic thinkers who oppose artificial birth control are aware of the theme of love covenant. But one might ask the question whether they have really played with this theme imaginatively, whether they have really let its full power enter into their reflections. Past Catholic history did at times contain a regrettable tone of downplaying marriage in favor of other vocations, and not all traces of this tone have disappeared in spite of the clear pro-marital tone of Vatican II and subsequent years. Thus, just as anti-birth control Catholics can wonder whether their dominant image of child as gift is really owned and played with by others, so too pro-birth control Catholics can wonder whether their dominant image of a love covenant expressed (partially) sexually is really owned and played with by others. Uncritically one-sided panegyrics about the beauty of sexual abstinence only strengthen the impression that the love covenant theme is not really heard by all.

I began by describing the birth control dispute as intractable and by stating that I could not make a simple prediction on the future course of the dispute. But my thought is that if both groups can exercise broad imagination, if both groups can genuinely open up to and play with all the pertinent images, perhaps new associations of images will become possible. Hopefully these will be imaginative associations which will help us to transcend the intractability of the present.

Two Newer Sexual Issues

A remarkably important development in twentieth century sexual ethics has been the growing awareness that human sexuality involves our entire personalities, not simply our physical make-up.[24] The more sexuality is spoken of in terms of themes like covenant fidelity, the more imperative it becomes to envision sexuality in terms of persons, not simply in terms of bodies or sexual organs. Contemporary theology does not forget or ignore the physical dimensions of sexuality, but it does move toward a much larger picture.

Several major challenges to our moral imaginations emerge from such a larger theological-anthropological approach to human sexuality. Two such challenges will be touched upon here. First, to the extent that our understanding of sexuality was too exclusively physical, the understanding of women was too exclusively physical. Three physical images of women predominated in many types of traditional thought. Women were seen as physical objects for the pleasure of men. Women were seen as a source of cheap labor, usually to be paid less than men, even for equal work. Women were seen as childbearers. This last role (of women as mothers) did not need to be understood in an exclusively physical sense, but sometimes it was.

These narrow physical images of women had a pervasive hold on the human imagination so that they were learned and made part of the self-concepts of many women (often with pain and repressed anger). At the same time these images led many men to see women as alien, inferior, and even evil beings. Studies have shown that elements of these images of women (with the corresponding images of men) were often part of the thinking of children in the very early years. Little girls already knew that their opportunities in life were different (and significantly more limited) than the opportunities which would be open to little boys.

I have spoken of this inadequate image of women as though it were something in the past tense. But regrettably, even though progress has been made, much of this image is still present. Much of it still colors relationships between the sexes. Men still conceive of women as sex objects, as inferiors in the workplace, etc. Here I am reminded of Carl Jung's notion that the collective memory of humanity is very long. Memory and imagination are closely related in human life. Both work with images, and both are partly sense functions. It takes a long time to outlive our images, even when these images are clearly inadequate. On women's issues, many men have learned the right language and the right theories, but they have not learned to imagine women differently, and thus, even with all good will, they still offend women.

Hence there is a real challenge to creative moral imagination, a challenge of coming up with powerful and viable images which adequately express the full humanity of women. Only with such images will we be ready, as a human community, to deal with the many ethical issues related to the women's rights movement. Such new and powerful images should not imply, at least in my judgment, that physical embodiment has no human meaning beyond biology. Granting this caution, it is clearly time to set aside past fears and move to an imaginative grasp of women and men as co-equals. If Jung is right about the collective human memory, it may take a few generations to work out an adequately imaginative theology of women. The time to begin is now.[25]

A second challenge of the larger and less physical approach to human sexuality is the challenge to us to work out new images of the sexuality of certain sexually forgotten groups such as the aged, the physically handicapped, and the retarded.[26] In this context the difficulty is that the image of sexual activity as being only for the young and physically healthy is extremely powerful in our society. So much in advertising, in television, in film, in art, and in literature depicts sexual activity as belonging only to the young and healthy. Thus we have a great difficulty in reflecting on the elderly, the handicapped, etc. as persons who are interested in sexual activity. We fear to imagine the elderly engaging in sexual acts, and we develop stereotypes (the "dirty old man") which label sex for the elderly as bad. Many people have a very hard time accepting the notion that their aging parents are still sexually active, with this fact sometimes contributing to the tendency of middle aged persons to treat their parents as children.

Often we do not even like to look at handicapped persons (prosthetic devices are sometimes as much for others as for the handicapped person), so that it becomes very difficult to imagine them as enjoying sex, even when they are personally able to do so. Much the same thing can be said about the sexual activities of the retarded.

Clearly, we need a new image of physical sexual activity as something which the aged, handicapped, and retarded are capable of enjoying. Once we let ourselves come to such a new image, we will be much more able to address with sensitivity the ethical questions which relate to the sexuality of these and similar groups. For instance, if we come to a better image of sexuality and the aging, the policies of nursing homes on the cohabitation of married couples, on courtship, and on marriage might become more open than they were in some instances in the past. Similarly we might be able to help reduce fear of sexual activity by the handicapped, and by those considering marrying them. Also, we might be able to make more realistic judgments as to when retarded persons ought to be free to marry, and when not. Many other examples could be cited as well.

In forming new images on the themes we are now considering, we must also be careful not to let our imaginations run in the opposite direction, so that we imagine groups such as the aged or handicapped too exclusively in sexual terms. One of my friends, who has a slight handicap and who is happy single, finds the literature for persons with the handicap to be a bit one-sided, in that the subject of how to be sexually active receives more attention than any other single issue. While homosexuality is clearly neither retardation nor a handicap, a similar type of sexual over-emphasis sometimes exists in the contemporary image of homosexual persons, with both many homosexuals and many persons who reject homosexual acts envisioning homosexual persons too exclusively in terms of sexual acts. It is good that many segments of society are more concerned for the human rights, etc. of homosexuals than was the case in the past. In the present context, my thought it that the disputes about homosexual actions and ethics may be able to be addressed more readily, if all people can develop an imagination which begins by seeing homosexuals as fully human persons, instead of beginning with the imagination of homosexual activities. On the basis of such an imagination, various issues related to the homosexual orientation can be addressed more adequately and with more nuance.

EXAMPLES FROM SOCIAL JUSTICE AND FROM PEACE ETHICS

Before we take up some specific examples from social justice, two points should be noted. First, it should be mentioned again that all imagining has a profoundly social character about it. In the two previous sections on medicine and sexuality, both the postive images (of covenant, resurrection, caring, childhood, etc.) and the unacceptable images (of the omnipotent doctor, of getting only what you pay for, of the woman as sex object, of the dirty old man, etc.) are socially shared images. Were these images only possessed by isolated individuals, they would not be as powerful as they are, either for good or for ill. This ties in with MacIntyre's point that because images are socially shared they lead us to virtue or to vice.[27] From this perspective, and without denying the importance of creative imagination by individual persons, moral imagination must be considered to be social.

Second, even from the point of view of specific moral issues, the division of moral theology into personal ethics (i.e., medicine and sexuality) and social ethics (war, economics, international relations, criminal justice, etc.) is never a fully adequate division. The major issues we have treated so far (death, health care, marriage and family life) have huge social ramifications, so that we can never adequately address them unless we can imagine them as social issues as well as personal issues.

However, for purposes of organization, it remains convenient to consider in a separate category those issues which relate to very large social systems, especially those issues which relate to the higher levels of government. We now turn to a sampling of such issues from the viewpoint of moral imagination.

Capital Punishment

Throughout most of human history, capital punishment has been accepted as a morally legitimate means of redressing major crimes.[28] Three major images—all in my judgment inadequate—have been used historically to legitimate captital punishment, with contemporary supporters of capital punishment still using these images today. The three images are as follows.

First, there was the image of revenge as a glorious act. The Old Testament and the medieval world both celebrated revenge in song and literature. When I was a child, revenge on the other side was often seen as a major object in little boys' games. Before I had any ethical concepts at all, I knew how to shout "revenge" as I charged the other side when playing Cowboys and Indians. Fundamentalist preachers even today place a lot of emphasis on the revenge passages in the Old Testament.

More careful reflection shows that revenge is not as glorious as was its depiction in song and cavalry charge. Study of the Christian concept of punishment points out that the purpose of punishment must be the ultimate reunion of the punisher and punished, i.e., the welcoming of the punished person back into the fold of society.[29] Thus punishment can never be a (glorious) end in itself but only a means to human growth. One of Gandhi's greatest insights was that violence is in the long run counter-productive because it only begets more violence. We may not succeed in totally eliminating all forms of violence, but we can no longer glorify revenge.

Second, there has been the long-standing theory that capital punishment would serve to deter other persons from committing serious crimes. Deterrence was often presented in ways which appealed to our imaginations and fears. Medieval rulers displayed the heads of beheaded victims on fenceposts or hurled these heads with catapults into the walled towns from which the criminals came.[30] Every once in a while some contemporary politician calls for modern executions to be done live and in color on television, so that executions will be more effective as deterrents to crime.

The main problem with deterrence images is that responsible studies have repeatedly failed to show that capital punishment actually does serve to deter crime.[31] The fact that capital punishment is not a proven method of preventing major crime (except on the part of the person who is executed) does not rule out other arguments for capital punishment, but like the imagery of revenge, the imagery of deterrence simply is not satisfactory as an argument for capital punishment.

Third, and perhaps most importantly, capital punishment has been justified on a ''good guys/bad guys'' approach to life, on what we might call a gnostic view of life. In such a view, the other (whether this other is a political enemy, a member of the other sex, a member of another race, a criminal, etc.) is made the source or locus of all evil. The other is demonized, i.e., pictured or imagined to be the devil incarnate. Any true human relationship with him or her becomes impossible. This view can be called gnostic because the major tenet of gnostic philosophy is a radical dualism which divides the world into good and evil. In gnostic thought the distinction between good and evil is perfectly clear. As the racially tinged metaphor puts it, all situations are clearly black and white.

We will see more of this demonizing dualism when we reflect on economic questions and arms policy. In the present context, such a gnostic dualism envisions the criminal to be a non-person toward whom we have no human responsibilities. Many past societies treated prisoners (and the mentally ill) virtually as animals. Such dualism also makes crime completely the responsibility of the criminal. All recognition of social inequities which lead to crime is excluded. In no way is crime our fault as a society. Once we have this kind of image of the criminal as a non-person and of ourselves as perfectly pure, capital punishment and all other dehumanizing approaches become completely acceptable without any questions being raised.

Sober reflection makes us realize that life is a good deal more complex. Without exonerating criminals (which is dehumanizing both for us and for the criminals),[32] we can see that crime has many roots and that to deal with crime we have to look at the nature of society as well as at the question of appropriate punishment of criminals. The gnostic image of the prisoner as a non-human demon is an incorrect basis from which to address the issues of capital punishment and criminal justice.

We should then set aside the unsatisfactory images of capital punishment as glorious revenge, as frightfully effective deterrence, and as dealing with demons. It is probably true that none of these images exists today in as raw a form as was the case in the ancient and medieval world. But we have already seen that the human recall of images, even bad ones, is very long lasting. We do not seem past the time when appeal to these images, often in very clever form, is used in setting public policies.

However, even if we do set these three images aside, criminal behavior remains a major human problem. It is reasonable to fear crime. It is reasonable to want to prevent crime. It is reasonable to be concerned for suitable punishment of criminals. The image of peace, of safety in the streets, is an image of genuine and true appeal to us. For these reasons, some in society still call for capital punishment, at least as a means of assuring that a specific murderer will not commit murder again.

Even among Christians, there are surely sincere and thoughtful persons who favor capital punishment.[33] But a very impressive majority of the mainstream Christian denominations today are opposing capital punishment.[34] Some denominations speak against capital punishment in all forms, while others do not theoretically rule out capital punishment, but oppose it as of now because we seem to have no just way of fairly enforcing capital punishment statutes, no just way to determine which criminals should be capitally punished and which not. This latter or "as of now" opposition is the position of the American Catholic bishops.[35] Recently Supreme Court Justice Powell spoke about the unsatisfactory character of existing capital punishment practices[36] (which have a tendency to involve long and contorted legal processes and which can work against the poor and against racial minorities), thus raising some of the same concerns raised by the Catholic bishops.

My own opinion is that it is probably not possible to construct a decisive logical argument against capital punishment. Can we then find a way to explain and give support to the instinct of the many Christian groups (and of many others as well) who are against capital punishment? So far we have appealed to moral imagination in a negative sense, seeking to do away with some popular and unacceptable images of capital punishment. I think moral imagination can also be used in a positive sense to help construct an argument against capital punishment.

Such a use of moral imagination begins with the following question: What happens imaginatively or symbolically when we deliberately put someone to death? Various answers might be possible, but, very clearly, the deliberate putting of someone to death has about it a profound hopelessness. Putting someone to death says that nothing else is possible for that person. It also says that nothing else is possible for society in the specific circumstances at hand. The human story is symbolized as a story without much hope, as a story which is not going anywhere except into an ongoing cycle of violence. Sometimes the intended killing of other human beings might not be avoidable (e.g., the killing of the person intending to murder one's child, when only killing will stop the evil deed). But even when justifiable, direct killing suggests hopelessness. It says something about those who do the deed, no matter how justifiable the killing may be in certain circumstances.

Thus, capital punishment always raises this question: Can we afford to say about ourselves what capital punishment says about us? Can we afford this particular instance of making the human story a story of violence and bloodshed? Can we afford to foster such a hopeless image of ourselves? If we abandon any hope for the individual criminal, do we not in the same act abandon at least some of our hope for making a better and more just world? Such are the questions which moral imagination raises in the context of capital punishment.

In this context, the prisoner, when alive and incarcerated, becomes a challenge to us, a symbol, a reminder of our need to look for ways to rebuild society, to make crime happen less, and to rehabilitate those who are criminals. The prisoner becomes a text which we must read and interpret as part of our move toward a more human future. At times it appears that the prisoners who might be considered for execution would prefer to be dead. If we were only considering the prisoner or the specific crime, death for such a prisoner might be very coherent. When we imagine on a larger scale, perhaps we need the text of the prisoner alive rather than the image of the prisoner dead. Christ, who called upon us to visit prisoners, may well have seen matters in this way.

A major issue of course is whether we have reasonable alternatives to capital punishment. I suggested earlier that the justification of the child defense (or self-defense or wife defense, etc.) killing is that there are no other alternatives. A big problem up to now is that the alternatives to capital punishment have been so poorly managed in many cases. We all know the stories of life imprisonment leading to parole after a few years, and of the sometimes unbelievable slowness and unfairness of the criminal justice system. I think what we really ought to do as moral imaginers is to dream up better alternatives to capital punishment, rather than to continue to accept the image of ourselves which is conveyed by capital punishment. Many of the reasonable alternatives may cost us more in dollars than capital punishment. But perhaps we need to pay out such dollars, rather than bear the even greater human cost which can be part of the image of humanity conveyed by capital punishment. It is also possible that, through creative imagination, sound alternatives might be developed which will not cost as much as many people fear they will.

These thoughts by no means solve the problem of capital punishment. Hopefully, however, I have shown that with imagination, some old themes might be set aside and some fresh approaches developed to enable us to approach the capital punishment issue in a better way.

World Hunger

Much good literature has been published on the subject of world hunger in recent years.[37] From a study of this literature, it is possible to learn a great many facts about world hunger. One can learn about the extent of hunger (which involves five hundred million to a billion people, depending on which statistics one uses and what degree of hunger one uses in assembling the statistics). One can learn about which regions of the world are the hardest hit by hunger (with India and Saharan Africa near the top of most lists).[38] One can also learn that, of all the groups which make up the human family, children are the hardest hit by hunger because nutrition is so crucial in the childhood years.[39]

Going further, one can learn many of the major causes of world hunger.[40] Bad weather (floods, droughts, etc.) often contributes to food shortages and hunger. High populations are often a factor in hunger. But it must also be noted that standards of living and programs of development have considerably more impact on population levels than do contraceptive policies, i.e., raising a country's standard of living will do much more than contraceptive devices to lower population growth.[41] The diet of people in the rich countries also has a great impact on world hunger, since it takes so much more grain to produce foods such as beef and beer than it does to nourish people directly with grain.[42] Energy consumption by the rich countries also helps cause world hunger, since many sources of energy could be used as sources for fertilizers.

Perhaps most of all, we can learn from factual study that poor economic distribution is the single most important factor helping to create world hunger.[43] Much of the research which has been done concludes that, at least as of now, the world does have the resources to feed all of its people. The problem is that present economic systems of distribution do not succeed in getting food supplies from the places where they are more adequate to the places which need them so much.[44] Nor do present systems of economic distribution do enough to help stimulate local production of food in countries which are hungry. Foreign aid helps some, but foreign aid has become so highly politicized that it is unable to address the problem as a whole.

Even the simple facts mentioned in these last few paragraphs make it clear that world hunger is an enormous problem. It may well be the most significant moral issue facing the world today, with only the nuclear arms issue possibly being an equally strong contender for that title. But for all its enormity, many of us have very little sense of world hunger as a moral issue. The issue is so big and so pervasive that we would prefer not to deal with it. To put this in another way, I think that, while we know the theory of world hunger, we fail almost completely in trying to imagine what world hunger is like. And without such moral imagination, world hunger is unable to assume its true significance as a moral issue.

To set these remarks in context, recall my comments in Chapter 1 that one of the most difficult problems in moral theology today is to find ways to help students appreciate the social side of moral issues. My experience over the years has been that it is generally much harder to keep students interested in major social problems than it is to keep them interested in courses on subjects such as sex or medicine. There have been some exceptions to this such as the tremendous student interest in the morality of the Vietnam War, but, by and large, social issues are so huge, so massive, that the human mind recoils from dealing with them. It seems easier to let oneself be blind, so as not to deal with the tremendous burden which can be connected with major social issues. No one knows any simple way to change all of this, but I do think that a moral theology which makes more use of imagination may be able to wake us up to the true meaning of social moral issues such as world hunger.

Thus, while it may not be pleasant, I think that we very much need to come up with genuine images of what hunger is like. Pictures and descriptions may be of some help. So may practices such as fasting. Some parishes and religious education programs have been promoting occasional meatless meals, meals which are not wasteful, meals which are efficient in terms of their impact on food distribution, etc. Such practices, because of their concreteness, can speak about world hunger, even to little children, in a way that theories will never accomplish.[45]

In a more specifically Christian sense, the symbolism of the Eucharist as food or nourishment has been used to call us to concern about world hunger and related social problems. Such an approach not only can help raise our consciousness of world hunger, but it can also serve to re-energize the meaning and power of the Eucharist in the lives of believers. The continuing popularity of the Eucharistic Congress hymn, *Gift of Finest Wheat*, comes at least in part from the hymn's ability to give a creative expression of both religious and moral concerns.

None of this denies that the world hunger problem calls for hard analysis by economists, agricultural experts, demographers, meteorologists, etc. But for the world to address its hunger problem, images and symbols are a primary and fundamental necessity.

Once we move ahead from our failure to imagine world hunger, we can find ourselves deeply challenged by the images which impress themselves upon us. For me the two most powerful and disturbing images of the problem of world hunger are, first, the seemingly endless series of pictures of little starving children with frail limbs and distended bellies, and, second, the almost as endless series of pictures of surplus grain rotting in warehouses (often in the United States), or pictures of farmers accepting money for not growing crops, or of farmers destroying milk which they cannot sell, at least at a viable price.

I am not an economist, and therefore I cannot understand or explain all the details of food distribution. But I think I do know out of moral imagination that somehow the images of massive starvation and massive food surpluses cannot morally exist together in the same world. There simply has to be a better way of doing things, and the challenge to humanity, once it has begun to imaginatively accept the scope of the hunger problem, is to find that better way. It may well be that as we really face the images of world hunger, we will have to abandon some of our cherished economic dogmas or principles. These principles may have worked very well in the past, but that does not take away world hunger's challenge to us to be free enough to imaginatively play with and even let go of our principles of distribution so as to come up with new understandings and new applications. There are many texts or stories which we must read in our times, texts which we must let interpret us as we interpret them. Perhaps no text demands a more imaginative reading than the text of world hunger.

International Economic Order

From a theoretical perspective it goes almost without saying that, as a world, we face many major ethical problems in the field of economics. Some of the issues we have already considered, such as world hunger and the worldwide delivery of basic health care, are essentially economic issues, and there are numerous other world economic issues as well. Nearly a century ago, Pope Leo XIII spoke of the right of all working people to earn a living wage, i.e., to live in a reasonable and frugal comfort.[46] Such reasonable and frugal comfort is still lacking to enormous numbers of people around the globe, to people who lack adequate shelter, clothing, and food. When discussing world population, we noted that the opportunity for education has a very large impact on birth rates and on population levels. But the lack of economic resources denies many persons the opportunity for much education.

Many other examples of economic injustice could also be cited. As far as the world's economic order is concerned, the basic moral principle is the principle of distributive justice, i.e., the principle that each person on this planet deserves a reasonable (not necessarily an equal) share of the economic goods which our world is capable of producing.[47] The issues we have just mentioned (world hunger, lack of health care, education, etc.) all can be understood as issues in which the principle of distributive justice is violated.

Moral imagination by itself may not be able to solve all these issues of world level economic injustice.[48] Moral imagination does, however, offer three important resources for dealing with international economic issues. In what follows, we shall touch on each of these three resources.

First, moral imagination can help us to form a true and vital vision of the moral nature of economic problems. Earlier, we have seen that the human mind is often blind to the world's larger moral problems. This is especially true of economic problems. We would rather not deal with them. We are so used to things being the way they are that we fail to grasp the seriousness of the world's major economic difficulties. We see economics as operating according to fixed laws so that we cannot do anything about it anyway. We give in too easily to uncritical interpretations of Christ's words, "The poor you will always have with you."

I think that with moral imagination at least some of this blindness about economic moral issues can be overcome. With moral imagination perhaps we can become free enough to take a thoughtful, even playful look at economic issues, free enough to see the moral injustice found in many economic practices. A key task of moral imagination in any area is to help us form a vision of what is really happening, a vision of what the moral issues really are. In economic issues, we especially need such moral vision. The Bible tells us about the importance of naming, particularly about the importance of being able to name demons. Once we can name a demon, we begin to have power over that demon, and we can become able to exorcise it. There are demons to be named in the economic order, and moral imagination can markedly enhance our power to name such demons.

Second, moral imagination can help those of us who have been raised in the United States and in the other capitalist countries to overcome the pre-conditioning which leads us to think that capitalist economics are the only viable and moral approach to economic problems, even in cultural and social conditions which are very different from our own. My point in saying this is not to attack capitalist economics as such. The point is that we are so conditioned by capitalist economic practices that we are often unfree to consider or play with other possible alternatives, particularly socialist alternatives. Economic life and structure is so basic to human existence that we can fail to recognize the degree to which our own economic experience impacts our thinking and limits our openness to economic choices which are not part of our own experience.

In this context, moral imagination might help us to suspend our usual pro-capitalist economic judgments so as to play with and give genuine consideration to a wide variety of economic alternatives. Such alternatives might well come into play both in new situations in our own culture (e.g., the cost of health care which could call for a more socialized approach to medicine) and in situations in other cultures (where a socialist economy might genuinely be the better alternative).

Over the course of the twentieth century, the official teaching of Roman Catholicism has become significantly more open to socialist forms of economic analysis.[49] But many Catholics in the capitalist countries have not been able to give a full acceptance to the developing economic approaches of their Church. The basic difficulty is that these Catholics cannot imagine what a non-capitalist economic system would be like. They (and others too) have invested capitalism with a religious fervor and aura which excludes any real consideration of other options. The other options may not be completely perfect, but in a world with so much economic injustice, what we need is a full and imaginative consideration of all the possibilities.

One might mention a parallel case in which the force of an existing practice is so strong that the existing practice may serve to block any real and imaginative consideration of other possibilities.

The parallel is the practice of celibacy in the Roman Catholic Church. Just as capitalism has accomplished great things over history in the West, so celibacy has accomplished great things over history for the Church. Just as our experience with the success of capitalism keeps many persons from really looking at and imagining other options in economics, so the great historical successes of celibacy keep many persons from really imagining whether other options might serve the Church better in changing cultures. If the Church does engage in genuine imagination on the subject of celibacy, the Church might still choose mandatory celibacy, or it might choose some form of optional celibacy. But, as with economic choices, whatever choice the Church makes on celibacy, it should be made on the basis of true moral imagination, not on the basis of a refusal to imagine the full range of human possibilities.

Third, when the circumstances are appropriate, moral imagination can help us to develop more flexible attitudes toward those who are already engaging in economic practices different from our own. As an offshoot of our difficulty in imagining economic policies other than capitalism, we have a fairly easy time in demonizing the leaders of countries with socialist economics, particularly when these countries are communist or thought to be sympathetic to communism. As a result we sometimes end up supporting foreign regimes or political parties whose policies are repressive, dehumanizing, and much less moral than are some socialist regimes or parties, even when these regimes or parties have ties to communism. With a more open moral imagination, perhaps we could come to see that, in some cases, our demonizing of those who hold different economic theories leads us to support less moral instead of more moral options.

Competent historians of recent years have shown that, in the last years of World War II, Chiang Kai-shek's regime was despotic, repressive, selfish, and almost completely incapable of meeting the needs of the Chinese people.[50] In that circumstance, the Chinese communists were the one group capable of providing a reasonably human form of government. From a larger human viewpoint, the Chinese communists were the obvious group to support. Had the West supported them, their form or style of communism could have evolved quite differently and along lines which the West might have seen as more acceptable. The entire history of the post-war world might have been different and better. But the fact is that fear and lack of imagination led the West, especially the United States, to glorify Chiang and to repress the facts of his incompetence and corruption. While all the details are not as clear at this point, one must at least wonder whether similar fears and similar weak imagination are at work in the policy of the United States toward Central America.

None of these statements about our need to imagine what is really happening in other countries is to be taken as meaning that capitalism (with its many historically outstanding accomplishments) is to be abandoned.[51] Nor do these statements mean that socialist economics are to be naïvely adopted, or socialist regimes naïvely supported. Socialist regimes can be as repressive as capitalist ones, and surely there are situations in which countries such as the United States should oppose these regimes. Moreover, there is no doubt that there are themes in the communist ideology (as opposed to its economics) which we would never accept. The point of moral imagination is not therefore an uncritical embrace of either socialism or communism.[52] The point is a genuinely imaginative search through all possible alternatives for the international economic order.

To the extent that there is an ''answer'' to the dilemma of the international economic order, that answer is in all probability a mixed economy involving both capitalist and socialist elements, with different emphases in different parts of the world due to differences in culture, in level of development, etc. Even in one country or culture, there will probably be different economic approaches to different issues due to the nature of the issues themselves. In a markedly capitalist country such as the United States, most people are favorable to Social Security which is a socialized system of retirement.

This notion of a mixed economy can be found in much theoretical writing from the entire course of our century. Catholic scholars such as John A. Ryan and authors from other traditions have proposed it. But the problems of economics are so great and so ongoing that even many years of rather sound theoretical writing have not served to relieve them even though progress has been made on some specific issues. Moral imagination is needed to supplement a moral theory of economics, as moral theory alone will never be enough to keep us alive to the challenges of a world economic order.

Nuclear Arms and World Peace

We noted in Chapter 1 that the nuclear disarmament movement is one of the most remarkable events taking place in the world today, with the involvement of the American Catholic hierarchy being an especially notable feature of this movement.[53] A great many things would have to be discussed to set forth a complete picture of the nuclear arms issue. Our purpose will be more narrow: we will seek to show the major ways in which moral imagination can help us in dealing with the nuclear arms question. Four major contributions of imagination to the nuclear debate will be cited. Each of these four contributions has parallels in the examples we have previously discussed. The crucial importance of the nuclear debate suggests that we review the contributions of imagination specifically in the nuclear context.

Imagining Nuclear Attack

First, a lively and morally realistic imagination will help us to get some kind of understanding of what a nuclear holocaust is really like, what it would mean for the world. We have been living in the nuclear age since 1945, meaning that nearly two full generations have grown up with their existence bracketed by the nuclear question mark, with fear for the future and civil defense drills as a staple of childhood. And yet for all of that, we have strikingly little awareness of what a full-scale nuclear war might do to the world. The tendency to avoid dealing with tough social issues has surely been present here. We do not like to think about what a nuclear attack would be like.

Fortunately, we have begun in recent years to see some imaginative efforts to help us understand what a nuclear war would be like. Jonathan Schell's *The Fate of the Earth* is perhaps the best known example of an effort to imagine a nuclear attack. The films, lectures, etc. of the organization known as Physicians for Social Responsibility (PSR) are another such effort. PSR's materials especially emphasize the medical consequences of a nuclear attack and the very limited potential of medicine in dealing with these consequences.[54] Morally sensitive imagination can and should produce more efforts of this type. To come to good moral judgments about nuclear arms, a key first step is imaginative, and thus painful, reflection on what a nuclear war would be like.

Reimagining the Just War Theory

Second, moral imagination, once it begins to grasp the nature of nuclear weapons, can raise profound and provocative questions about the standard application of the just war theory. For centuries, the principles of the just war theory have served civilization quite well.[55] The standard application of the just war theory considered the question of when a specific war was just, and the question of when, within a war, certain weapons might be used or not used, in accord with the principle of proportionate reason. The standard application, however, never asked (or ever needed to ask) whether there were some weapons whose very nature was such that their use could never be considered moral, no matter how just the cause of the war, and no matter what the specific nature of the military situation might be.

Beginning from this point, the issue of nuclear arms raises new and previously unasked questions for the just war theory. If one holds that nuclear arms could never be used offensively or on a first strike basis, could nuclear arms be used defensively, after the "other side" had first used them? Could a country possess nuclear arms merely as a threat or deterrent, intending never to use them, but stocking them to keep the country's opponents from going to war? Could persons of conscience work in plants which manufacture nuclear weapons? Could persons serve in the military forces of countries which plan to use nuclear weapons? Could even limited wars be justified in the nuclear age, where there is always the threat of escalation to the nuclear level? Are the non-military uses of nuclear energy moral in a world such as ours?[56]

Moral imagination can offer much assistance in addressing these new questions. With moral imagination, we can avoid a retreat to the stock answers of the past. With moral imagination, the standard application of the just war theory can be suspended so that people can freely and creatively reassess the just war theory to see what this theory might mean and call for in the nuclear age. From this imaginative perspective, the questions just listed can really be asked as questions, not just mouthed as theoretical concerns. The answers, especially to the last couple of questions, are not clear. Imaginative association of the many aspects of our knowledge of nuclear weapons can help move us toward some further vision and clarity.

Imagining Concrete Steps to Disarmament

The first two contributions of moral imagination to the nuclear debate have been fundamental in nature. We have seen how imagination can help us grasp the basic meaning of nuclear weapons and the basic meaning of the just war theory in the nuclear era. The third contribution relates more to the immediate situation in the world as of now. If we agree (as the American bishops seem to)[57] that a long-term defense policy is immoral if it plans on the ongoing use and possession of nuclear weapons for first strike, defensive, or even deterrent purposes, how do we get from the present situation of massive nuclear arms stockpiles to long-term worldwide defense policies which are moral?

From the outset it must be granted that this is an extraordinarily difficult question. Relations between nations are sensitive and fragile. Even if all people everywhere clearly want to go to a post-nuclear world, mistaken judgments as to how to get there could lead to a nuclear catastrophe before a post-nuclear world is achieved. The American Catholic bishops, while creative even on this level, were also cautious in the tone with which they addressed the issues we are now considering.[58]

Several comments are in order on this practical question of how to get to a post-nuclear world. First, even here, true moral imagination is called for. We must be willing to think new thoughts, to formulate and try new approaches which may never have been attempted before. Too often, nothing but the old wisdom of "we must protect ourselves" seems to emerge as nations and people struggle with the problem of getting to a post-nuclear world. To paraphrase a song from the musical *The King and I*, those who think only of toughly protecting themselves might end up protecting themselves out of all they own and are.

Second, on a practical question such as nuclear disarmament, moral imagination and discernment of spirits come quite close together. The effort to think imaginative new thoughts about getting to the post-nuclear age is very much a question of listening for what the

Spirit says, a question for a morality based on holiness. Much of the anti-nuclear leadership around the world has come from religious sources. Religion, with its powerful and long-standing use of symbols and images, may be in an especially able position when it comes to thinking imaginative new thoughts about practical directions to lead the world into a post-nuclear age.[59] Isaiah's prophecy that, through the word of the Lord, we will turn our swords into plowshares and our spears into pruning hooks (Is 2:4) is but one example of the many powerful and imaginative religious visions of peace.

Third, while imagination and all forms of moral argument still have a great way to go on the question of specific steps toward disarmament, some matters of consensus do seem to be emerging. Specifically, it seems to be emerging that the enormous buildup of nuclear arsenals which has marked the past decade or so cannot continue. The already famous shift in the bishops' pastoral from the word "curb" back to the word "halt"[60] may not offer any concrete program for disarmament, but the shift clearly does oppose any massive continued buildup of nuclear weapons.

It is to be noted that the emerging anti-buildup consensus is a consensus about what specific steps ought not to be taken rather than a consensus about which steps should be taken. Moral imagination and moral discernment will often work in this fashion by seeing that certain images (e.g., of a just peace and of a massive arms buildup) cannot co-exist with one another. This means that moral imaginers will sometimes take up the role of being protesters against unjustifiable policies. Protest will never be enough, as moral imagination must stretch from protest onward to creative solutions. But protest will on many occasions be a task for moral imagination.

The Humanness of the Other Side

On several previous issues, we have seen that the tendency of opposing sides in serious disputes is to demonize one another so that serious dialogue toward creative solutions becomes almost impossible. The Western countries may not be as explicit in their demonizing as was Ayatollah Khomeini when he called the United States the great satan, but we demonize our opponents nonetheless. In particular, in the context of the nuclear arms issue, the United States demonizes the Russians and their society, while Russia demonizes the United States and its society. Naïve carelessness about the intentions of the two sides toward each other is of course out of place. But, still, an exercise of moral imagination might help the United States and Russia to form a new vision of each other, a vision in which both sides, along with admittedly very different economies, philosophies of history, and views of religion, are able to discover that they share many common elements in the human story.

Both sides share a concern for families, homes, and hearth. Both sides have a love for art, for music, and for literature. Both sides share a concern for technological progress and a love for athletic competition. Both have suffered war and both fear what would happen to them in a future war. Perhaps, if we could come to a fresh imaginative understanding of each other based on these points where our stories touch, it might not be quite so difficult to come to some new proposals for disarmament. An imaginative grasp of each other might help the United States and Russia to at least a little more trust, and without such increased trust very little, in the way of concrete progress toward nuclear disarmament, seems possible. Neither side need give up its genuine concerns about the philosophies and social problems of the other. But an imaginative setting of these problems into an at least partly common human story might make an important difference.

Surely more moral issues could be mentioned and further imaginative angles could be raised on the issues already cited. To close the chapter, we can note a hopeful theme which emerges from our practical examples of moral imagination. The theme is that moral imagination, when used in the manner discussed above, can help give the "person in the street" a handle with which to reflect upon some of the great problems of our times, difficult though these problems may be. Without moral imagination there is a danger that the only people who will feel qualified to discuss these problems are the technical experts. We need such experts and their opinions, but for true moral dialogue we also need to find ways to keep the ordinary members of society from becoming robots (à la Orwell's *1984*), who are totally without input on society's great moral dilemmas. The use of moral imagination on issues such as those considered in this chapter is one very important means of keeping open a broadly based social-moral dialogue.

6

Imagination and Education
for Moral Living

Throughout this book, the theme of education for imagination has been mentioned in passing on a number of occasions when various issues were being discussed. In this final chapter, the educational issues related to moral imagination will be addressed more directly. Five education related issues will be addressed: imagination and liberal education in general, imagination and moral development theory, imagination and education for sexual responsibility, imagination and education for social justice, and imagination and the moral education of adults. After treating these issues, the chapter will close with some brief summary thoughts on the overall significance of imagination for moral theology.

IMAGINATION AND LIBERAL EDUCATION OF YOUTH

Some General Comments

Throughout this book, my uses of the two terms imagination and moral imagination have sometimes overlapped. In general I have used the one word imagination when referring to the basic character and structure of human imagination, and I have used the term moral imagination to refer to situations in which human imagination functions in a specifically moral or ethical context. The overlap between the two terms exists because moral imagination is not a different process from imagination in general; rather, it is the same process operating in a specific context, namely the ethical context. Thus, when I have spoken about imagination in relation to ethics, I have used the single term imagination when I wished to stress the

147

fundamental structure of the person's imagining, but I have used the term moral imagination when I wanted to stress the ethical or moral context in which the imagining is taking place.[1]

What all this implies for the present section on education and imagination is that children, youth, and adults must be able to imagine well in a basic sense in order to imagine well in the moral area of life. Moral imagination is not so much a special set of imagining skills as it is the consistent applying of one's basic imagining skills when making moral choices. General education of our young to help them be imaginative thus becomes a crucial foundation for moral imagination.

I write these lines at a time when the quality of education has become a major issue for public discussion, at least in the United States. Recent reports, such as the study prepared by the National Commission for Excellence in Education,[2] have raised profound questions and concerns about the quality of education in the United States. Education thus seems likely to become a major issue in presidential elections and other public fora in the forthcoming years. My experience and that of colleagues with whom I have spoken seems to corroborate the concerns raised in the recent educational reports. Many young people reach the higher levels of education today with a rather limited ability to express themselves, either in speech or in writing. Their creative urge to learn does not seem to have been developed satisfactorily.

It is not my purpose here to get into a discussion of the political issues related to education of our young. On the more political issues, I would simply and briefly say that I believe that as a society, our stress on technical and material productivity has led us to undervalue, both economically and socially, the work of those who teach our children. Some redress seems called for, both in terms of financial compensation, and, perhaps even more importantly, in terms of the esteem and social recognition we give to those who teach. Some of the other countries in the West (such as Canada) handle the compensation and recognition of teachers considerably differently than does the United States. With a little imagination, better ways of esteeming our teachers could be found.

On another political issue, I think it must be said that both public and private education have a critically important role to play in a strong and free society. If at least some education is private, there is a good level of assurance that genuine freedom of thought will endure. But education is an unavoidable public responsibility as well. I grant the traditional and still central role of local government in education. But, in an ever more complex society such as ours, it is difficult to see how this public responsibility can be adequately met unless the federal government takes on a very significant role.

A Plea for the Liberal Arts

To turn now to my more direct concerns about education for imagination and creativity, I want to make a very strong plea for the importance of the liberal arts as a keystone to the fostering of genuine imagination and genuine concern for the quality of human life. Ever since the launching of Sputnik I in 1957, there has been a high concern in the West for technical education so as to keep up with or be ahead of the Russians. Technical education is very important, but if it is emphasized to the denigration of the liberal arts, everyone suffers. If we lack the imagination and the wisdom to use our technologies well, technical knowledge can all too easily lead us astray, no matter how good the technical knowledge happens to be.

The term liberal arts includes a whole host of imagination enhancers: language, history, social studies, music, art, dance, to name just a few. While all of these imagination enhancers are important, I would like to give special stress to two areas: basic language skills and classics, whether of literature, music, or art.

Basic Language Skills

As I see it, the importance of language skills comes from the fact that humans do more of their imagining in language than in any other single form. The whole process of metaphorical thinking involves seeing images (in words or language) which do not quite fit our past experiences, so that we have to stretch ourselves (i.e., we have to imagine) in order to know what a metaphor means. Surely experiences of visual art, music, and dance can stimulate the same imaginative stretching as linguistic metaphors. But language is the most basic of the skills which we use to grow imaginatively through metaphor.[3]

When I speak of the importance of language skills for imagination, the tendency might be to think about the ability to form an overall vision of the meaning of a text, be that text a novel, a play, a poem, or a scholarly treatise. Such overall linguistic vision and ability is important, but it has its roots in something even more basic: a disciplined knowledge of grammar, sentence structure, spelling, etc. These very basic skills are what young people so often seem to be missing today. It is with these skills that a person must begin in order to pick up the subtleties of individual metaphors, and only with the ability to get at individual metaphors will persons be able to move on—imaginatively—to the deeper meanings of texts as a whole.[4]

Some of the moral writers we discussed earlier spoke about virtue as springing from a shared human understanding.[5] Language too springs from a shared human understanding. This is the main reason why, both in language and in morality, all persons must begin with a disciplined effort to know the shared human values which are the foundations of language and morality. It may seem paradoxical that creative imagination begins from discipline, but without the effort to know our foundations, people will have nothing out of which to build a creative imagination, either linguistically or morally.

Today, with the tremendous emphasis on visual media (television, video games, computers) there is a common and most regrettable tendency to forget about language as a basic entry point into the process of human imagination. The trend to be satisfied with sloppy use of language needs to be reversed for many reasons. In our context a key reason is that sloppy language practices can contribute to sloppy and unimaginative moral reflection.

Another point to be made about language skills and imagination is that a knowledge of more than one language can be of very great value for the human imagination. When a person knows more than one language, he or she immediately has a much greater sense of the subtleties of words, and therefore a sharpened ability to form new combinations of words as well as new images of other sorts. Unlike the situation in other countries, many children in the United States learn only English, and as adults they can become almost tyrannical in their expectation that everyone else know English. In our rapidly changing culture, such a monolithic approach to language needs to be overcome if we are to achieve creatively imaginative dialogue on the social and moral issues we face as a society.

The present Holy Father, Pope John Paul II, is probably the most remarkable contemporary example of someone whose multiple language skills enable him to communicate with and challenge the religious imaginations of enormous numbers of people. Of course John Paul II's message is heard because of its religious character. Nonetheless, John Paul II's natural gifts, as the most multilingual Pope in history, are a highly important element in his ability to fire the religious imaginations and enthusiasm of so many. Few persons will ever be in John Paul II's position, but multilingual skills can enhance the imaginative capacities of all people.

The Use of Classics in Education

Above we have been arguing that imagination comes out of a shared language foundation, based on rules of grammar, spelling, etc. Imagination also comes from another highly notable common foundation, the foundation of a commonly shared experience of great works of literature, art, music, etc. Earlier we saw that moral imagination can wander astray, and is sometimes in need of discipline. The same "wandering astray" problem can exist with all types of imagination, so that imagination needs discipline, needs a chance to develop a sense for what is good.

In education, the use of classics is a critically important way of disciplining the imagination. If works of literature, art, and music have stood the test of time, often the time of centuries, such works are very likely to convey sound and disciplined imaginative creativity. The education of our children and young people ought to include the hearing, reading, seeing, and studying of such classics. It is not my intention here to propose a list of required classics, but it is hard for me to see how education can be complete if it does not include the reading of authors such as Shakespeare, the looking at paintings by masters such as Leonardo da Vinci, Michelangelo, and Picasso, and the listening to the music of composers such as Beethoven and Copland. To the extent that education bypasses artists such as these for the sake of technology, something is wrong and sound imagination may be dying.

Of course there will be ongoing debates as to which works are truly classics, and a healthy flexibility is to be encouraged on this matter. There is also a need to be open to classics when they emerge in new forms of art such as the film. Similarly there is a need to be open to classics which emerge from other cultural settings (e.g., from black culture), and to modern classics as they emerge in the more traditional art forms. The point is that across the ages and in our own time, societies learn to see certain works of art as giving appropriate and imaginative expression to deeply shared human values. These works of art are classics, and a major task of education will be to share our classics with the young.[6]

It should be noted too that there are religious classics as well as secular classics. Passages in the Scriptures, certain writings of saints and mystics, and works of art and music have all emerged as religious classics. The sharing of these classics with the young ought to be a major element in the religious education of the young, because there will be little in the way of creative religious imagination without the sharing of such classics.[7]

In this context, I fully support the liturgical changes which have taken place during the Vatican II period. The changes, however, have cast the Catholic community into a difficult period liturgically. One important function (not the only or even the most important function) of liturgy is to convey religious classics to people. It may be a generation or two before the new liturgy is fully able to do this. Vatican II recalled to our consciousness a great many rich biblical images of the Church (choice vineyard, holy city, new Jerusalem, spouse of the Lamb, etc.). These images are not capable of being fully explained on the basis of logic alone. These images also can have much impact on moral development and decisions. For many reasons it is crucial that the renewed liturgy patiently continue its efforts to find suitable means of sharing such images with us.

A Note on the Sciences and Imagination

In the last few paragraphs I have laid great emphasis on the liberal arts as a crucially necessary element in the development of imagination in children and young people. But what about the sciences and imagination? Are the sciences completely free of imagination? Are the sciences pure logic with no creativity? A close study of the sciences shows that there can be a great deal of awe and wonder in the sciences. Many scientists have had a markedly religious spirit, and have deepened their faith through their scientific research. Close study also shows that many of the great scientific breakthroughs of the past have been the result of creative and imaginative efforts and methods.[8] It goes without saying that our young people need to learn the sciences as well as the arts. And without doubt our young people can be taught science in a way which stimulates the imagination.

A caveat however needs to be added. The imagination and creativity which we find among scientists do not stem from the traditional scientific method per se. This method has been locked into an overly rationalist approach. Rather, the creativity of the sciences comes from the fact that the scientists themselves are creative people, who have used more than the traditional scientific method. Their creativity and imagination has come from the whole range of their life experiences and education, not simply from their use of the closed scientific method, which in itself does not have the openness to metaphor which we find in the arts. Many scientists have begun to recognize this, and as a result we are beginning to see the emergence of new and more creative approaches to science. We must educate young people in the sciences, but I do not see it as satisfactory to educate them in the traditional scientific method alone.

Earlier, I spoke about the spiritual as well as the scientific values which motivated John A. Roebling when he designed the Brooklyn Bridge. As a young student in Berlin from 1828–31, Roebling studied a great deal of science and engineering. But he studied other subjects as well, most notably philosophy. His vision was technical and scientific as it needed to be, but it was more than scientific. While in Berlin, Roebling was a student of Hegel.[9] A theologian friend of mine said he was surprised that the Brooklyn Bridge had stood up so long, since Hegel's thinking was so centered upon spirituality and so detached from matter. Roebling was a thorough student of engineering and his bridge has stood up. But Roebling's most genuine success (as with all the great scientists) took place because he could imagine. He was more than a scientist.

IMAGINATION AND MORAL DEVELOPMENT THEORY

We turn now from the general question of developing imagination through liberal education to the more specific question of how imagination can relate to the development of moral values in children and youth. To approach this more specific question, we shall consider one of the most notable developments in ethics in recent years, the emergence of the cognitive structural theory of moral development. This theory has its roots in the work of the Swiss psychologist Jean Piaget a half century ago, and it has become especially influential in our times because of the work of the Harvard psychologist Lawrence Kohlberg.[10] James Fowler has developed Kohlberg's work in a Christian/religious faith context and made some significant modifications to it, as we shall see in the course of our reflections.[11]

My comments on the cognitive structural approach to moral development will be divided into three sections: first, a brief summary of Kohlberg's work; second, a review of the major criticisms of Kohlberg; third, a consideration of how an emphasis on moral imagination might supplement Kohlberg's approach.

A Brief Look at Kohlberg's Approach

Kohlberg sees the moral development of each person as a process which passes through three levels, with each level containing two stages for a total of six stages of moral development. As the individual develops morally, he or she passes in an ordered fashion from one stage to the next, by acquiring the reasoning processes of the next higher stage. The individual can only develop one stage at a time, since he or she can only understand the reasoning pattern of the next higher stage, not of stages higher than the next stage.[12] Some individuals develop only to a certain point and never reach the highest stages of moral development. Most commonly, individuals who stop developing morally stop their development at stage four.[13]

Detailed descriptions of Kohlberg's six stages can be found elsewhere.[14] To summarize very briefly, in stage one the purpose of moral behavior is to avoid punishment, while in stage two the purpose of moral behavior is to achieve pleasure. These two stages constitute the first or pre-conventional level. The second or conventional level of moral behavior includes stages three and four. In stage three, moral behavior is aimed at pleasing one's group and at winning acceptance by the group. In stage four, moral behavior is done for the good of the group, with a realization that laws are valuable because they foster the good of the group. The sense of group in stage four is more developed than in stage three, with government and the social structures necessary for government often becoming a major focus.

In stages five and six, which together make up the post-conventional level, law no longer stands as an end in itself but rather as a means to the common good. Thus, if action in accord with law fails to serve the common good, it can be replaced with other action. Personally, I have always found it difficult to work out a fully clear distinction between the two post-conventional stages, i.e., stages five and six. Both of these stages stress universal or common good oriented values. In stage six there seems to be greater personal ownership of these values, and greater concern that these values be fully universal, applying to all people.

While the basic structure of Kohlberg's six stages has remained steady over the years, Kohlberg has from time to time suggested modifications to his stages, to deal with new questions. To address the problem of the difficult transition from stage four (with its concern for law) to stage five (with its willingness to go beyond law in certain carefully chosen circumstances), Kohlberg at one period proposed an in between or rebellious anti-law stage called stage four and one half.[15] To address the problem of how religious motivation fits into his moral development model, some scholars hold that Kohlberg has raised the possibility of a stage seven.[16]

Some Criticisms of Kohlberg

In the early years after Kohlberg's work became known, his stage theory of cognitive moral development was received with a good deal of enthusiasm by many religious and moral educators. Some of this first enthusiasm may have been naïve and oversimplified, too ready to label every person as a stage two, three, or whatever. Today, after a couple of decades of reflection, many religious and moral educators still find Kohlberg's work to be important and helpful. At the same time, over the past ten years a number of noteworthy criticisms of Kohlberg's theory have emerged among Christian educators and other ethical thinkers. Five major criticisms of Kohlberg will be discussed here.

The first criticism is that Kohlberg's approach lays too much stress on discursive reason as the key to moral decisions. In this context, the critics argue that Kohlberg is too Kantian, more concerned with principles than with the concrete reality of moral decisions.[17] Kohlberg's sharp distinction between form and content and his consistent concern with only the form (and not the content) of moral choices are two factors which inspire the criticism of Kohlberg as excessively rationalist in his approach to ethics. Following the Roman Catholic tradition, I believe that reason does play a major role in ethics and that some of Kohlberg's critics on this point may be too anti-rational. At the same time, a major thesis of this book is that morality involves more than the logical side of life. Thus, the criticism of moral development theory as one-sidedly rational rings true with the purposes of the present book.

The second criticism is that Kohlberg, in his emphasis on reason and principles, lays too much stress on justice as the essential moral value, while at the same time presenting a notion of justice which is too narrow and too individualistic. None of Kohlberg's critics would deny that justice is a crucially important moral notion. The critics would, however, assert that there are many other central moral notions such as love and care, so that an approach to moral development cannot be based on justice alone.[18]

At the same time, when Kohlberg does speak about justice, he seems to refer largely to what traditional Roman Catholic ethics called commutative justice, i.e., the justice which governs the relationships between two private individuals. Kohlberg's moral dilemmas will often help advance children's thinking about one-to-one issues of justice, but the dilemmas do not seem to get as readily at the larger issues of justice. Kohlberg does on occasion open up what the Catholic tradition called legal or general justice—what citizens owe to the state as a matter of justice—but his concept of justice seems to make only very few openings to what the tradition described as distributive justice, i.e., to the issue of what nations and the world owe to all people. What Kohlberg does do with his concept of justice is a valuable contribution to moral education. But I believe that the critics are correct in arguing that he could bring in themes other than justice and that he could develop a broader and more social notion of justice.

A third criticism focuses on a key element said to be missing in Kohlberg's theory, the element of affectivity. In particular, James Fowler's writings stress this theme of affectivity and criticize Kohlberg for not developing it sufficiently.[19] There is some controversy on this affectivity theme between the proponents of Kohlberg and the proponents of Fowler. Walter Conn holds that while Kohlberg may not explicitly speak about affectivity very often, affectivity is surely an important element in his total overview. Fowler, in Conn's opinion, says a lot on the theoretical level about the importance of affectivity, but without really making affectivity an important de facto element in his approach to faith development.[20]

In any case, regardless of whether Kohlberg or Fowler does a better job of incorporating affectivity into a cognitive structural theory of moral development, affectivity clearly is important in moral education, along with moral reasoning. Moreover, affectivity is often missing, at least in many of the popular interpretations of Kohlberg's theory. Earlier, we saw that imagination is not the same as affectivity, because imagination involves thoughtful reflective activity as well as an affective component. Affectivity and imagination do relate closely, however, so that critics who call for more affectivity in a theory of moral development sometimes call for moral imagination as well. This is especially the case in the work of James Fowler and Craig Dykstra.[21]

The fourth criticism is that Kohlberg's model of moral development is too male, too much based on how young boys think, reason, and move from one moral stage to another. Kohlberg's emphasis on logical moral principles or laws is seen as the major sexist or overly male theme in his writings. The most important critic of the sexism in Kohlberg's model is Carol Gilligan, who worked with Kohlberg for some time. Gilligan has published her criticisms in several articles and in her recent and much discussed book, *In a Different Voice*.[22] Gilligan's main point is that both young girls and mature women enrich the human moral dialogue by emphasizing different themes than the logical law-and-order themes which mark so much male moral dialogue. This does not mean that logic and law are unimportant in moral life, but it does mean that there are other themes which should be included in order to come to a whole picture of moral development.

As Gilligan sees it, the most important single factor in the moral perspective of young girls and women is the factor of human relationships, the factor of what a given course of behavior will do to the quality of human relationships between persons.[23] Consistently in her research, Gilligan found this relationship factor coming to the fore in the moral decisions of girls and women. She believes that Kohlberg's stages, since they are designed to look for the way in which a person reasons morally, will often see girls and women as morally underdeveloped, whereas, in actual fact, girls and women can be equally or more developed morally, though in a different style (or as Gilligan puts it, in a different voice).

Personally, I would not want to overly dichotomize the moral thinking of the sexes, so that we conceive of men as doing all of the logical moral thinking, and women as doing all of the relational-intuitive moral thinking. Members of both sexes can and should engage in both types of moral thinking and deciding. Nonetheless, I think that Gilligan is definitely on to something in her critique of Kohlberg. Girls and women do have highly important perspectives to contribute to moral living, perspectives which Kohlberg's models can tend to miss.

Criticisms of Kohlberg similar to that of Gilligan would also seem to be in order from members of different racial, economic, ethnic, and cultural groups. Besides being too male, Kohlberg's dilemmas might also be said to be too capitalist, too middle class, too Western.

The fifth criticism of Kohlberg comes from those who find his system wanting because of its lack of an explicitly Christian perspective. In many respects, this criticism is the correlative or flip side of the first criticism which castigated Kohlberg's emphasis on reason and his lack of concern for the content of moral decisions. This fifth criticism is very concerned about content, and it wants to make the content an explicitly Christian content. The Christian story, symbols, and traditions are seen as centrally important to ethics by this fifth criticism. Those interested in moral imagination will find themselves quite at home with many of the concerns of the fifth criticism.[24]

I think that this fifth criticism raises some valid concerns about Kohlberg's work, but I also think there are two important cautions to be made about the criticism. First, I believe that some of Kohlberg's critics can tend to be opposed to a legitimate secular ethic and to call for too large a gap between secular and religious/Christian approaches to ethics. Roman Catholicism may have relied too much on the natural in some of its past approaches to ethics, but the core insight of Aquinas—that natural and religious approaches to ethics are both legitimate and can work together—needs to be preserved. Many of Kohlberg's critics recognize this point, but it could be made more clearly.

Secondly, I agree strongly that any sound ethics must have content as well as form. This book's stress on stories, symbols, etc. springs from a deep awareness of the importance of content. However, I do not think that content for ethics need come from Christian sources alone. Secular insights and insights from other religious traditions can also offer us ethical content. If we leave the Brooklyn Bridge and move to another part of New York Harbor our eyes might fall on the Statue of Liberty with all of its symbolism of the United States as offering welcome to the cold, the tired, and the poor. The symbolism of the statue offers an ethical content, a content which is perhaps best summarized in Emma Lazarus' poem to which I just alluded. Recently, and sadly, I have listened to both a President and a former President speak out about the dangers of more immigrants coming to the United States. Ethics can come from secular stories as well as religious stories, but there is no absolute guarantee that either will be well heard, especially if we lack moral imagination.

To close this summary of some of the major criticisms of Kohlberg's work, it might be helpful to ask about the exact status of the several criticisms mentioned. Do these criticisms totally undercut Kohlberg's work, so that we should scrap his system and start over again to construct a theory for the moral education of our young people? Or do the criticisms have the viewpoint that Kohlberg's work is basically sound and useful, but in need of supplementation by the several issues raised in the criticisms? As best I can assess it, most of Kohlberg's critics believe in the basic value and usefulness of Kohlberg's stage theory. They simply want to supplement his approach with some perspectives which he misses or emphasizes only slightly: Christian perspectives, feminist perspectives, social justice perspectives, and affective perspectives.

Donald M. Joy has recently edited a helpful collection of Christian criticisms of Kohlberg.[25] Nearly all of the authors in the Joy volume have a "keep, but modify and supplement" approach to Kohlberg's stage theory. The one notable exception in the volume is Craig Dykstra who does want to do away with Kohlberg's stage theory.[26] Interestingly, Dykstra is also one of the Kohlberg critics who most stresses moral imagination. Personally, I agree with the majority of critics who want to retain Kohlberg's work but modify it. Thus, in the next section, my question will be "How can moral imagination enhance Kohlberg's work?" rather than "How can moral imagination replace Kohlberg?"

Moral Development Theory and Moral Imagination

Each of the five criticisms of Kohlberg has its own particular interest and objectives, so that each of the criticisms ought to develop its own particular ways of supplementing Kohlberg. At the same time, moral imagination would seem to offer important resources to each of the five criticisms. The development of a sound Christian moral imagination in our young people can be a highly significant aid in their moral development and moral education. Moral imagination can thus serve as a very useful complement to Kohlberg's theories.

For instance, moral imagination can help moral development to transcend the excess rationalism which can mark some approaches to Kohlberg's stage theory. A stress on moral imagination will not lead young people to irrationalism (imagination, as we have seen, involves mental operations), but it will help moral development avoid becoming so scientific and legalistic that our young people cannot address the real problems of the real world.

Similarly, moral imagination can help young people include their affectivity and their femininity (which ultimately is present in both sexes) together with their reason as they approach moral questions. Imagination can also help young people have a taste for stories (both secular and religious) as a source for moral identity and moral decisions. The Christian child with moral imagination may well pass through Kohlberg's stages, but he or she will pass through them as someone whose whole existence is rooted in the story of Jesus of Nazareth. The child will reason, but with a vivid imaginative awareness of the Gospel story.

In light of the fact that moral imagination relates well to all of the major criticisms of Kohlberg, I am not inclined to favor the working out of another separate critique of Kohlberg based on moral imagination. Rather, as Christian and moral educators continue to use Kohlberg and to supplement his work in light of the existing critiques, I think Christian and moral educators should keep in mind that the development of moral imagination can and should be a major factor in all of the efforts to supplement Kohlberg, from whatever critical perspective one is working. Kohlberg's work is very valuable; it can be even more valuable if supplemented by perspectives which incorporate moral imagination.

IMAGINATION AND SEXUAL EDUCATION OF YOUTH

The Basic Importance of Sexual Imagination

Having spoken about liberal education in general and about basic moral education, we will now consider two concrete areas in which the development of imagination can assist the moral development of the young. The first concrete area to be considered will be the relationship between imagination and the sexual education of youth. When I have told people that I have been working on a book about imagination and moral theology, the response has very often been a laugh, a smile, or some comment about sexuality. While these responses may well reflect an excessive tendency to connect moral theology exclusively with sexuality, it is an undisputed fact that we humans do engage in a great deal of imagining in the sexual area of life. Thus, the question of how we might help young people develop morally appropriate sexual imaginations is an important question. Herein we shall consider the positive importance of imagination for responsible sexual development, and the problems of imagination when it represses all sexual images or is excessively concerned with sexuality.[27]

On the positive side, the fact is that all of us form images of a sexual sort, and all of us playfully associate these images in various ways, as we come to judgments about which sexual behaviors are morally good and which are morally wrong. This process of imagining about sexuality, of using our imaginations to appreciate the beauty, goodness, and wonder of sexuality, is essential to the wholesome sexual development of our young people. Great literature and great art, which convey the meaning and beauty of sexuality, are for this reason an appropriate part of the education of youth, though it is important to carefully select the right time and context for the use of such literature and art. Some sexual imagery is contained in the

Scriptures, particularly in the Old Testament. This imagery can be used beneficially in the development of an appropriate sexual imagination in the young.

The Problem of Repressed Sexual Imagination

Problems can ensue when sexual imagination is not developed along the lines just mentioned. A first and sometimes very serious problem can ensue when all sexual imagination is repressed. If young people are educated in a context which is very fearful of all sexual imagery, the young may never be able to learn the true beauty of sexuality. If their imaginations fail in this way, the young may very well have great difficulty in relating to persons of the other sex. Major sexual aberrations, such as the sexual abuse of children, may very well come from the type of repressive imaginative failure I have just described.[28] If one does not learn to imagine appropriate forms of sexual behavior, the human sexual drive may sometimes emerge in such highly inappropriate ways. While the homosexual orientation is not simply to be lumped together with problems such as child abuse, at least one major study has suggested that the homosexual orientation springs from a sexual imagination which is limited in the formative years.[29]

To illustrate my point about repressed sexual imagination, I am going to suggest a simple example. The example is limited because it relates to my perspective as a male, but I think it can make the point. When a man meets or is working with an attractive woman, I think he needs to be able to use his imagination somewhat along the following lines: "Mrs. (or Sister or Miss) So-and-So is very attractive to me in a sexual sense; were I married to her, sexual communion would be a wonderful human experience. Of course I am not married to her, so we will get on with our work, our socializing, or with whatever else is taking place."

If a man has been educated to be free enough to imagine along these lines, I think he will be able to have a suitable relationship with the woman in question. His interest will move beyond the level of sexual fantasies to concern for the woman's character, intelligence, life direction, maturity, etc. Moreover, any woman or man who learns to imagine sexually with a "moving beyond" framework will develop a disciplined sexual imagination, an imagination which will discern that some sexual images are never morally acceptable, and that other images are not acceptable because of the life commitments of the persons who are imagined as acting sexually. Such men and women will also have the freedom to look at other men and women as co-equal and dignified human beings, even when no particular sexual attraction is present.

On the other hand, if the man of the above example has repressed his sexual imagination so that he cannot let himself be aware of the woman's sexual attractiveness, he will almost inevitably be afraid of the woman. His fear will manifest itself in withdrawnness, hostility, or some other unacceptable response. Obviously, there is care and control needed in educational approaches to developing the sexual imagination of the young. But care and control are not the same as seeking to eliminate sexual imagination in the young. The elimination of sexual imagination can only be counter-productive for the reasons just stated.

Excess or Arrested Sexual Imagination

An opposite problem to the difficulty of repressed sexual imagination is the problem of those whose imagining never moves beyond the sexual level, whose imagining concentrates on sexual expression to the exclusion of everything else. The Roman Catholic tradition used to speak about "bad thoughts" ("bad images" might say it better), when discussing this area, and the area remains an area of genuine moral concern.

In my previous example, I suggested that a person needs to be free to fantasize sexually before moving on to other images when actual expression of a given sexual fantasy is not appropriate. But if the person can never move beyond sexual images, his or her life adjustment will be quite unsatisfactory. If all men can think about when relating to women is their physical sexual beauty, these men are almost as limited imaginatively as are the men who are afraid to even let themselves be aware of sexual images. In this circumstance, men see women only as sexual objects, and men therefore have a very inadequate basis for reaching out to women in a human sense. Regrettably this problem is all too common in many societies, both traditional and modern.

In terms of education of youth, the key to transcending this kind of excess or arrested sexual imagination is to find ways of waking up all levels of imagination in the young. If the young learn to appreciate images from great art, music, literature, etc., their imagination will take on a large focus, rather than simply a physical sexual focus. If the young learn (from the arts and from personal experiences) to develop images of the other sex, in which the heroism, commitment, competence, etc. of the other sex are dominant themes, it seems quite unlikely that their sexual imaginations will remain arrested. For these reasons, liberal education can be seen as crucial for sexual justice as well as for social justice.

In this context, the specific nature of the evil in pornography becomes clear. The problem with pornography is not that it portrays the human body as beautiful, for the body is beautiful. The problem with pornography is that it concentrates so exclusively on the physical, sexual aspect of our humanity that other aspects of our humanity are forgotten. For this reason, pornography is very especially a problem for the young whose notion of our humanity is still in the process of being shaped. Pornography can so slant the development of human imagination that it can deny young people the opportunity to develop the whole range and power of human imagination. Thus, pornography must be challenged by responsible adults. But the challenge must be a challenge which seeks to stretch the range of young people's imagining to higher levels, not a challenge which rejects sexual imagination in every respect.[30]

All of this suggests that education for sound sexual imagination must be a part of a much larger educational process, a process which is thoroughly intertwined with the whole purpose of liberal education as we discussed it earlier. The real key to sexual imagination, in my judgment, is to be found in the concept of balance. The balance which moral educators should seek is a balance which sensitively develops sexual imagination for the sake of the good which it can present to us. But, at the same time, such a balance should never rest with sexual imagination alone. It should seek to hold out to the young an imaginative grasp of all levels of human existence. Such a balance will be difficult to achieve, and it must respect the differences in age, culture, life experience, etc. which will be found in different children and young people. But whatever the difficulties, balanced imagining, rather than repression or excess sexual preoccupation, ought to be our goal in educating the sexual imagination.

IMAGINATION IN THE YOUNG AND SOCIAL JUSTICE

From the outset, the issue of social justice has been a significant concern of this book. I stated in the first chapter that it can be difficult to get people to look upon social problems as moral issues, and I suggested that imagination might help people be more conscious of social justice issues. In Chapter 5 I tried to show that our approaches to a number of specific social problems might be improved through moral imagination. So far, however, we have not looked at the specific question of imagination and the education of children and young people for social justice. This question will be considered now.

I pointed out earlier that Kohlberg's moral development theory is very concerned with justice and fairness. In one-on-one justice situations, Kohlberg's model accomplishes a great deal. Cases such as the classic case of children dividing a piece of pie into two (''you cut and I'll choose'') are very manageable under Kohlberg's approach. But the deeper questions of social justice will often be untouched in Kohlberg's model until people reach the fifth and sixth stages, and, according to the usual interpretation of Kohlberg, many persons never reach those states. Why is it that Kohlberg's model (and many other approaches to moral education as well) does not get at the larger questions of social justice quite so easily?

As I see it, the basic reason why many approaches to ethics (including Kohlberg's) have trouble educating children and young people for social justice is that large numbers of children and youth, especially in our own culture, have no concrete experience of structural social injustice with the result that they cannot relate in any real way to major social problems. This lack of experience is especially acute in white middle and upper class boys. If the child or youth is a girl, poor, or a member of a racial, ethic, or religious minority, she or he may have something of an experiential basis out of which to relate to social justice issues, but even some children in these groups can have a very limited experience base for social justice in our kind of society.

From this perspective, imagination can be seen as a very important help in educating children and the young for social justice. Abstract presentations about social justice issues will not be enough to motivate children to concern for social justice. Instead, we must find ways to create true experiences of social injustice in children and youth. If these true experiences cannot be created in actual fact, they must be created imaginatively—by getting the children and youth to experience imaginatively what social injustice is like.

Some fine work has already been done along these lines using a variety of strategies and approaches.[31] While some of the authors working on educating the young for social justice have not specifically mentioned imagination, their pedagogies clearly involve appeals to imagination, even if these appeals are only implicit. In what follows, I will mention four imagination-oriented approaches which I believe can help children become more conscious of social moral issues. The four approaches are: first, providing concrete social justice experiences; second, using games to teach social justice; third, the use of audio-visual media; fourth, the use of ascetic practices as a motivator for social justice.

Providing Concrete Social Justice Experience for Youth

First, parents, pastors, teachers, and counselors can look for opportunities to create for children and youth actual experiences involving social stresses and social justice questions. While such experiences may seem difficult to provide, numbers of such experiences would seem to be achievable with the use of a little imagination. Children, for example, can often be given opportunities to meet and socialize with children of other races, other religions, and other socio-economic situations. When they do meet, and have a chance to play together, children of different races, etc. can often form understandings of each other more easily than adults who are beset with various types of cultural baggage and prejudice. Such childhood experiences can help children avoid false cultural stereotypes as they grow toward adulthood.[32]

Another opportunity to give children actual social justice experience can be found whenever a parish or other group is planning a social project such as taking food to the poor, visiting the elderly or the retarded, etc. When such projects are being planned, ways to include the children and the teenagers in the projects should be part of the plan whenever possible. Too often there is a tendency to shelter children and teenagers from such projects, even though such projects can be a very important element in the social moral development of children and teenagers.

Still another potential experience for social justice learning by children is even closer to home. I refer to the matter of sexism. If, in family living, parents can avoid projecting narrow sex-role stereotypes, and if, both at home and in school, the sex stereotypes of our society can be subjected to enlightened criticism, a most important type of actual social learning can be afforded to children and youth. Children and youth can thus be helped to form an imaginative new vision of sexual justice and equality. In the final analysis, the issue of justice between the sexes may be the single most important social learning experience for the young. Childhood contacts with other races, economic groups, etc. may often be sporadic even though important. But contact with members of both sexes will be more or less constant for most children and youth. Such contact can thus be a crucial experience for learning social justice.

The actual social justice experiences I have just cited obviously relate to only a tiny fraction of all the social justice issues which exist worldwide. But if we use our imaginations to provide those actual social justice experiences which can be made available to children and the young, the hope is that our children will be able to apply the lessons of their youthful experiences to the other social questions they will become conscious of later in life.

Games and Social Justice

It is a basic fact of life that children like to play games and learn from playing games. It is also a fact that imagination is in many respects a play-oriented process. We have noted this play theme many times in our comments on imagination. Thus, it seems that one of the best ways to help children begin to grasp those social problems which they cannot directly experience is through games and game type activities. Through games the nature of economic oppression, racial injustice, etc. can be brought home concretely to children's imaginations. Such games will often involve role playing which gets the children to take on the identities of the poor, racial minorities, etc. I do think that such games need to be used carefully, and that persons skilled in child and adolescent psychology ought to be involved in the design of socially oriented games. But the fact remains: children like imaginative play, and they can learn about social justice through such play.

Audio-Visual Media and Social Justice

For the larger and more global social justice issues, films and other audio-visual media seem to be one of the very best ways to spark the moral imaginations of children and adolescents (and of adults for that matter). Such audio-visual media can speak to children and young people in two ways. First, the media can give children and teenagers a concrete visual awareness of actual social issues (such as world hunger, the medical aspects of a nuclear attack, the problems related to drug abuse, and the inadequacies of our criminal justice system in helping the victims of rape). Out of such awareness, a whole new level of social concern can emerge. Social principles which before were stale and meaningless can become matters of vital concern.

Second, audio-visual social media can reach youthful imagination by depicting the work of truly charismatic persons who are engaged in the struggle for social justice. Movies of the Dom Helder Camaras, the Dorothy Days, the Martin Luther Kings, the Cesar Chavezes, and the Bruce Ritters of this world can have a very marked impact on the moral imaginations of young people. The fact that such people truly and effectively act for social justice serves to put flesh and blood on the 1971 synod of bishops' famous proclamation that action in behalf of social justice is a constitutive dimension of the preaching of the Gospel.[33]

Asceticism and Social Justice

One of the interesting aspects of the American bishops' recent pastoral letter on the nuclear arms question can be found in the pastoral's invitation to voluntary Friday fast and abstinence as a sign of our concern about the nuclear question.[34] The bishops' fast and abstinence invitation has a different spirit than some of the past legalist approaches to fasting and abstinence, and in my judgment stems from a very important pastoral/theological insight, namely that our attitude toward justice and our personal lifestyle are highly interconnected. This insight applies to all persons, but it is especially important to young people who are in their formative years.

Thus, if young people can be invited to engage in symbolic gestures such as fasting and abstinence, they can in the process be open to still another imaginative form of learning, to a learning which faces up to the evil of social injustice by voluntarily accepting some aspects of that evil. If a concern for social justice remains purely theoretical, it is all too likely to be an empty and remote concern. But if young people can personally take on some aspects of an injustice (e.g., by being a bit hungry because some people have to be a lot hungry), they (and all of us too) have a new imaginative connection with social issues.

This ascetic approach seems especially valuable as a teaching tool for children because we live in such a consumer oriented, wasteful, energy absorbing society.[35] The broadest social changes will not come about unless we all change. Voluntary ascetic practices are our little steps toward that change. Some might suggest that with such small ascetic practices we are only playing games in the face of the huge social problems which beset the world. This may well be true, but, as we have seen already, much moral learning can take place through game playing (with ''playing'' being understood in the sense it has had throughout this book).

No doubt education of the young for social justice will remain a long and difficult struggle. But at least some progress is possible along the lines just mentioned. This progress will come from many factors, but the use of moral imagination is clearly a key element in the several steps which can help our young people be more sensitive to social justice concerns.

A Note on Imagination and the Moral Education of Adults

When we think about moral education, it is natural that our attention turns to issues related to the moral education of children and adolescents. We should not forget, however, that adults are also very much in need of moral education. According to Kohlberg's paradigm, only a small number of adults reach the highest stages of moral reasoning. Even apart from Kohlberg, it is obvious that many adults have rather limited moral perspectives. In some respects, the task of morally educating adults may be even more of a challenge than is the moral education of children because of the ''set on one's ways factor'' which can often be a part of adult life.

In a larger sense, most of what has been said throughout this book about the nature of moral imagination can be seen as relevant to the moral education of adults. The basic imagination structure we saw in Chapter 4—forming images, playfully associating them, and making judgments about appropriate connections of images— should be an important objective in the moral education of adults. More specifically, many themes from the preceding sections of this chapter can be as relevant to the moral education of adults as well as to children and adolescents. Adults need to keep cultivating the interests which are sought after by a liberal education. The imagination-related strategies which I suggested for adjusting to sexual fantasies and the four approaches to raising social consciousness can all be useful with adults. Adults may, however, have a harder time letting go, and thus it is more of a challenge for them to be good game players than it is for children.

At this point, I do not intend to present a detailed overview of the principles for adult religious or moral education. I do however want to make a case for moral imagination and to explain why I think moral imagination can be a very significant factor in the moral education of adults.

I mentioned above that one of the main difficulties which inhibits the moral growth of adults is that adults tend to be living in a somewhat stable pattern of adjustment so that they do not so easily open themselves up to new patterns of thought or new judgments on how to approach moral issues. Kohlberg recognizes this fact when he posits that some kind of cognitive disequilibrium is necessary to move people to new levels of moral awareness. I believe that Kohlberg is correct in suggesting that moral growth in adults often involves crises, but he may lean a bit too much toward understanding adult moral growth as a change in one's logical pattern of moral analysis.

In this context, I believe that it may well be more possible to stimulate adult moral growth through fresh images than through new logical patterns. If we can open adults to a new vision, to new symbolisms, to a new sense of the human dream and the human story, such adults might very well be able to move to new levels of moral awareness, levels which will include whatever logical pattern adjustments are necessary. For instance, if adults can be helped to form an image of the Church as a story-formed peace community which follows after Christ, the Prince of Peace, such adults may be more free, still using due care and caution, to work toward an adequate nuclear arms policy. If Catholic piety can develop for us a vision of Mary which avoids stereotypes and follows Vatican II's integration of Mary more fully into the Church, new understandings of women and men as equals might become more possible. If the image of God as Father can become a more powerful sign of the common humanity we all share, perhaps we can hope for a more personally owned, and not just legally imposed, form of racial justice. To accomplish this the image of God the Father will need to become less sexist, and to be used in conjunction with complementary images of God as female.

Yes, adult moral growth will be difficult. It will involve crises and disequilibrium. But such growth will be considerably more likely, in my judgment, if we can appeal to adult imagination as well as to adult logic.

Some Concluding Comments

A summary of all the judgments made in this book could be presented at this time. But I prefer to conclude by asking a simple question: In light of all that I have said, what is the present status of imagination in moral theology or Christian ethics? While several types of responses might be possible, I think the most helpful phrase with which to categorize moral theological imagination is H.R. Niebuhr's well-known phrase "partial answer."[36] I will comment on each of the two words.

Imagination is an "answer" because it offers very important resources to moral theology. With its interest in stories, metaphors, vision, playfulness, prayerful reflection, and a virtuous lifestyle, imagination can offer moral theology many highly important resources, resources which might well be missed on the basis of moral logic or moral principles alone. Imagination as a moral resource can help us not only in seeing what we ought to do; imagination can also help motivate us to do the good which we see. Images have power which can move or "motor" us to action.[37]

But imagination is only "partial" as an answer. In and of itself, it cannot be set forth as a complete treatise on moral theology. Imagination can offer poor or fanciful images which will need correction by moral principles. Imagination is partial because it must be engaged in dialogue with moral principles. Only on the basis of such dialogue will we achieve a truly adequate approach to fundamental moral theology.

Finally, to the extent that imagination is a partial or part answer, it is a part answer that none in the recent past have heard very well, because we are living in an age which has been so dominated by a one-sided approach to science, technology, and discursive rationality. Thus, at the present time we very much need to attend to the perspectives on moral matters which can be offered by imagination. The more we can do this, the better and richer our approach to moral theology will be.

Notes

1. The best summary of the work of Vatican II on moral theology can be found in Josef Fuchs, *Human Values and Christian Morality* (Dublin: Gill and Macmillan, 1971), pp. 1–75. The major work which best expresses the spirit of Vatican II, especially its biblical emphasis and its reunion of the moral life and the spiritual life, is Bernard Häring, *Free and Faithful in Christ* (cf. abbr. *F&F*).

2. A summary of discernment literature through the mid 1970's can be found in Philip S. Keane, "Discernment of Spirits: A Theological Reflection," *American Ecclesiastical Review* 168 (1974), pp. 43–61. More contemporary thinking on discernment can be found in James M. Gustafson, *Ethics from a Theocentric Perspective* (cf. abbr. *ETP*), pp. 327–342. A helpful connection of discernment with story, character, vision, etc. can be found in James A. Donahue, "Religious Institutions as Moral Agents: Toward an Ethics of Organizational Character," *Issues in the Labor-Management Dialogue: Church Perspectives*, ed. by Adam J. Maida (St. Louis: The Catholic Health Association, 1982), pp. 139–159.

3. Much will be said about moral development in Chapter 6. A simple basic text reflecting the Catholic interest in the theme is Ronald Duska and Mariellen Whelan, *Moral Development: A Guide to Piaget and Kohlberg* (New York: Paulist Press, 1975).

4. Important examples of contemporary writing on the natural law include Franz Böckle, *Fundamental Moral Theology* (New York: Pueblo Publishing Co., 1980), pp. 180–247, and Charles E. Curran, *Themes in Fundamental Moral Theology* (Notre Dame, Ind.: University of Notre Dame Press, 1977), pp. 27–80. Most of the major recent writings on the double effect can be found in *RMT No. 1: Moral Norms and the Catholic Tradition* or in Richard A. McCormick and Paul Ramsey, eds., *Doing Evil To Achieve Good: Moral Choice in Conflict Situations* (Chicago: Loyola University Press, 1978).

5. In addition to Häring's *F&F* and Böckle's *Fundamental Moral Theology,* other new full length works in this area include Timothy E. O'Connell, *Principles for a Catholic Morality* (New York: Seabury Press, 1978), and Daniel C. Maguire, *The Moral Choice* (cf. abbr. *TMC*).

6. Many of these four developments can be found in the *SCDF's Declaration on Certain Questions Concerning Sexual Ethics,* Dec. 29, 1975. The English text was published by the *USCC* (Washington: 1976). Books which have reflected this kind of thinking, sometimes in a controversial fashion, include: Anthony Kosnik, *et al., Human Sexuality: New Directions in American Catholic Thought* (New York: Paulist Press, 1977); André Guindon, *The Sexual Language* (cf. abbr. *TSL*); and Philip S. Keane, *Sexual Morality: A Catholic Perspective* (New York: Paulist Press, 1977).

7. Cf. Bishop Francis Mugavero, "Pastoral Letter: The Gift of Sexuality," *Origins* 5 (1976), pp. 581–586; Archbishop John R. Quinn, "A Pastoral Letter on Homosexuality," *Origins* 10 (1980), pp. 106–108. See also the report of the task force of the archdiocese of Baltimore on ministry to lesbian and gay Catholics, in *Origins* 11 (1982), pp. 549–553.

8. For the recent official Catholic teaching on death and dying see *SCDF, Declaration on Euthanasia,* May 5, 1980 (in *Origins* 10 [1980], pp. 154–157). On abortion, see *SCDF, Declaration on Procured Abortion,* November 18, 1974 (in *Origins* 4 [1974], pp. 385–392). Much of the Catholic (and other) writing on abortion is summarized and critiqued in Richard A. McCormick, *How Brave a New World?* (Garden City, N.Y.: Doubleday, 1981), pp. 117–206.

9. To anticipate a point to be made shortly in the text, much of this new work on medicine and ethics is being done in an ecumenical context, involving Catholic, Protestant, Jewish, and philosophical ethicists. Key sources for the issues mentioned are Warren T. Reich, ed., *Encyclopedia of Bioethics,* 4 vols. (New York: Macmillan and Free Press, 1978); Tom L. Beauchamp and LeRoy Walters, eds., *Contemporary Issues in Bioethics* (cf. abbr. *CIB*); and Thomas A. Shannon, ed., *Bioethics* (cf. abbr. *Bio*).

10. Two important recent Catholic works on social ethics in America are Charles E. Curran, *American Catholic Social Ethics:*

Twentieth Century Approaches (Notre Dame, Ind.: University of Notre Dame Press, 1982); and John A. Coleman, *An American Strategic Theology* (New York: Paulist Press, 1982).

11. September 14, 1981. Eng. tr.: *On Human Work*. In *Origins* 11, pp. 225–244.

12. *NCCB, The Challenge of Peace* (cf. abbr. *TCP*).

13. Three of the more well-known non-clerics now writing moral theology are Margaret Farley, R.S.M., Daniel C. Maguire and William E. May.

14. Cf. abbr. *ETP*.

15. The first well-known Protestant medical ethics text was Joseph Fletcher, *Morals and Medicine* (Princeton: Princeton University Press, 1954).

16. For a spectrum of Protestant (as well as some Catholic) reflection on the nuclear issue see *Christianity and Crisis* 41 (1982), pp. 370–398. This is a special issue titled *In Amsterdam Thinking About the Bomb*. It reports testimony from a World Council of Churches hearing on nuclear arms.

17. The best source describing this movement to a common middle ground is James M. Gustafson, *Protestant and Roman Catholic Ethics* (cf. abbr. *PRC*).

18. Most significant of the Protestant writers on the virtue theme is Stanley M. Hauerwas whose work will come up often in this book—e.g., his *Vision and Virtue* (cf. abbr. *VV*).

19. For this notion of forgetting the real meaning of some of our basic truths, cf. Karl Rahner, ''Forgotten Truths Concerning the Sacrament of Penance,'' *Theological Investigations* (cf. abbr. *TI*) 2, pp. 135–136.

20. Cf. Chapter 5, pp. 120–123.

21. In *TCP*, nos. 8–12, the bishops are very clear in making the distinction between principles and concrete applications.

22. For a classic article which set forth the traditional Catholic position, see Gerald Kelly, ''The Duty of Using Artificial Means of Preserving Life,'' *TS* 11 (1950), pp. 203–220.

23. Profound questions about how theology works are at stake here. Some would hold that theological opinions which diverge from the magisterium ought only to be given private expression to the Vatican, preferably in Latin. Others seem to suggest that theologians

are free to say anything about anything. Neither of these approaches is satisfactory.

24. Of the much important work which has been done on rape, I believe the most significant text is Susan Brownmiller, *Against Our Will: Men, Women and Rape* (New York: Simon and Schuster, 1974).

25. Cf. Paul Ramsey, "On (Only) Caring for the Dying," *The Patient as Person: Explorations in Medical Ethics* (New Haven: Yale University Press, 1970), esp. pp. 157–164.

26. Cf. the sources cited in note 4 above. My own latest comments are in Philip S. Keane, "The Objective Moral Order: Reflections on Recent Research," *TS* 43 (1982), pp. 260–278.

27. Hauerwas, "The Self as Story: A Reconsideration of the Relation of Religion and Morality from the Agent's Perspective," *VV*, pp. 68–89; *idem*, "Towards an Ethics of Character," *VV*, pp. 48–67; *idem*, "A Story-Formed Community: Reflections on *Watership Down*," *A Community of Character* (cf. abbr. *CC*), pp. 9–35; Alasdair MacIntyre, *After Virtue* (cf. abbr. *AV*), esp. pp. 190–209.

28. Edward Shils, *Tradition* (Chicago: University of Chicago Press, 1981); Daniel Callahan, "Tradition and the Moral Life," *The Hastings Center Report* 12, no. 6 (1982), pp. 23–30.

29. For Ramsey and other authors on this point, see the special issue titled *Focus on Liturgy and Ethics* in *JRE* 7 (1979), pp. 139–248.

30. Häring, *F&F* 2, pp. 102–152.

31. Daniel C. Maguire, *TMC*, pp. 189–217.

32. Maguire, *TMC*, pp. 343–369. Stanley Hauerwas, *Truthfulness and Tragedy* (cf. abbr. *TT*), esp. pp. 57–70, 147–202.

33. Specifics on these developments in philosophy, systematic theology, and Scripture will be found in Chapter 3.

34. Cf. Paul Ricoeur, *Interpretation Theory: Discourse and the Surplus of Meaning* (Fort Worth: Texas Christian University Press, 1976).

35. Tracy, *The Analogical Imagination* (cf. abbr. *AI*).

36. Examples of Rahner's writings on this theme include "Priest and Poet," *TI* 3, pp. 294–317; and "Poetry and the Christian," *TI* 4, pp. 357–367.

37. Gustafson's phrase is "A Preference for the Reformed Tradition," *ETP*, p. 157.

CHAPTER 2

1. Plato's theory of forms can be found throughout his famous Dialogue, *The Republic (GDP*, pp. 118–422). A more succinct exposition of Plato's thinking about the forms can be found in his Dialogue, *Phaedo* (*GDP*, esp. pp. 482–487). For an overview of Plato's thought, see Gilbert Ryle. "Plato," *EP* 5, pp. 314–333.

2. Plato, *The Republic,* Book 10 (*GDP*, pp. 393–409).

3. For a clear example of the later Plato's move away from the theory of forms see his Dialogue, *Parmenides.* In *The Dialogues of Plato*, vol. 2 (New York: Random House, 1937), esp. pp. 93–95.

4. For a clear statement of Augustine's use of the Platonic tradition in relationship to Christianity, see his *Confessions,* Book 7, Chapter 9, Sec. 13–14. In *Saint Augustine: Confessions* (New York: Fathers of the Church, 1953), pp. 176–179.

5. For Augustine's mature thinking on the senses/intellect issue see his *De Trinitate*, Book 15, Chapter 12. Eng. tr.: *The Trinity* (Washington: The Catholic University of America Press, 1963), pp. 480–483.

6. *Confessions,* Book 10, Chapter 6, Sec. 9–10. In *Saint Augustine: Confessions,* pp. 270–272.

7. *De Trinitate*, Book 3, Chapter 9, Sec. 16. *The Trinity*, p. 112. "The world itself is pregnant with the causes of unborn beings."

8. René Descartes, *Discourse on the Method of Rightly Conducting the Reason.* In *The Philosophical Works of Descartes* (Cambridge: Cambridge University Press, 1970 [originally 1911]), esp. pp. 100–106.

9. Immanuel Kant, *CPuR,* pp. 143ff.

10. Kant, *Groundwork of the Metaphysic of Morals* (New York: Harper and Row, 1964), pp. 64–68.

11. For most readers, Aristotle's *Metaphysics* is probably the most readily available source for reading of his move away from Plato. Key sections of *Metaphysics* are found in Aristotle, *On Man and the Universe* (New York: Walter J. Black, 1943), pp. 3–37. For an overview, see G. B. Kerferd, "Aristotle," *EP* 1, pp 151–162.

12. In *On Man and the Universe,* pp. 84–244.

13. St. Thomas Aquinas, *ST* I, q. 78, a. 3–4.

14. *ST* I, q. 79, a. 2–3.

15. *ST* I, q. 84, a. 7, ad 3. The theme of *excessus* is a major focal point of Karl Rahner's interpretation of Thomas in his doctoral dissertation. Karl Rahner, *Spirit in the World* (cf. abbr. *SW*), esp. pp. 146–226.

16. In our context Maritain's most important work showing a neo-Thomist dynamism is his *Creative Intuition in Art and Poetry* (cf. abbr. *CIAP*). The most seminal of the Transcendental Thomists is Joseph Maréchal, especially in *Le Point de Départ de la Métaphysique* (3rd ed. Paris: Desclée de Brouwer, 1944). English selections in *A Maréchal Reader* (New York: Herder and Herder, 1970).

17. Rahner, *SW*, p. 385.

18. John Henry Newman, *An Essay in Aid of a Grammar of Assent* (London: Longman's, Green, 1906), pp. 258–329.

19. *Ibid.,* pp. 343–383.

20. *Ibid.,* p. 360.

21. *Ibid.,* p. 354.

22. An excellent summary of the history of aesthetics can be found in Monroe C. Beardsley, ''Aesthetics, History of,'' *EP* 1, pp. 18–35.

23. Plato, *The Republic,* Book 10. In *GDP*, pp. 394–408.

24. *GDP*, p. 407.

25. David Hume, *A Treatise of Human Nature*, ed. by L.A. Selby-Bigge (Oxford: Clarendon Press, 1967 [reprint of 1888 ed.]), Book 1, Part 4, Sec. 3, p. 225.

26. Plato, *The Republic*. *GDP*, pp. 179–280.

27. For a summary of this see Monroe Beardsley, *op. cit.*, pp. 21, 24–25.

28. Clive Bell, *Art* (New York: G.P. Putnam's Sons, 1958 [orig. 1913]), esp. pp. 47–55.

29. The best source for Aristotle's thinking on aesthetics is his short work *Poetics*. Eng. tr.: *Aristotle on the Art of Poetry* (Ithaca, N.Y.: Cornell University Press, 1947).

30. Cf. Beardsley, *op. cit.,* p. 26.

31. Cf. Rudolph Allers, ''St. Augustine's Doctrine on Illumination,'' *Franciscan Studies* 12 (1952), pp. 27–46.

32. Aquinas' term *claritas* is found in *ST* II–II, q. 145, a. 2, and in *ST* II–II, q. 180, a. 2. The term *"resplendentia formae"* appears in *De Pulchro et Bono,* which may have been written by either Aquinas or Albert the Great. Cf. Beardsley, *op. cit.,* p. 23.

33. Henri Bergson, *Creative Evolution* (New York: Modern Library, 1944 [orig. 1911]).

34. For roots of the theory of transcendentals in Thomas, see *ST* I q. 6, 11, 16.

35. Kant, *CPuR,* p. 143.

36. For a summary of ancient and medieval approaches to biblical exegesis, cf. Raymond E. Brown, *The Sensus Plenior of Sacred Scripture* (Baltimore: St. Mary's University, 1955), pp. 29–67.

37. Three vols. New Haven: Yale University Press, 1955 (orig. 1923–29). Also important in this context are the works of Susanne K. Langer, e.g., *Philosophy in a New Key: A Study in the Symbolism of Reason, Rite, and Art,* 3rd ed. (Cambridge, Mass.: Harvard University Press, 1957), and *Feeling and Form* (New York: Charles Scribner's. 1953).

38. David Hume, *Of the Standard of Taste and Other Essays,* ed. by John W. Lenz (Indianapolis: Bobbs-Merrill, 1965).

39. While Croce nuanced his position over the years, perhaps the clearest statement of his view can be found in *Aesthetic* (Boston: David R. Godine, 1979 [orig. 1902]). Robin G. Collingwood, *The Principles of Art* (Oxford: Oxford University Press, 1958 [orig. 1937]).

40. John Dewey, *Art as Experience* (cf. abbr. *AE*).

41. Aristotle, *Poetics*, Chapter 6. In *Aristotle on the Art of Poetry*, p. 17.

42. Edmund Burke, *A Philosphical Inquiry into the Origin of Our Ideas of the Sublime and the Beautiful*, ed. by James T. Boulton (Notre Dame, Ind.: University of Notre Dame Press, 1968 [orig. 1757]).

43. Coleridge's pertinent work will be discussed later (cf. note 54).

44. Dewey, *AE*, esp. pp. 272–297.

45. For a summary of how these three approaches function in ethics, cf. Kai Nielsen, "Ethics, Problems of," *EP* 3, pp. 127–130.

46. Plato, *Laws*, 653–654. In *The Dialogues of Plato* vol. 2, pp. 432–434.

47. Plotinus, *Enneads*. I, vi. In *The Essential Plotinus: Representative Treatises from the Enneads* (Indianapolis: Hackett Publishing Co., 1975), pp. 33–44.

48. Cf. Beardsley, *op. cit.*, p. 26.

49. In Shelley, *A Defense of Poetry*. Cited in John Hospers, "Aesthetics, Problems of," *EP* 1, p. 50.

50. Baumgarten, *Meditationes Philosophicae de Nonnullis ad Poema Pertinentibus*, 1735.

51. Francis Bacon, *Advancement of Learning* (Totowa, N.J.: Rowan and Littlefield, 1973 [orig. 1605]).

52. Hobbes, *Leviathan* (New York: Simon and Schuster, 1964 [orig. 1651]), p. 5. On p. 4 is Hobbes' famous description of imagination as a "decaying sense." Kant, *CPuR*, pp. 142–143.

53. Cf. note 25 above.

54. Coleridge's views on imagination can be found in his *Biographia Literaria*, Chapter 13 (New York: E.P. Dutton, 1906 [orig. 1817]), pp. 153–160.

55. Gilbert Ryle, *The Concept of Mind* (London: Hutchinson & Co., 1949), esp. pp. 257–258.

56. One of the very best presentations of the Roman Catholic approach to the notion of mystery in theology is Karl Rahner's "The Concept of Mystery in Catholic Theology," *TI* 4, pp. 36–73.

57. Cf. Karl Rahner, "The Theology of the Symbol," *TI* 4, pp. 211–252. For a survey of Paul Ricoeur's work on the notion of symbol, cf. Loretta Dornish, "Symbolic Systems and the Interpretation of Scripture: An Introduction to the Work of Paul Ricoeur," *Semeia* 4 (1975), pp. 3–21.

58. Dewey, *AE*, p. 46.

59. For sources on discernment of spirits, cf. Chapter 1, note 2.

60. Cf. Karl Rahner, "On the Question of a Formal Existential Ethics," *TI* 2, pp. 232–234; *idem*, "The Church's Limits: Against Clerical Triumphalists and Lay Defeatists," *The Christian of the Future* (New York: Herder and Herder, 1967), p. 56.

61. For an overview on mysticism, cf. Heribert Fischer *et al.*, "Mysticism," *Sacramentum Mundi* 4 (New York: Herder and Herder, 1969), pp. 136–152.

62. Cf. Sidney Spencer, *Mysticism in World Religion* (Baltimore: Penguin Books, 1963).

63. Cf. Jacques Maritain, *CIAP*, pp. 172–174.

64. Of special note in the recent Catholic past is the Vatican II notion of a universal call to holiness. Second Vatican Council, *Lumen Gentium* (*The Constitution on the Church*), Chapter 8.

65. Cf. Karl Lehmann, "Transcendence," *Sacramentum Mundi* 6 (New York: Herder & Herder, 1970), p. 278.

66. Aristotle, *Nichomachean Ethics,* book 6. In *On Man and the Universe*, pp. 169–178.

67. Daniel C. Maguire, "*Ratio Practica* and the Intellectualistic Fallacy," *JRE* 10 (1982), pp. 22–39.

68. For a contemporary evaluation of the usefulness of probabilism, cf. Richard M. Gula, *What Are They Saying About Moral Norms?* (New York: Paulist Press, 1982), pp. 101–104).

69. Karl Rahner echoes these sentiments in "The Dignity and Freedom of Man," *TI* 2, p 254: " . . . the historical way of acting of Christians in society, the State, and the Church, has inevitably the character of a bold venture, of uncertainty, of walking into the dark, of 'not knowing what we should pray for', of praying for gracious guidance from above to lead us beyond that which can be calculated in advance, of 'art' (in contrast to theory)." For careful reflections of the life of faith as a creative art, cf. Joseph Powers, "Faith, Mortality, Creativity: Toward the Art of Believing," *TS* 39 (1978), pp. 656–678.

70. For contemporary Catholic writing on conscience, cf. Charles E. Curran, "Conscience," *Themes in Fundamental Moral Theology* (cf. Chapter 1, note 4), pp. 191–231; Timothy E. O'Connell, *Principles for a Catholic Morality* (cf. Chapter 1, note 5), pp. 83–97.

CHAPTER 3

1. Important new feminist works in theology and ethics include Elizabeth Schüssler Fiorenza, *In Memory of Her: A Feminist Theological Reconstruction of Christian Origins* (New York: Crossroads Publ., 1983); Rosemary Radford Ruether, *Sexism and God-Talk: Toward a Feminist Theology* (Boston: Beacon Press, 1983); Carol Gilligan, *In a Different Voice* (cf. abbr. *IDV*). Gilligan's work will be considered below in Chapter 6.

2. Cf. Chapter 2, note 16.

3. For the basic methodological works of Rahner and Maréchal, cf. Chapter 2, notes 16 and 15. For Rousselot (who was tragically killed during World War I), cf. *L' Intellectualisme de Saint Thomas* (Paris: Gabriel Beauchesne, 1924). For Bernard Lonergan,

cf. *Insight: A Study of Human Understanding* (London: Longman's, Green, 1957).

4. Leslie Dewart, "On Transcendental Thomism," *Continuum* 6 (1968), p. 390.

5. *Op. cit.*, esp. pp. 139–45.

6. Rahner, *SW*, p. 64.

7. Cf. Chapter 2, note 15.

8. Rahner, *SW*, p. 103, and throughout.

9. For Lonergan's frequent use of this phrase and its variants, cf. *Insight,* p. 776.

10. Rahner, *SW*, p. 385.

11. For an excellent historical overview of the emergence and development of the hermeneutic question, cf. the section titled "Studies in the History of Hermeneutics," in Paul Ricoeur, *Hermeneutics and the Human Sciences* (cf. abbr. *HHS*), pp. 43–128.

12. Ricoeur, *HHS*, pp. 43–44.

13. Ricoeur develops this notion of a hermeneutics of suspicion especially in his work on Freud and Hegel. Cf. Don Ihde, "Editor's Introduction," *The Conflict of Interpretations* (cf. abbr. *CI*), pp. xv-xvi. Also see Ricoeur, *CI*, p. 148.

14. Cf. Hans-Georg Gadamer, *Truth and Method* (cf. abbr. *TM*), pp. 242–245.

15. Paul Ricoeur, *HHS*, pp. 45–48.

16. *HHS*, pp. 48–53.

17. For Husserl's own thinking on phenomenology see Edmund Husserl, *The Idea of Phenomenology* (The Hague: Martinus Nijhoff, 1964 [orig. 1907]); *idem, Ideas: General Introduction to Pure Phenomenology* (New York: Humanities Press, 1931 [orig. 1913]). For Ricoeur's explanations of Husserl, cf. Paul Ricoeur, "Phenomenology and Hermeneutics," in *HHS*, pp. 101–128.

18. Paul Ricoeur, "Existence and Hermeneutics," *CI*, p. 3.

19. Martin Heidegger, *Being and Time* (New York: Harper and Row, 1964), esp. pp. 182–195.

20. For the notion of a hermeneutical arc, cf. Paul Ricoeur, *HHS* pp. 161, 164.

21. *TM*, esp. pp. 91–99.

22. *TM*, esp. pp. 238–253.

23. *TM*, p. 419; Paul Ricoeur, "The Hermeneutic Function of Distantiation," *HHS*, p. 141.

24. *HHS*, pp. 36, 59–62, 90, 117, 132.

25. Most important is Paul Ricoeur, *The Rule of Metaphor* (cf. abbr. *RM*). Also very helpful are some of Ricoeur's shorter pieces including "Metaphor and the Central Problem of Hermeneutics," *HHS*, pp. 165–181; "Creativity in Language" (cf. abbr. *CL*); "The Metaphorical Process as Cognition, Imagination, and Feeling" (cf. abbr. *CIF*).

26. In addition to the last named article, very helpful is Mary Schaldenbrand, "Metaphoric Imagination: Kinship through Conflict," *Studies in the Philosophy of Paul Ricoeur* (cf. abbr. *SPR*), pp. 58–81. In the same volume, Ricoeur himself offers some significant comments on Schaldenbrand's interpretation of his work, *SPR*, pp. xiii–xiv, xvi–xvii. The closing paragraph of "Metaphor and the Central Problem of Hermeneutics," *HHS*, p. 181, is also most helpful.

27. Paul Ricoeur, "What Is a Text? Explanation and Understanding," *HHS*, pp. 145–164.

28. Cf. Paul Ricoeur, "The Hermeneutic Function of Distantiation," *HHS*, pp. 131–144.

29. *HHS*, pp. 111–113.

30. *RM*, pp. 216–221; *HHS*, pp. 167–168, 171.

31. *HHS*, pp. 160–162.

32. *CL*, pp. 124–133.

33. *TM*, p. 440. The fact that both Rahner and Gadamer relied so much on the early Heidegger no doubt serves to explain some of their similarities. Gadamer's famous notion of "effective historical consciousness" (*TM*, pp. 305–341) and Rahner's notion of "performance" (*SW*, p. 64) both reflect the Heideggerian concern for historical being.

34. *HHS*, pp. 166–176.

35. *CL*, pp. 120, 130.

36. *CL*, pp. 130–133; *HHS*, pp. 180–181.

37. For the two movements, cf. *HHS*, pp. 171–181.

38. *CL*, pp. 132–133; *HHS*, p. 176.

39. "Preface," *SPR*, p. xvii.

40. *SPR*, p. xiii.

41. "For Ricoeur's exposition of these three themes, cf. *CIF*, pp. 147–155.

42. Schaldenbrand, *SPR*, pp. 79–80.

43. Ricoeur does touch this theme briefly in *CIF*, pp. 155–158. For a critique see Robert C. Solomon, "Paul Ricoeur on Passion and Emotion," *SPR*, pp. 1–20.

44. *AI*, pp. 99–135. Cf. *TM*, pp. 253–258.

45. *AI*, pp. 154–178.

46. *AI*, p. 100.

47. *AI*, p. 104.

48. *AI*, pp. 376–398.

49. *AI*, pp. 408–414.

50. *AI*, esp. pp. 454–455.

51. In addition to Tracy's *AI*, other recent systematic-spiritual works touching on imagination include: John Coulson, *Religion and Imagination: In Aid of a Grammar of Assent* (Oxford: Oxford University Press, 1981); John W. Dixon, *Art and the Theological Imagination* (New York: Seabury Press, 1978); Julian Hartt, *Theological Method and Imagination* (New York: Seabury Press, 1977); Kathleen R. Fischer, *The Inner Rainbow: The Imagination in Christian Life* (New York: Paulist Press, 1983); Urban T. Holmes, *Ministry and Imagination* (New York: Seabury Press, 1981); John Shea, *Stories of Faith* (Chicago: Thomas More Press, 1980); Amos Niven Wilder, *Theopoetic: Theology and the Religious Imagination* (Philadelphia: Fortress Press, 1976). Older, but still of much significance are the two books of William F. Lynch, *Christ and Apollo: The Dimensions of the Literary Imagination* (New York: Sheed and Ward, 1960); *idem, Images of Hope* (cf. abbr. *IH*). Also Ray Hart, *Unfinished Man and the Imagination: Toward an Ontology and a Rhetoric of Revelation* (New York: Herder and Herder, 1968). From an anthropological/philosophical viewpoint Jacob Brownowski's *The Origins of Knowledge and Imagination* (New Haven: Yale University Press, 1978) is most valuable. For the perspective of religious sociology cf. Andrew M. Greeley, *The Religious Imagination* (New York: William H. Sadlier, 1981).

52. *TM*, pp. 44–49.

53. For Rahner's work along these lines, cf. Chapter 1, note 32. For Heidegger cf. Heidegger's *Poetry, Language, Thought* (New York: Harper and Row, 1975).

54. Evanston, Ill.: Northwestern University Press, 1973 (orig. 1953).

55. Paul Ricoeur and Mikel Dufrenne, *Karl Jaspers et la philosophie de l'existence* (Paris: Seuil, 1947).

56. Roger Scruton, *Art and Imagination: A Study in the Philosophy of Mind* (London: Routledge and Keegan Paul, 1982 [orig. 1974]).

57. For a presentation of modern brain research (with illustrations and copious references), cf. Sally P. Springer and Georg Deutsch, *Left Brain, Right Brain* (San Francisco: W.H. Freeman and Company, 1981).

58. *HHS*, pp. 157–164.

59. James M. Gustafson, "Context Versus Principles: A Misplaced Debate in Christian Ethics," *Christian Ethics and the Community* (Philadelphia: United Church Press, 1971), pp. 117–125.

60. Charles E. Curran, "A Methodological Overview of Fundamental Moral Theology," *Moral Theology: A Continuing Journey* (cf. abbr. *CJ*), pp. 38–44.

61. Hauerwas, *VV*, pp. 30–47, 222–240.

62. Häring, *F&F*, 1, p. 7.

63. *VV*, p. 34.

64. The full title of the article in question is "The Significance of Vision: Toward an Aesthetic Ethic," *VV*, pp. 30–47. Iris Murdoch is referred to repeatedly in the article.

65. See especially Gustafson's rewording of Romans 12:1–2. *ETP*, pp. 327–328.

66. Gregory Baum, ed., *Journeys: The Impact of Personal Experience on Religious Thought* (New York: Paulist Press, 1975). For Shea, see above, note 50.

67. Hauerwas, *CC*, pp. 9–35. Richard Adams, *Watership Down* (New York: Avon Books, 1972).

68. MacIntyre, *AV*, pp. 200–203.

69. *AV*, esp. p. 207.

70. Maguire, *TMC*, pp. 349–358.

71. H. Richard Niebuhr, *Radical Monotheism and Western Culture* (New York: Harper and Row, 1970).

72. Karl Rahner, "Everyday Things," *Belief Today* (New York: Sheed and Ward, 1967), pp. 29–31; *idem*, "A Spiritual Dia-

logue at Evening: On Sleep, Prayer, and Other Subjects,'' *TI* 3, pp. 220–236.

73. Häring, *F&F* 2, pp. 145–148. Cf. also MacIntyre, *AV*, p. 196.

74. *TT*, pp. 57–70.

75. *TT*, pp. 184–202.

76. Maguire, *TMC* pp. 356–365; MacIntyre *AV*, p. 196.

77. Häring, *F&F* 2, pp. 102–115.

78. Joseph Pieper, *In Tune with the World: A Theory of Festivity* (New York: Harcourt, Brace, and World, 1965); Hugo Rahner, *Man at Play* (New York: Herder and Herder, 1972); Harvey Cox, *The Feast of Fools: A Theological Essay on Festivity and Fantasy* (Cambridge, Mass.: Harvard University Press, 1969).

79. New York: Oxford University Press, 1980.

80. Paul Ramsey, ''Liturgy and Ethics,'' *JRE* 7 (1979), pp. 139–171.

81. Donald Saliers, ''Liturgy and Ethics: Some New Beginnings,'' *JRE*, pp. 173–189.

82. William Frankena, *Ethics* (Englewood Cliffs, N.J.: Prentice-Hall, 1963), esp. pp. 52–54. *idem*, ''Prichard and the Ethics of Virtue,'' *Perspectives on Morality: Essays by William K. Frankena*, ed. by K.E. Goodpaster (Notre Dame, Indiana: University of Notre Dame Press, 1976), esp, p. 160. Frankena clearly does want to revive the theology of virtue and move away from an excessively obligation oriented approach. But obligation still seems the prime factor for him.

83. *AV*, esp. pp. 169–209.

84. Cf. Chapter 2, note 67.

85. *AV*, p. 178.

86. *ETP*, p. 338. *Idem, Can Ethics Be Christian?* (Chicago: University of Chicago Press, 1975), pp. 40–47.

87. Cf. the entire first volume of *F&F*.

88. Stanley Hauerwas and Paul Wadell, ''Review of *After Virtue*,'' *The Thomist* 46 (1982), pp. 313–323, esp. p. 320.

89. Maguire, *TMC*, pp. 189–217; Rubem A. Alves, *Tomorrow's Child: Imagination, Creativity, and the Rebirth of Culture* (New York: Harper and Row, 1972); Stanley Hauerwas and Philip Foubert, ''Disciplined Seeing: Imagination and the Moral Life,'' *New Catholic World* 225 (1982), pp. 250–253; Philip Rossi, *To-*

gether Toward Hope (cf. abbr. *TTH*). Rossi's very worthwhile text became available just as this text was being completed. Kathleen Fisher's *The Inner Rainbow* (cf. note 50 above) has a broader focus but contains a helpful summary chapter on moral theology and imagination.

90. *TMC*, pp. 189–217.

91. Knox, *Enthusiasm: A Chapter in the History of Religion* (New York: Oxford University Press, 1961); Pieper, *Leisure: The Basis of Culture* (New York: Random House, 1963).

92. Cf, note 88 above.

93. Lonergan, *Insight* (note 3 above), pp. 3–6.

94. *TMC*, pp. 197–199.

95. MacIntyre, *AV*, pp. 6–34. For Ricoeur, cf. note 43 above. For Hauerwas, cf. "Disciplined Seeing" (note 89 above). Ricoeur's use of the Wittgensteinian term "Seeing As" might also be cited in this context. Cf. *RM*, pp. 212–214.

96. "Disciplined Seeing," esp. p. 253.

97. Alves, *Tomorrow's Child*, pp. 182–205; For one of the many examples of this in Maguire's thought, cf. his example on abortion (in *TMC*, pp. 209–212). Maguire returns to abortion in a recent article, "Abortion: A Question of Catholic Honesty," *The Christian Century* (Sept. 14–21, 1983), pp. 803–807. For a critique of Maguire's approach to abortion cf. Richard A. McCormick, "Notes on Moral Theology: 1983," *TS* 45 (1984), pp. 105–108.

98. For a summary of the work of Gunkel and his followers, cf. Alexa Suelzer, "Modern Old Testament Criticism," *The Jerome Biblical Commentary* (Englewood Cliffs, N.J.: Prentice-Hall, 1968), pp. 598–600.

99. James Muilenberg, "Form Criticism and Beyond," *Journal of Biblical Literature* 88 (1969), pp. 1–18.

100. James A. Sanders, "Adaptable for Life: The Nature and Function of Canon," *Magnalia Dei: The Mighty Acts of God* ed. by F.M. Cross, Werner Lemke and Patrick D. Miller (Garden City, New York: Doubleday, 1976), pp. 531–560. *Idem, Torah and Canon* (Philadelphia: Fortress Press, 1972). Walter Brueggemann, *The Creative Word: Canon as a Model for Biblical Education* (Philadelphia: Fortress Press, 1982).

101. Crossan, "Waking the Bible: Biblical Hermeneutic and Literary Imagination," *Interpretation* 32 (1978), pp. 269–285.

102. Sandra M. Schneiders, "Faith, Hermeneutics, and the Literal Sense of Scripture," *TS* 39 (1978), pp. 719–736. *Idem,* "The Paschal Imagination: Objectivity and Subjectivity in New Testament Interpretation," *TS* 43 (1982), pp. 52–68.

103. Brueggemann, in *The Creative Word,* cites Ricoeur a dozen times.

104. Brueggemann, *The Prophetic Imagination* (Philadelphia: Fortress Press, 1978). The grief theme appears throughout, but note esp. pp. 44–61. For Brueggemann on story, cf. *The Creative Word,* pp. 15–27. Crossan, *op. cit.,* pp. 273–276, 278–280; Muilenberg, *op. cit.,* p. 7.

105. Brueggemann, *The Creative Word,* pp. 7, 10–12.

106. In Brueggemann, *The Prophetic Imagination,* cf. esp. pp. 44–50, including an interesting use of Rubem Alves. Schneiders, "The Paschal Imagination," esp. p. 65. See also Schuyler Brown, "Exegesis and Imagination," *TS* 41 (1980), esp. p. 749.

CHAPTER 4

1. The past two chapters contained a great many specific citations of the authors discussed. In this chapter, which is more a statement of my own position, I will usually offer only general indications in the notes as to the authors who have inspired my thinking (leaving it to the reader to check back into my more detailed citations of these authors in the previous two chapters). There will of course be some specific citations (in those cases where I raise a previously uncited theme which is to be attributed to an author).

2. The reflections so far have roots in Rahner's transcendental epistemology which he develops most completely in *SW*.

3. The theme of suspension of judgment is essential to Ricoeur's whole notion of metaphor and it also ties in with Gadamer's notion of play. These notions in turn have some rooting in the phenomenological notion of *epoché*. Cf. Ricoeur, *HHS*, p. 116; Ricoeur, *CIF*, p. 153.

4. Paul Ricoeur, "From Existentialism to the Philosophy of Language," *Philosophy Today* 17 (1973), p. 92; see also Loretta Dornish, "Symbolic Systems and the Interpretation of Scripture," *Semeia* 4 (1975), pp. 7, 16.

5. Ricoeur, *HHS*, pp. 142–144, 158–162.

6. In *SPR*, pp. xvii.

7. For the history the building of the Brooklyn Bridge cf. David McCullough, *The Great Bridge* (New York: Simon and Schuster, 1972). See also McCullough, "The Great Bridge and the American Imagination," *New York Times Magazine* (March 27, 1983), pp. 28–34.

8. Cf. Chapter 2, note 25.

9. *CPuR*, pp. 142–143.

10. After having worked out much of the epistemology in this section with an awareness of Rahner, I delightedly discovered that, in a quite recent article honoring Bernard Häring, Rahner himself has articulated an approach to the derivation of moral norms in which he relies on his basic epistemology and thus uses terms such as conversion, image, visualization, representational model, etc. Thus Rahner himself sees that his long-standing metaphysics of imagination applies to morality as well as to all other areas of human knowing. Cf. Karl Rahner, "On Bad Arguments in Moral Theology," *TI* 18, pp. 74–85. Josef Fuchs (in *Personal Responsibility and Christian Morality* [Washington: Georgetown University Press, 1983], p. 99) seems to suggest the same line of argument when he speaks of our "active creativity" in moral matters.

11. For a twentieth century treatment of *sensus communis*, cf. Gadamer, *TM*, pp. 19–29.

12. Ricoeur is quite clear on the visual or pictorial as an essential element in imagination. Cf. *CIF*, p. 144.

13. Cf. Rahner's theme that even angels, whom we traditionally describe as "pure spirits," are created beings and must have a relatedness to materiality. Karl Rahner, "The Unity of Spirit and Matter in the Christian Understanding of Faith," *TI* 6 (1969), esp. pp. 58–59.

14. This of course is the theme of association of images and ideas which reaches back to authors such as Locke, Hume, and Coleridge. Granted that we need to judge carefully to avoid poor associations, association seems an essential staple to all truly imaginative thinking.

15. William F. Lynch's stress on an imagination which is able to wish, wait, and be filled with hope (while not being willful or seeking to absolutize reality) is what I mean by an imagination which works in concert with the human will. Cf. Lynch, *IH*, pp.

129–157, 243–256; Cf. also Hauerwas' and Foubert's notion of imagination as disciplined seeing (Chapter 3, note 89).

16. Cf. André Guindon, *TSL*, pp. 223–249; Harvey Cox, *The Feast of Fools,* esp. pp. 59–97.

17. See above, Chapter 3, note 8.

18. Gadamer, *TM*, pp. 239–240; See also Ricoeur, *HHS,* pp. 66–71.

19. Cf. John Dewey, *AE*, pp. 24–57.

20. This is a key statement. While I have been tremendously helped in this book by scholars such as Rahner and Ricoeur, I ultimately see my position as rooted in an Aristotelian-Thomistic realism.

21. Cambridge: Cambridge University Press, 1953.

22. I would in no way deny that many catechisms of the past accomplished a great deal of good. I think it is arguable, however, that many catechisms did not help people accomplish ownership of the principles which the catechisms taught.

23. Cf. Ricoeur, *CL*; also cf. Rahner, "On Bad Arguments in Moral Theology," *TI* 18, pp. 78–83.

24. Cf. Rahner's famous dictum that dogmas are much less end points and much more beginning points for theological discussion. Rahner, "The Prospects for Dogmatic Theology," *TI* 1, p. 10.

25. Cf. Karl Rahner, "On Bad Arguments in Moral Theology," *TI* 18, p. 82.

26. For a survey of current literature on moral theology and the magisterium, cf. *RMT No. 3: The Magisterium and Morality.* See also Karl Rahner, "Magisterium and Theology," *TI* 18, pp. 54–73.

27. Cf. *PRC*, pp. 128–137.

28. A key point here is to remember that, granting its special role, the magisterium has to make use of theology to express itself, so that the magisterium, as any theological procedure, needs to rely on theological skills such as imagination.

29. Cf. Chapter 3, notes 96–97.

30. MacIntyre, *AV*, esp. pp. 204–207.

31. My purpose here is not to object to the valuable role which Christians and the Church can play as critics of society. My purpose is to call for more. On the Church's role as critic, cf. J.B. Metz, "The Church and the World in the Light of a 'Political Theology',"

Theology of the World (New York: Herder and Herder, 1969), pp. 107–140.

32. Cf. abbr. *IH*. Philip Rossi, in *TTH*, also makes strong connections between hope and imagination.

33. Cf. *Lumen Gentium (The Constitution on the Church)*, no. 7.

34. Absolute future: Karl Rahner, "The Question of the Future," *TI* 12, p. 182; Power of the Future: Wolfhart Pannenberg, *Theology and the Kingdom of God* (Philadelphia: Westminster Press, 1969), p. 56; Future of Man: Edward Schillebeeckx, *God the Future of Man* (New York: Sheed and Ward, 1968); Omega Point: Pierre Teilhard de Chardin, *The Phenomenon of Man* (New York: Harper and Row, 1961), pp. 257–263.

35. These thoughts tie closely to the main insight of contemporary Transcendental Thomism: not only is what we humans know remarkable; that we know (and how we know it) is also remarkable.

36. Ricoeur, *RM*, pp. 212–213.

37. On the specific theme of decision making as an art, cf. the quote from Rahner cited in Chapter 2, note 69.

38. The point here is not that artistic judgment and ethical judgment are the same. Aquinas distinguishes these two judgments with artistic judgment being *recta ratio factibilium* and moral judgment (prudence) being *recta ratio agibilium*. One of these can be present without the other which explains artists who live immoral lives, etc. But, for Aquinas, both artistic judgment and ethical judgment are forms of practical reason, e.g., in the same family of human skills. Cf. Vernon J. Bourke, "Thomas Aquinas, St.," *EP* 8, p. 113.

39. For a helpful perspective on how pre-Vatican II Catholics and Protestants differed in their use of Scripture, cf. James Gustafson's comparison of the great social thinkers John A. Ryan and Walter Rauschenbusch (*PRC*, pp. 21–29). For a brief description of the older Catholic notion of "proof-texting" when using Scripture, cf. Charles E. Curran, *Catholic Moral Theology in Dialogue* (Notre Dame, Ind.: University of Notre Dame Press, 1976), pp. 26–27.

40. Major sources for this debate include *RMT No. 2: The Distinctiveness of Christian Ethics;* James M. Gustafson, *Can Ethics Be Christian?* (Chicago: University of Chicago Press, 1975); Josef

Fuchs, *Personal Responsibility and Christian Morality* (cf. note 2 above), pp. 51–111.

41. Of the authors we have considered, this point is made especially articulately by Hauerwas. Cf. Hauerwas, "Toward an Ethics of Character," *VV*, pp. 48–67. Cf. also Hauerwas, *Character and the Christian Life: A Study in Theological Ethics* (San Antonio: Trinity University Press, 1975).

42. For the theme of imagination as a communal task, cf. Lynch, *IH*, pp. 159–176; cf. also Philip Rossi, *TTH*, esp. p. 107.

43. Cf. Lynch, *IH*, pp. 177–186.

44. Cf. Karl Rahner, "Theological Remarks on the Problem of Leisure," *TI* 4, pp. 385–389; Josef Pieper, *Leisure: The Basis of Culture*, pp. 56–64.

45. Two excellent histories which illustrate this point are Theodore H. White, *In Search of History: A Personal Adventure* (New York: Harper and Row, 1978), pp. 83–319; Barbara W. Tuchman, *Stilwell and the American Experience in China: 1911–1945* (New York: Macmillan, 1970).

46. For a summary of the traditional Scholastic approach to certitude, cf. J.S. Hickey, *Summa Philosophiae Scholasticae* 1 (New York: Benziger Brothers, 1933), pp. 179–186. Some authors such as Austin Fagothey spoke of "prudential certainty" instead of "moral certainty." *Fagothey's Right and Reason: Ethics in Theory and Practice* 7th ed., rev. by Milton A. Gonsalves (St. Louis: C.V. Moseby, 1981), p. 60.

47. Newman, *Grammar of Assent* (cf. Chapter 2, note 18), p. 360. Cf. Lonergan's notion of "emergent probability" (in *Insight* [cf. Chapter 3, note 3], pp. 123–128).

48. H. Richard Niebuhr, *The Responsible Self: An Essay in Christian Moral Philosophy* (New York: Harper and Row, 1963), esp. pp. 60–61.

CHAPTER 5

1. For a statement of the traditional Catholic approach, cf. Chapter 1, note 22.

2. For anthologies of the periodical literature on medical ethics and care for the dying, cf. *CIB*, pp. 269–380; *Bio*, pp. 129–168;

195–232; Thomas Mappes and Jane Zembaty, *Biomedical Ethics* (cf. abbr. *BE*), pp. 342–355, 367–398. Also highly important is the recent U.S. Government Report: President's Commission for the Study of Ethical Problems in Medicine and Biomedical and Behavioral Research, *Deciding To Forego Life-Sustaining Treatment: A Report of the Ethical, Medical, and Legal Issues in Treatment Decisions* (Washington: U.S. Government Printing Office, March 1983).

3. For a Christian theological view of death, cf. Karl Rahner, *On the Theology of Death*, 2nd ed. (New York: Herder and Herder, 1965). Cf. also Norbert Greinacher and Alois Müller, eds., *Death and Dying (Concilium* 94 [1974]).

4. Cf. Paul Ramsey, "On (Only) Caring for the Dying" (cf. Chapter 1, note 25), pp. 113–164; Arthur Dyck, *On Human Care: An Introduction to Ethics* (Nashville: Abingdon, 1977).

5. For discussions of paternalism (which some are now calling parentalism), cf. Tom Beauchamp and James Childress, *Principles of Biomedical Ethics,* 2nd ed. (New York: Oxford University Press, 1983), pp. 168–179; James F. Childress, *Priorities in Biomedical Ethics* (Philadelphia: Westminster Press, 1981), pp. 17–33.

6. Cf. Theodore Maynard, *A Fire Was Lighted: The Life of Rose Hawthorne Lathrop* (Milwaukee: Bruce Publishing, 1948).

7. Two of the most important issues in the Christian approach to death and dying are the issues of pastoral care for the dying and liturgical celebration of dying and death. For some of the important recent work on these issues, cf. J. Donald Bane, *et al.,* eds., *Death and Ministry: Pastoral Care of the Dying and the Bereaved* (New York: Seabury Press, 1975); James L. Empereur, *Prophetic Anointing: God's Call to the Sick, the Elderly, and the Dying* (Wilmington, Del.: Michael Glazier, Inc., 1982).

8. For the Veterans Administration guidelines, cf. Circular 10–83–140, August 25, 1983, Veterans Administration, Dept. of Medicine and Surgery, Washington 20420. For the Vatican statement, cf. Chapter 1, note 8. For discussions of hospice care, cf. Robert W. Buckingham, *The Complete Hospice Guide* (New York: Harper and Row, 1983); David Skelton, "The Hospice Movement: A Human Approach to Palliative Care," *Canadian Medical Association Journal* 126 (1982), pp. 556–558; David H. Smith and Ju-

dith A. Granbois, ''The American Way of Hospice,'' *The Hastings Center Report* 12, no. 2 (April 1982), pp. 8–10.

9. For the historical development of the notion of the right to health care, cf. Carleton B. Chapman and John M. Talmadge, ''The Evolution of the Right to Health Concept in the United States,'' *Ethics in Medicine: Historical Perspectives and Contemporary Concerns*, ed. by Stanley Joel Reiser, Arthur J. Dyck, and William J. Curran (Cambridge, Mass.: MIT Press, 1977). For a most helpful study of the changing nature of medicine in general, cf. Paul Starr, *The Social Transformation of American Medicine* (New York: Basic Books, 1982).

10. For the contemporary ethical debate on the distribution of health care, cf. *CIB*, pp. 381–434; *BE*, pp. 516–587; Charles E. Curran, ''The Right to Health Care and Distributive Justice,'' *Transition and Tradition in Moral Theology* (Notre Dame, Ind.: University of Notre Dame Press, 1979), pp. 139–170.

11. Pope John Paul II, *Laborem Exercens* (*On Human Work*). no. 19 (*Origins* 11 [1981], p. 239). The Pope spoke in terms of the right of workers to health care benefits.

12. On preventive care, cf. Dan E. Beauchamp, ''Public Health as Social Justice,'' *BE*, pp. 551–559.

13. For a review of health insurance systems in various parts of the world, cf. Stefan Riesenfeld, ''Health Insurance,'' *Encyclopedia of Bioethics* 2, pp. 637–643; John G. Cullis and Peter A. West, ''Economic Aspects of a Public Health Care System: The U.K.,'' *Economics of Health: An Introduction* (Oxford: Martin Robinson, 1979).

14. For selections of major articles on the ethics and priorities in medical research, cf. *Bio*, pp. 235–307; *BE*, pp. 500–514; *CIB*, pp. 503–532.

15. At the time of the publication of the *SCDF's Declaration on Sexual Ethics* (December 29, 1975), some Catholic theologians did raise questions about the methodology with which the document was drawn up and about its philosophical understanding of moral norms. Few Catholic scholars however seemed to question the Congregation's underlying concern about pre-marital intercourse, especially when the pre-marital intercourse is casual. Cf. the roundup of scholarly reactions presented by Richard McCormick in his ''Notes

on Moral Theology: 1976," *TS* 38 (1977), pp. 100–114. Mc-
Cormick's own comments on the *Declaration* vis-à-vis pre-marital
intercourse can be found in "Sexual Ethics—An Opinion," *National Catholic Reporter*, January 30, 1976, p. 9.

16. By way of giving the Metropolitan Opera's centennial
equal time with the Brooklyn Bridge, it was hard not to notice that
so much of the great music used for the Met's centennial gala dealt
with love, especially with love in marriage. This does not mean that
music, art, literature, etc. should never deal with themes which de-
part from Christian moral standards (cf. Karl Rahner, "Poetry and
the Christian," *TI* 4, p. 366), but it does suggest that the arts can be
powerful and imaginative educators for human values such as mari-
tal fidelity.

17. For reflections on the importance of covenant (with references to many helpful sources), cf. *TTH*, pp. 149, 191.

18. Cf. the address of the Holy Father to the bishops of the
United States in Chicago on October 5, 1979, no. 5, in *Pilgrim of
Peace: The Homilies and Addresses of His Holiness Pope John Paul
II on the Occasion of His Visit to America* (Washington: *USCC*,
1979), pp. 118–119.

19. In his recent writing, Karl Rahner, while not moving in
quite the same direction as my present comments, has sought to find
some way of moving "behind" the position against position sort of
argument which has marked so much recent theology on contraception and related issues. Cf. Rahner, "On Bad Arguments in Moral
Theology," *TI* 18, pp. 76–78.

20. For a discussion of the many questions related to *in vitro*
fertilization, cf. Leon R. Kass, " 'Making Babies' Revisited," *Bio*,
pp. 445–472; Charles E. Curran, "*In Vitro* Fertilization and Embryo
Transfer," *CJ*, pp. 112–140; on care for defective newborns, cf.
James Gustafson, "Mongolism, Parental Desires, and the Right to
Life," *Bio*, pp. 129–155; Richard A. McCormick, "To Save or Let
Die," *Bio*, pp. 157–167.

21. Second Vatican Council, *Gaudium et Spes* (*Pastoral Constitution on the Church in the Modern World*), no. 51.

22. For an excellent statement of this theme of the child as gift,
cf. Stanley Hauerwas, "Having and Learning To Care for Retarded
Children," *TT*, pp. 147–156.

23. Cf. Pope John Paul II, "Homily at Capitol Mall," nos. 5 and 6, in *Pilgrim of Peace*, pp. 177–178.

24. For developments of this viewpoint, cf. *TSL*, pp. 7–220; James Nelson, *Embodiment: An Approach to Sexuality and Christian Theology* (Minneapolis: Augsburg Publishing House, 1978), pp. 11–129. The Vatican's *Declaration on Sexual Ethics*, no. 1, shows the same awareness.

25. For major recent theological works about women, cf. Chapter 3, note 1. For a key new work on women of a more general nature, cf. Susan Brownmiller, *Femininity* (New York: Simon and Schuster, 1983).

26. Cf. James Nelson, *op. cit.*, pp. 211–235.

27. *AV*, pp. 190–209.

28. For the history of Roman Catholic teaching on capital punishment, cf. Francesco Compagnoni, "Captial Punishment and Torture in the Tradition of the Catholic Church," *Concilium* 120 (1979), pp. 39–53. For Thomas Aquinas' support of the death penalty, cf. *ST* II–II, q. 64, a. 2. Pope Pius XII's support of capital punishment can be found in his Address to the Italian Association of Catholic Jurists, December 5, 1954 (*Acta Apostolicae Sedis* 47 [1955], 60–85); Eng. tr.: "Crime and Punishment," *Catholic Mind* 53 (1955), pp. 364–384. For an anthology of the growing opposition to capital punishment in more recent centuries, cf. Philip E. Mackey, ed., *Voices Against Death: American Opposition to Capital Punishment, 1787–1975* (New York: Burt Franklin and Co., 1976). For general background on the history and theological issues related to criminal justice cf. L. Harold DeWolf, *Crime and Justice in America* (New York: Harper and Row, 1975); Gerald Austin McHugh, *Christian Faith and Criminal Justice: Toward a Christian Response to Crime and Punishment* (New York: Paulist Press, 1978).

29. Cf. Karl Rahner, "Forgotten Truths Concerning the Sacrament of Penance," *TI* 2, esp. p. 142.

30. Cf. Barbara W. Tuchman, *A Distant Mirror: The Calamitous Fourteenth Century* (New York: Albert A. Knopf, Inc., 1978), p. 135.

31. This conclusion is stated in different ways. A panel of the National Research Council simply states that there is not sufficient

evidence to show that criminal sanctions deter crime. Cf. Alfred Blumstein, Jacqueline Cohen, and Daniel Nagel, eds., *Deterrence and Incapacitation: Estimating the Effects of Criminal Sanctions on Crime Rates* (Washington: National Academy of Sciences, 1978), esp. p. 15. Critics of capital punishment argue the case more strongly, holding that there is positive evidence that the prospect of the death penalty does not deter homicide or promote police safety. Cf. Thorsten Sellin, "Homicides in Retentionist and Abolitionist States" and "The Death Penalty and Police Safety," in Sellin, ed., *Capital Punishment* (New York: Harper and Row, 1967), pp. 135–154; Hugo Adam Bedau, "The Case Against the Death Penalty," in Mackey, *op. cit.*, pp. 303–305.

32. Cf. McHugh, *op. cit.,* esp. p. 81.

33. Notable for example is the fact that thirty-one Catholic bishops in the United States opposed the bishops' 1980 statement on capital punishment (cf. note 35 below) while one hundred and forty-five supported it. Bishop Joseph Madera of Fresno, California was the most articulate of the opposing bishops.

34. For an anthology of the impressive denominational opposition to capital punishment, cf. National Interreligious Task Force on Criminal Justice, Work Group on the Death Penalty, *Capital Punishment: What The Religious Community Says,* 1978 (Room 1700-A, 475 Riverside Drive, New York, N.Y. 10115). Perhaps the most important scholar/opponent of capital punishment is Hugo Adam Bedau. Cf. his *The Case Against Capital Punishment* (New York: American Civil Liberties Union, 1975). (Reprinted in Mackey, *op. cit.*, pp. 301–312.) See also Bedau, ed., *The Death Penalty in America* 3rd. ed. (New York: Oxford University Press, 1982).

35. *NCCB*, "Statement on Capital Punishment," November 13, 1980, in *Origins* 10 (1980), pp. 373–377. The "as of now" phrase should not obscure the fact that the bishops come across as strongly and clearly against capital punishment. They do not however hold that capital punishment would be unjustifiable in any society, and they make it clear (p. 375) that their opposition is based on conditions in contemporary American society. On January 15, 1983 Pope John Paul II recommended clemency and mercy for those condemned to death, especially for political prisoners, but he did not

rule out capital punishment in every conceivable circumstance. "A Voice for the Voiceless," Address to the Diplomatic Core, no. 5. Cf. *Origins* 12 (1983), p. 549.

36. Justice Powell's remarks (which especially concerned the legal cumbersomeness of the U.S. approach to capital punishment) were made in an address at Savannah, Georgia to the judges of the 11th circuit. Cf. *The New York Times,* May 10, 1983, I, p. 16.

37. Helpful sources include Arthur Simon, *Bread for the World* (New York: Paulist Press, 1975); Ronald J. Sider, *Rich Christians in an Age of Hunger: A Biblical Study* (New York: Paulist Press, 1977); Commission on International Development Issues, Willi Brandt, chair, *North—South: A Program For Survival* (Cambridge, Mass.: MIT Press, 1980); Robert L. McCan, *World Economy and World Hunger: The Response of the Churches* (Frederick, Md.: University Publications of America, 1982); William Byron, ed., *The Causes of World Hunger* (New York: Paulist Press, 1982).

38. McCan, *op. cit.,* pp. 1–3; Sider, *op. cit.,* pp. 31–36.

39. Sider, *op. cit.,* pp. 36–37.

40. For a summary overview of the causes, cf. Byron, *op. cit.,* pp. 1–15.

41. For the ties between population and development, cf. Peter Henriot, "Global Population in Perspective: Implications for U.S. Policy Response," *TS* 35 (1974), pp. 48–70.

42. Cf. Sider, *op. cit.,* pp. 42–45.

43. Cf. McCan, *op. cit.,* pp. 3–7; Arthur Simon, "The Basic Cause: Poverty," in Byron, *op. cit.,* pp. 15–27.

44. The Pope's January 1983 speech to the diplomats (cf. note 35 above) clearly points out the connection between world hunger and world economics (no. 7, p. 550).

45. For pertinent educational strategies, cf. Padriac O'Hare, ed., *Education for Peace and Justice* (San Francisco: Harper and Row, 1983); James and Kathleen McGinnis, *Parenting for Peace and Justice* (Maryknoll, New York: Orbis Books, 1981).

46. Pope Leo XIII, *Rerum Novarum (The Condition of Labor),* no. 34.

47. For the most significant scholarly work on the concept of distributive justice in the twentieth century, cf. John A. Ryan, *Distributive Justice: The Right and Wrong of Our Present Distribution of Wealth* (New York: Macmillan, 1916, 1927, 1943). For a current

study of Ryan, cf. Charles E. Curran, *American Catholic Social Ethics* (cf. Chapter 1, note 10), pp. 26–91.

48. For an overview of the international economic scene from the perspective of Christian ethics, cf. J. Philip Wogaman, *The Great Economic Debate: An Ethical Analysis* (Philadelphia: Westminster Press, 1977). Another notable analysis of the world socioeconomic order can be found in Robert Heilbronner, *An Inquiry into the Human Prospect: Updated and Reconsidered for the 1980's* (New York: W.W. Norton. 1980).

49. For a review of the development of Roman Catholic social and economic thought, cf. John Coleman, "Development of Church Social Teaching," *Origins* 11 (1981), pp. 33–41.

50. For sources, cf. Chapter 4, note 45.

51. Precisely because strong and credible logical arguments can be made for capitalism, logic alone will never resolve the disputes between those thinkers in the West who are rigidly capitalist and those who are more flexible in their approach to economic issues. For example, the difference in economic outlook between a Michael Novak (in *The Spirit of Democratic Capitalism* [New York: Simon and Schuster, 1982]) and someone such as Daniel Maguire (in *A New American Justice: Ending the White Male Monopolies* [Garden City, N.Y.: 1980]) may never be overcome through discursive reason. But what about the possibilities for a creative, affective, imaginative sharing of symbols?

52. For a contemporary American Catholic viewpoint on Marxism, cf. Arthur F. McGovern, *Marxism: An American Christian Perspective* (Maryknoll, N.Y.: Orbis Books, 1980).

53. In addition to the U.S. bishops' pastoral (cf. abbr. *TCP*), key sources from the ever growing body of material on nuclear disarmament include: Jonathan Schell, *The Fate of the Earth* (New York: Alfred A. Knopf, 1982); George F. Kennan, *The Nuclear Delusion: Soviet-American Relations in the Atomic Age* (New York: Pantheon Books, 1982); and Alan Geyer, *The Idea of Disarmament! Rethinking the Unthinkable* (Elgin, Ill.: The Brethen Press, 1982).

54. For Schell, cf. note 53. PSR's address: 639 Mass. Ave., Cambridge, Mass., 02139. The ABC television movie *The Day After* had not yet aired at the time of this writing, but it may come to have significant importance as a visual/imaginative expression of the aftermath of a nuclear attack. For a fascinating commentary on

Schell, cf. Langdon Gilkey, David Tracy, Paul Ricoeur, and Stephen Toulmin, "On Thinking About the Unthinkable," *University of Chicago Magazine* (Fall 1983), pp. 4–9, 28–31.

55. For a study of the history of the just war theory, cf. Roland H. Bainton, *Christian Attitudes Toward War and Peace: A Historical Survey and Critical Re-evaluation* (Nashville: Abingdon Press, 1960). For a critique of some of the major just war theorists of the past two decades, cf. James F. Childress, "Just War Theories: The Bases, Interrelations, Priorities, and Functions of Their Criteria," *TS* 39 (1978), pp. 427–445.

56. For a review of the current scholarly debate on just war in the nuclear age, cf. Richard A. McCormick, "Notes on Moral Theology: 1982," *TS* 44 (1983), pp. 94–114.

57. *TCP*, nos. 142–161, 172–188. Here the bishops rely heavily on Pope John Paul's message to the U.N.'s 1982 Special Session on Disarmament which held that deterrence was not moral as an end but only as a means to disarmament.

58. *TCP*, nos. 189–199.

59. Cf. the bishops' call for prayerfulness, *TCP*, nos. 290–296.

60. *TCP*, no. 191.

CHAPTER 6

1. Throughout *TTH*, Philip Rossi makes much use of the two terms imagination and moral imagination. Rossi uses the specific term moral imagination when imagination is operative in the context of "what ought to be" (pp. 44–45) and also when imagination is related to moral themes such as mutuality and vision (p. 169). For Rossi (as for myself) I do not believe that the distinction between imagination and moral imagination is fully adequate, but rather that moral imagination is human imagination operating in the moral sphere. He too has the sections (e.g., p. 156) where the two terms are readily interchanged. For Rossi's earlier work on moral imagination, cf. *TTH*, p. 182, n. 4.

2. National Commission on Excellence in Education, *A Nation at Risk: The Imperative for Educational Reform* (Washington: U.S. Government Printing Office, April 1983).

3. In this context, recall the importance of language and its understanding to many of the great scholars we have considered in this book. For Rahner, the arts which use words transcend other arts because of their linguality. (Cf. "Poetry and the Christian," *TI* 4, pp. 357–367.) The whole of Part Three of Gadamer's *TM* (pp. 345–447) stresses the centrality of language. For Ricoeur, cf. *CL*.

4. Cf. Ricoeur's point that one must first be able to grasp the individual metaphors so as to move on to the understanding of longer texts. With an understanding of longer texts one can then understand the individual texts more deeply, but the first understanding of individual short texts is a crucial starting point. Cf. Ricoeur, *HHS*, pp. 170–181.

5. Cf. MacIntyre, *AV*, pp. 190–209; Rossi, *TTH*, pp. 108–109.

6. For philosophical-theological reflection on the classical, cf. Gadamer, *TM*, pp. 253–258; Tracy, *AI*, pp. 99–135.

7. For the notion of theology as interpretation of religious classics, cf, *AI*, pp. 154–219, as well as the entire second half of the book.

8. Cf. Thomas Kuhn, *The Structure of Scientific Revolutions* (Chicago: University of Chicago Press, 1970).

9. Described in McCullough, *The Great Bridge*, p. 42.

10. From Kohlberg's lengthy bibliography, two helpful recent statements of his position are "The Cognitive-Developmental Approach to Moral Education," *Readings in Moral Education*, ed. by Peter Scharf (Minneapolis: Winston Press, 1978), pp. 36–51; *Essays on Moral Development*, 2 vols. (San Francisco: Harper and Row, 1981, 1983). For a helpful popular summary of Kohlberg, cf. the work of Ronald Duska and Mariellen Whelan (cited in Chapter 1, note 3).

11. For Fowler, cf. Jim Fowler and Sam Keen, *Life Maps: Conversations of the Journey of Faith* (Minneapolis: Winston Press, 1978); James W. Fowler, *Stages of Faith: The Psychology of Human Development and the Quest for Meaning* (San Francisco: Harper and Row, 1981).

12. Cf. Kohlberg, "The Cognitive-Developmental Approach," p. 37.

13. Cf. Duska and Whelan, p. 75.

14. For a short summary by Kohlberg himself, cf. "Cognitive-Developmental Approach," pp. 50–51.

15. Duska and Whelan, pp. 70–75. Paul J. Philibert points out that Kohlberg talked about stage 4 1/2 in 1973–74 and not thereafter. Cf. Philibert, "The Motors of Morality: Religion and Relation," *Moral Development Foundations* (cf. abbr. *MDF*), p. 89.

16. Cf. the discussion and critique of this in Donald M. Joy, "Kohlberg Revisited: A Supra-Naturalist Speaks His Mind," *MDF*, pp. 46–48.

17. Cf. (among others) Charles E. Curran, "A Methodological Overview of Fundamental Moral Theology," *CJ*, p. 48; Craig Dykstra, "What Are People Like? An Alternative to Kohlberg's View," *MDF*, pp. 153–162. For Dykstra's overall critique of Kohlberg, cf. his *Vision and Character: A Christian Educator's Alternative to Kohlberg* (New York: Paulist Press, 1981).

18. Cf. Joseph Reimer, "Beyond Justice: Moral Development and the Search for Truth—A Contemporary Midrash," *MDF*, pp. 63–76.

19. Cf. Fowler, *Stages of Faith,* pp. 101–103. Immediately after this, Fowler (citing William Lynch among others) goes on to criticize the lack of a stress on imagination in Kohlberg (pp. 103–105).

20. Walter E. Conn, "Affectivity in Kohlberg and Fowler," *Religious Education* 76 (1981), pp. 33–48.

21. Cf. the sources cited in notes 17 and 19.

22. Cf. abbr. *IDV*.

23. *IDV,* pp. 24–63.

24. Cf. Donald M. Joy, "Kohlberg Revisited," *MDF*, pp. 39–48; 53–58; Hauerwas (in *CC*, pp. 129–152) is quite critical of Kohlberg's rationalism and lack of concern for narrative, etc. On p. 130 he lists the perspectives a Christian would want to add to Kohlberg's cognitive-structural theory of development.

25. Cf. abbr. *MDF*.

26. Dykstra. "What Are People Like?" *MDF*, esp. pp. 156–157.

27. For an overview treatment of sexual fantasies, cf. *TSL*, pp. 223–249.

28. For a statistical and behavioral profile of child abusers, cf. Herant A. Katchadourian and Donald T. Lunde, *Fundamentals of*

Human Sexuality, 2nd. ed. (New York: Holt, Rinehart and Winston, 1975), pp. 340–342.

29. Cf. Sheldon Kranz, *The H Persuasion: How Persons Have Permanently Changed from Homosexuality through the Study of Aesthetic Realism* with Eli Siegel (New York: Definition Press, 1971). Some would argue that the "true" homosexual orientation can never be changed. My point is not to agree with all of the above work's conclusions, but to point to its aesthetic/imaginative interpretation of homosexuality.

30. For arguments against pornography by several women writers, cf. Laura Lederer, ed., *Take Back the Night: Women on Pornography* (New York: Morrow, 1980).

31. E.g., Kathleen and James McGinnis, *Parenting for Peace and Justice* (cf. Chapter 5, note 45). Also very helpful, while less explicit on the justice issues, is Gloria Durka and Joanmarie Smith, eds., *Aesthetic Dimensions of Religious Education* (New York: Paulist Press, 1981).

32. *Parenting for Peace and Justice,* esp. Chapters 4 and 6.

33. Synod of Bishops Second General Assembly, *Justice in the World* (Nov. 30, 1971), no. 6. In Joseph Gremillion, *The Gospel of Peace and Justice: Catholic Social Teaching Since Pope John* (Maryknoll, New York: Orbis Books, 1976), p. 514. For commentary, cf. Charles M. Murphy, "Action for Justice as Constitutive of the Preaching of the Gospel: What Did the 1971 Synod Mean?" *TS* 44 (1983), pp. 298–311.

34. *TCP,* no. 298.

35. For a basic theological overview of the meaning of asceticism, cf. Karl Rahner, "The Passion and Asceticism," *TI* 3, pp. 58–85.

36. Cf. H.R. Niebuhr, *Christ and Culture* (New York: Harper and Row, 1956), p. 40.

37. Cf. Paul Philibert, "The Motors of Morality," *MDF,* pp. 87–110.

Abbreviations

AE	John Dewey. *Art as Experience*. Capricorn Books. New York: G.P. Putnam's Sons, 1958.
AI	David Tracy. *The Analogical Imagination: Christian Theology and the Culture of Pluralism*. New York: Crossroad Publishing, 1981.
AV	Alasdair MacIntyre. *After Virtue: A Study In Moral Theory*. Notre Dame, Ind.: University of Notre Dame Press, 1981.
BE	Thomas A. Mappes and Jane S. Zembaty, eds. *Biomedical Ethics*. New York: McGraw-Hill, 1981.
Bio	Thomas A. Shannon, ed. *Bioethics: Basic Writings on the Key Ethical Questions That Surround the Major, Modern Biological Possibilities and Problems*. Ramsey, N.J.: Paulist Press, 1981.
CC	Stanley Hauerwas. *A Community of Character: Toward a Constructive Christian Social Ethic*. Notre Dame, Ind.: University of Notre Dame Press, 1981.
CI	Paul Ricoeur. *The Conflict of Interpretations: Essays in Hermeneutics*. Evanston, Ill.: Northwestern University Press, 1974.
CIAP	Jacques Maritain. *Creative Intuition in Art and Poetry*. Cleveland: World Publishing Co., 1954.
CIB	Tom L. Beauchamp and LeRoy Walters, eds. *Contemporary Issues in Bioethics*. 2nd ed. Belmont, Cal.: Wadsworth Publishing Co., 1982.
CIF	Paul Ricoeur. "The Metaphorical Process as Cognition, Imagination, and Feeling," *Critical Inquiry* 5 (1978), pp. 143–159.
CJ	Charles E. Curran. *Moral Theology: A Continuing Journey*. Notre Dame, Ind.: University of Notre Dame Press, 1982.
CL	Paul Ricoeur. "Creativity in Language: Word, Poly-

semy, Metaphor,'' *The Philosophy of Paul Ricoeur: An Anthology of His Work.* Ed. by Charles E. Reagan and David Stewart. Boston: Beacon Press, 1978, pp. 120–133.

CPuR   Immanuel Kant. *Critique of Pure Reason.* New York: Macmillan, 1929. (New Edition: New York: St. Martin's Press, 1965.)

EP   *The Encyclopedia of Philosophy,* ed. by Paul Edwards. 8 vols. New York: Macmillan and Free Press, 1967.

ETP   James M. Gustafson. *Ethics from a Theocentric Perspective. Volume One. Theology and Ethics.* Chicago: University of Chicago Press, 1981.

F&F   Bernard Häring. *Free and Faithful in Christ: Moral Theology for Clergy and Laity.* 3 vols. New York: Seabury Press, 1978–1981.

GDP   *Great Dialogues of Plato,* ed. by Eric Warmington and Philip G. Rouse. New York: New American Library, 1956.

HHS   Paul Ricoeur. *Hermeneutics and the Human Sciences,* ed. and trans. by John B. Thompson. Cambridge: Cambridge University Press, 1981.

IDV   Carol Gilligan. *In a Different Voice: Psychological Theory and Women's Development.* Cambridge, Mass.: Harvard University Press, 1982.

IH   William F. Lynch. *Images of Hope: Imagination as Healer of the Hopeless.* Baltimore: Helicon Press, 1965.

JRE   The Journal of Religious Ethics.

MDF   Donald M. Joy, ed. *Moral Development Foundations: Judeo-Christian Alternatives to Piaget and Kohlberg.* Nashville: Abingdon Press, 1983.

NCCB   National Conference of Catholic Bishops.

PRC   James M. Gustafson. *Protestant and Roman Catholic Ethics: Prospects for Rapprochement.* Chicago: University of Chicago Press, 1978.

RM   Paul Ricoeur. *The Rule of Metaphor: Multi-Disciplinary Studies in the Creation of Meaning in Language.* Toronto: University of Toronto Press, 1977.

RMT   Charles E. Curran and Richard A. McCormick, eds. *Readings in Moral Theology.* 4 vols. New York: Paulist

Press, 1979-1984.

SCDF	Sacred Congregation for the Doctrine of the Faith.
SPR	Charles E. Reagan, ed. *Studies in the Philosophy of Paul Ricoeur*. Athens, Ohio: Ohio University Press, 1979.
ST	St. Thomas Aquinas. *Summa Theologica*.
SW	Karl Rahner. *Spirit in the World*. New York: Herder and Herder, 1968.
TCP	*NCCB. The Challenge of Peace: God's Promise and Our Response*. A Pastoral Letter on War and Peace. May 3, 1983. Washington: *USCC*, 1983. Citations by numbered sections.
TI	Karl Rahner. *Theological Investigations*. 20 vols. London: Darton, Longman, and Todd, 1961–1983. (Also New York: Crossroad Publishing.)
TM	Hans-Georg Gadamer. *Truth and Method*. New York: Continuum Publishing Corp., 1975.
TMC	Daniel C. Maguire. *The Moral Choice*. Garden City, N.Y.: Doubleday, 1978.
TS	*Theological Studies*.
TSL	André Guindon. *The Sexual Language: An Essay in Moral Theology*. Ottawa: University of Ottawa Press, 1976.
TT	Stanley Hauerwas. *Truthfulness and Tragedy: Further Investigations into Christian Ethics*, with Richard Bondi and David B. Burrell. Notre Dame, Ind.: University of Notre Dame Press, 1977.
TTH	Philip Rossi. *Together Toward Hope: A Journey to Moral Theology*. Notre Dame, Ind.: University of Notre Dame Press, 1983.
USCC	United States Catholic Conference.
VV	Stanley M. Hauerwas. *Vision and Virtue: Essays in Christian Ethical Reflection*. Notre Dame, Ind.: Fides Press, 1974.

Index

Abstraction 80–82, 85, 90, 108
Aesthetics 15, 17, 21, 28–36, 40,
    42, 50, 54, 56, 60–62, 65,
    77, 86
Aeterni Patris 48
Agent intellect 25–26, 34, 49
Albert the Great 30, 61, 178
Alves, R. 73–74, 187–88
Analogy 37, 59–60
Antinomianism 9, 59
Appropriateness (and judgment)
    108–109, 113, 162
Aquinas, Thomas 23–26, 30, 33–
    36, 44, 48, 56, 61, 72, 79–
    80, 84, 86, 158, 177–79,
    190–91, 196, 206
Aristotle 21, 23–26, 29–30, 32,
    44, 72–73, 89, 109, 177–79,
    181–190
Art, arts 17–18, 22–23, 27–34, 38,
    40, 42–43, 46, 48, 53–54,
    59, 65, 67, 73, 84, 88–89,
    99, 101, 105–06, 121, 128,
    146, 149, 151–53, 161, 164
Association 30, 86–87, 100, 106–
    08, 126, 144
Augustine 10, 21–22, 30, 33, 177

Bacon, F. 27, 180
Barth, K. 60
Baum, G. 66, 185
Baumgarten, A.G. 27, 34, 180
Beardsley, M. 178–179
Beauchamp, T. 174, 193, 204

Beauty 15–17, 27–28, 34, 61–62,
    67–68, 71–72, 84, 88, 120,
    161–164
Bedau, H.A. 197
Bell, C. 28, 178
Bergson, H. 30, 179
Bernard, St. 40
Bible: interpretation and morality
    5–6, 9, 15, 31, 50–51, 65, 75
    –78, 93, 102–03, 114, 121–
    22, 125, 130, 138, 145, 162
Birth control 123–26
Bishops, U.S. Catholic 5, 12, 104,
    132, 142, 144–45, 168, 197,
    200, 206
Brain, hemispheres of 1, 62–63
Broca, J. 62
Brownmiller, S. 176, 196
Brownowski, J. 184
Brueggemann, W. 76–77, 187–188
Burke, Edmund 32, 179

Callahan, D. 15, 67, 176
Canonical criticism 76
Capital punishment 130–34
Carrier, W. 73
Cassirer, E. 31
Catharsis 32–33
Censorship 27–28, 89
Certainty 46
Character 15–16, 34, 61, 70–73,
    103–04
Children as gift 124–25
Childress, J. 193, 200

Church teaching 94–95, 104, 176, 190

Classic 59–61, 89, 96–97, 151–52

Coleman, J. 175, 199

Coleridge, S.T. 33, 35, 51, 179–80, 189

Collingwood, R. 31, 33, 35, 61, 179

Comedy 15, 67, 71, 77, 82

Conn, W. 157, 202

Conscience 46

Cost of health care 5, 116–120, 139

Coulson, J. 184

Covenant 9, 114–15, 121–23, 125–26

Cox, H. 69, 186

Creativity 3, 11, 16–17, 23–26, 29, 41, 44, 46–47, 57–61, 65, 67, 72–73, 93–98, 102–03, 106, 116, 119, 134, 136, 143–45, 149–53, 189

Croce, B. 31, 33, 35, 51, 61, 179

Crossan, J. 76–77, 187

Curran, C. 64–65, 173–74, 181, 185, 191, 194–95, 199, 202, 204–05

Dax, M. 62

Death and dying 5, 9–10, 12–13, 68, 111–116, 133

Demonization 131, 138, 145–46

Descartes, R. 23, 28, 36, 50, 177

Dewey, J. 31–33, 38, 179, 190, 204

Dilthey, W. 32

Discernment 3, 39–41, 101–02, 109, 144–45

Discursive and non-discursive 14–21, 27, 38–39, 41–43, 63–64, 67, 70, 75, 155, 172

Dixon, J. 184

Dornish, L. 180, 188

Double effect, 4, 14, 68

Dufrenne, M. 61, 185

Duska, R. (and Whelan, M.) 173, 201–02

Economics and justice 137–141

Emotion, affectivity 32–33, 59, 74, 84, 86–90, 100, 156–57, 160

Empereur, J. 193

Epikeia 8

Epistemology 21–26, 31, 33–34, 49, 54, 57, 60, 85

Excessus ad esse 25, 34, 49, 178

Experience, priority of 88–90

Fancy 27, 35, 83, 95, 172

Fiorenza, E. 181

Fisher, K. 184, 187

Form Criticism 75–76

Forms, formalism 21–24, 28–29, 32, 38, 61, 156

Forms, splendor of 30, 61

Fowler, J. 154, 156–57, 201–02

Frankena, W. 71, 186

Fuchs, J. 173, 189, 192

Fundamental moral theology 3–4, 6

Gadamer, H-G. 15, 53–56, 59, 61, 65, 69, 77, 87, 182–83, 189–190, 201, 206

Gandhi, M. 130

Gilligan, C. 157–58, 181, 205

Gilson, E. 48

Glory, doxology 15, 68–69

Greeley, A. 184

Guindon, A. 174, 190, 206

Gula, R. 181

Gunkel, H. 75, 187

Gustafson, J. 6, 20, 64–65, 72, 173, 175–76, 185, 191, 195, 205

Häring, B. 15, 64–65, 67–69, 72, 173, 176, 185, 189, 205
Hart, R. 184
Hartt, J. 184
Hauerwas, S. 15, 64–66, 68, 72–74, 77, 175–76, 185–87, 190, 192, 195, 202, 204, 206
Hawthorne, R. 114
Hegel, G. 153
Heidegger, M. 49, 53–55, 61, 182–84
Heilbronner, R. 199
Hermeneutic circle 52, 59
Hermeneutics 4, 49–59, 61, 77
Hermeneutics of suspicion 51, 57, 182
Hobbes, T. 35, 180
Holmes, U. 184
Homosexuality 5, 129
Hume, D. 27, 31, 35, 58, 83, 178–79, 189
Humor 67–68
Hunger 134–37, 168–69

Ignatius of Loyola 40
Illative sense 26
Illumination 30
Imagination:
  in Kant 23
  in Aquinas 24–26
  history of 34–36
  in Rahner 56
  in Ricoeur 57–59
  in moral theology 73–75
  in Scripture study 77–78
  and senses 84–86
  and intelligence 84–86
  and intuition 86–90
  and emotion 86–90
  and experience 86–90
  and moral principles 90–95
  and moral imagination 147–48
Imitation and art, 27, 29–30
Interpretation 50–51, 55, 59–60, 76, 93
Intuition 24–25, 29–31, 33, 35, 42, 48, 51, 59, 63, 74, 80, 86–90, 158

John Paul II, Pope 5, 116, 123–25, 150–51, 194–98, 200
Joy, D. 159, 202, 205
Just war 10, 92, 98, 143–44

Kant, I. 21, 23, 30, 33, 35, 44, 48–54, 58, 61, 71, 74, 83, 156, 177, 179–80, 205
Keane, P. 173–74, 176
Knox, R. 73, 187

Laborem exercens 5, 116, 194
Langer, S. 179
Language 4, 49, 53–55, 63, 71, 76, 88, 96, 149–51, 201
Leo XIII, Pope 18, 137, 198
Liberal arts 51, 88, 96, 149–54, 164, 170
Literature 16–17, 35, 51, 54, 59, 61, 71, 88–89, 106, 121, 128, 146, 151, 161, 164
Liturgy 15, 27, 38, 69–70, 94–95, 125, 152
Locke, J. 30, 35, 189
Logic and morality 14–15, 23, 26, 36, 40–41, 44–46, 56, 63, 65, 70, 88, 102, 108, 114, 119, 121–22, 132, 156–58, 170
Lonergan, B. 48–49, 73–74, 181–82, 187

Lynch, W. 98, 184, 189, 192, 205

MacIntyre, A. 15, 66–68, 71–72, 74, 97, 129, 176, 185, 187, 190, 201, 204
Maguire, D. 15, 44, 67–68, 72–74, 77, 174–76, 181, 185–87, 199, 206
Mappes, T. (and Zembatty, J.) 193–94
Maréchal, J. 48–49, 178–81
Maritain, J. 26, 48, 178, 180, 204
Marriage 9, 120–23, 195
Marxism 27, 199
May, W.E. 72, 175
McCormick, R. 173–74, 187, 195, 200, 205
McCullough, D. 189, 201
McGinnis, J. and K. 198–203
McGovern, A. 199
McHugh, G. 196–97
Medical ethics 5–7, 9, 12, 18, 68, 111–120
Mercy killing 13
Merleau-Ponty, M. 53
Metaphor 55–58, 61, 63, 81–82, 93, 101, 123, 148, 150, 153
Meyers-Briggs 35
Moore, G. 90
Moral development and education 3, 11, 17–18, 29, 34, 39, 89, 91, 147–72
Moral imagination defined 79–84
Moral principles 8–11, 14, 17–18, 21, 37, 42, 44, 55–56, 68, 90–95, 100, 102–03, 112, 115, 119–20, 143, 171–72
Muilenberg, J. 76–77, 187
Murdoch, I. 65, 185
Music 17, 28, 63, 88–89, 106, 121, 146, 149, 151, 164

Mystery 36–37, 40, 80, 90, 102, 124
Mysticism 23, 30, 41–44

Narrative 15, 17, 66–67, 71–72, 77, 89
National commission (education) 148
Natural law 4, 7, 68, 99–100, 102, 107, 158
Niebuhr, H.R. 67, 109, 171, 185, 192, 203
Niebuhr, R. 60
Nelson, J. 196
Neo-Platonists 22
Newman, J.H. 23, 26, 33, 49, 109, 178, 192
Nuclear arms 5–7, 10, 12, 67, 92, 104, 135, 142–46, 168, 171

O'Connell, T. 174, 181
Origen 30
Orwell, G. 146

Paternalism 8–9, 114
Phantasm, conversion to 79–82
Phenomenology 4, 52–55, 61
Philibert, P. 202–03
Philodemus 28
Physicians for Social Responsibility 142, 199
Piaget, J. 154
Pieper, J. 69, 73, 186
Pius XII, Pope 196
Plato 21–24, 27–28, 33–34, 177–79
Play 54–55, 60–61, 65, 69, 81–85, 91–93, 100, 106–09, 113, 115, 118–19, 123, 125–26, 138–39, 161, 166–70
Plotinus 30, 34, 179

Poetry 17, 48, 51, 61, 67, 88, 121
Polysemy 56, 92
Pornography 164
Powell, L., Justice 132, 198
Powers, J. 181
Practical Reason 26, 44–45, 72–73, 109
Prejudice 54, 87
Probabilism 44–46, 181
Productive imagination 35–36, 58, 83, 88
Protestant ethics 6–7, 19–20, 40

Rahner, H. 69, 156
Rahner, K. 17, 26, 36, 48–49, 60–61, 67, 87, 175–76, 178, 180, 182–85, 188–89, 193, 195, 196, 201, 203, 206
Ramsey, P. 15, 69–70, 173, 176, 186, 193
Rape 12, 168
Rationality 15–16, 22–24, 32–33, 47, 71–72, 76, 78, 154–56, 160
Rationes seminales 22
Rausehenbusch, W. 191
Reproductive imagination 35
Rerum novarum 5, 198
Retarded and handicapped 68, 124, 128, 195
Ricoeur, P. 15, 50, 53, 55–58, 60–61, 63, 65, 74, 76–77, 81–82, 92–93, 101, 176, 180, 182–85, 187–191, 200–01, 204–06
Roebling, J. and W. 82–83, 155
Romanticism 33–35, 51–52
Rossi, P. 73, 186–87, 191–92, 200, 206
Rousselot, P. 48, 181
Ruysbroeck, J. 40

Ryan, J.A. 141, 191, 198–99
Ryle, G. 36, 177, 180

Sacramental theology 21, 36–39, 94
Saliers, D. 70, 186
Sanders, J. 76, 187
Schaldenbrand, M. 58, 183, 184
Scheler, M. 53
Schell, J. 142, 199–200
Schleiermacher, F. 50–52
Schneiders, S. 76, 188
Science 18, 51, 54, 56, 61, 63, 66, 68, 88, 92, 99, 101, 152–53, 172
Scripture see Bible
Scruton, R. 61, 185
Second naïvete 81, 98
Sense knowledge 22, 24–25, 34–36, 79–80, 84–86, 100
Sexual education 161–164
Sexual ethics 4–5, 9, 12, 18, 107, 120–129
Shaftesbury, Lord 33–34
Shannon, J. 174, 204
Shea, J. 66, 184
Shelly, P. 34, 180
Shils, E. 15, 67, 176
Sin 3
Social ethics 5, 7, 11–12, 81, 96–97, 108, 129–46, 158–59, 165–69
Socialism 27, 139–41
Socrates 24
Spirituality 3, 15, 21, 25, 37, 39–44, 101–03, 121, 153
Sublime 52
Starr, P. 194
Story 15–16, 66, 81, 89, 94–98, 103–04, 113–15, 137, 158–60, 171

Surplus of meaning 15, 59, 176
Suspension of judgment 54, 58, 81–83, 85, 91, 100, 106–07, 118–19, 123, 139, 143
Symbol, symbolism 31, 37–39, 88, 94–98, 103, 105, 115, 123, 133, 136, 145, 158–59, 170–71
Systematic theology 15, 19, 59–60

Taste 29, 31, 89, 160
Teachers, esteem for 148
Teilhard 99, 191
Text 55–57, 93, 133–34, 137, 150
Tracy, D. 15, 59–60, 176, 184, 200–01, 204
Tragedy 15, 67–68, 71, 77, 82, 94
Transcendental Thomism 4, 26, 48–50, 56, 59–61, 187, 191
Transcendental thought 23, 30, 32, 80, 87
Tuchman, B. 192, 196

Unemployment 13

Vatican II 3–5, 7, 48, 98–99, 102, 126, 152, 171, 180, 195
Viae 43–44
Victorines 22
Virtue 7, 15–17, 34, 50, 70–73, 95, 97, 103–04, 129, 150
Vision 16, 59, 63–70, 73–74, 81, 96, 100–101, 104, 117, 138, 145–46, 150, 153, 170
Von Ranke, L. 52, 75

Wainwright, G. 69–70
Walters, L. 174, 204
Watership Down 66
White, T.H. 192
Wilder, A. 184
Wittgenstein, L. 101, 187
Women, 4, 12, 47, 126–27, 157–58, 160, 163, 171
Wordsworth, W. 33